The Sit-Ins

THE CHICAGO SERIES IN LAW AND SOCIETY
Edited by John M. Conley and Lynn Mather

Also in the series:

The Sit-Ins

*Protest and Legal Change
in the Civil Rights Era*

CHRISTOPHER W. SCHMIDT

The University of Chicago Press   Chicago and London

The University of Chicago Press, Chicago 60637
The University of Chicago Press, Ltd., London
© 2018 by The University of Chicago
Published 2018
Printed in the United States of America

27 26 25 24 23 22 21 20 19 18   1 2 3 4 5

ISBN-13: 978-0-226-52230-2 (cloth)
ISBN-13: 978-0-226-52244-9 (paper)
ISBN-13: 978-0-226-52258-6 (e-book)
DOI: 10.7208/chicago/9780226522586.001.0001

Library of Congress Cataloging-in-Publication Data

Names: Schmidt, Christopher W., 1974– author.
Title: The sit-ins: protest and legal change in the civil rights era /
    Christopher W. Schmidt.
Other titles: Chicago series in law and society.
Description: Chicago: The University of Chicago Press, 2018. | Series:
    Chicago series in law and society
Identifiers: LCCN 2017028434 | ISBN 9780226522302 (cloth:
    alk. paper) | ISBN 9780226522449 (pbk: alk. paper) | ISBN
    9780226522586 (e-book)
Subjects: LCSH: African Americans—Civil rights—History—20th
    century. | African Americans—Civil rights—Southern States—
    History—20th century. | Civil rights demonstrations—United
    States—History—20th century. | Civil rights demonstrations—
    Southern States—History—20th century. | Southern States—Race
    relations. | African Americans—History—1877–1964.
Classification: LCC E185.61 .S33 2018 | DDC 323.1196/0730904—
    dc23
LC record available at https://lccn.loc.gov/2017028434

♾ This paper meets the requirements of ANSI/NISO Z39.48-1992
(Permanence of Paper)

To my parents, James and Margaret Schmidt

If you come down to the pool room
And you can't find me no where,
Just come on down to the Albany Movement,
I'll be waitin' down there.

If you come down to the Albany Movement
And you can't find me no where,
Just come on down to the drug store,
I'll be sittin'-in there.

If you come down to the drug store
And you can't find me no where,
Just come on down to the jail house,
I'll be waitin' down there.

If you come down to the jail house
And you can't find me no where,
Just come on up to the court room,
I'll be waitin' up there.

If you come down to the court room
And you can't find me no where,
Just come up to the Supreme Court,
I'll be winnin' up there.

—"I'LL BE WAITIN' DOWN THERE," ALBANY, GEORGIA, 1962[1]

Contents

Introduction

These students are not struggling for themselves alone. They are seeking
to save the soul of America. They are taking our whole nation back to those
great wells of democracy which were dug deep by the Founding Fathers in
the formulation of the Constitution and the Declaration of Independence.
In sitting down at the lunch counters, they are in reality standing up for the
best in the American dream. They courageously go to the jails of the South
in order to get America out of the dilemma in which she finds herself as a
result of the continued existence of segregation. One day historians will
record this student movement as one of the most significant epics of our
heritage. MARTIN LUTHER KING JR.[1]

It began with a conversation. Four young African American men, in their first year at North Carolina Agricultural
and Technical College, in a dormitory room, discussing
their hopes and their frustrations. It was late 1959, and
then it was early 1960, and of the many topics they talked
about in these "bull sessions," the one they kept returning to was the challenge of leading a dignified life in the
Jim Crow South. The experience of living with racial segregation had left them "exhausted," one later recalled.
They talked, and they talked some more. And then, in the
words of one of the students, "we just got tired of talking
about it and decided to do something."[2]

Late in the afternoon of February 1, 1960, the four
students—Ezell Blair Jr., Franklin McCain, Joseph McNeil,
and David Richmond—entered the Woolworth store in
downtown Greensboro. They browsed for a few minutes,

purchased some small items, and then sat down at the lunch counter. "I'm sorry," the waitress told them, "we don't serve colored in here." Like most department stores in the American South, the Greensboro Woolworth welcomed African American customers but with one restriction: they were not allowed to sit at the lunch counter. The students pointed out that their money had been accepted at the nearby merchandise counter and asked why they were being refused at this one. "What do you mean?" asked Blair. "This is a public place, isn't it? If it isn't, then why don't you sell membership cards? If you do that, then I'll understand that this is a private concern." "But they wouldn't serve us," McNeil recounted. "So we just sat there until the lunch counter closed. Then we came on back to school."[3]

They returned the following morning, this time with reinforcements. The group of twenty or so students, including four women, went through the same routine. They made small purchases in the store, then took seats at the lunch counter and requested service. They were refused again. The students talked quietly among themselves; some used the time to keep up with their schoolwork. Police officers kept watch on the scene, as did local newspaper reporters. Around midday, about an hour and half after they arrived, the group went back to campus. The next morning, they were back again. By the end of the week, an estimated two hundred students had joined the Greensboro protests.[4]

What happened in Greensboro during the first week of February 1960 was remarkable. The American South in 1960 was a world in which Jim Crow still reigned, the prerogatives of white supremacy maintained by law, custom, and violence. Racial inequities defined life for blacks in the South, ranging from the most fundamental aspects of American citizenship—disfranchisement, separate and unequal education, a racially oppressive criminal justice system—to the corrosive day-to-day reminders of how the whites who held the levers of power viewed their black fellow citizens: separate water fountains, the casual use of first names or "boy" when addressing black men, whites-only lunch counters. Against this backdrop, for young black men and women to demand service at these lunch counters was a leap into uncharted and potentially dangerous territory. "Sure, we were scared, I suppose," Blair told a reporter. "We didn't know what to expect." They thought they might be arrested; they feared worse. The Greensboro sit-in campaign was a bold—some said reckless—act of concerted defiance against racial injustice.[5]

Greensboro was not the first time African Americans challenged discrimination at a lunch counter by sitting down, requesting service, and, when denied, refusing to leave. There was a long if sporadic history of this kind of protest. What separated the sit-ins that took place in Greensboro in February 1960 from all that came before was what happened next. The Greensboro protests became a national news event, and they inspired thousands to march, picket, boycott, sit-in, even to go to jail—actions few would have imagined doing before being moved by the images of young men and women quietly sitting on stools at a lunch counter. A week of remarkable events in Greensboro turned into an inspired frontal assault on racial practices throughout the South. The sit-ins became a movement.

The sit-ins first spread to other North Carolina cities: Durham, Winston-Salem, Charlotte, Raleigh. On February 11, students in Hampton, Virginia, brought the sit-in movement to the first city outside North Carolina. Next was Rock Hill, South Carolina. In Nashville, Tennessee, and Tallahassee, Florida, students already had been planning their own sit-in protests, and the news from Greensboro spurred them to act. By the end of February, students had organized sit-ins in thirty cities across seven states. A month later, sit-ins had taken place in forty-eight cities in eleven southern states.[6]

There was a repetitive quality to the sit-ins. Having identified a protest tactic that was powerful and easily replicated, students across the South performed the same basic routines again and again through the winter and spring of 1960. Put on nice clothes. Collect a few course books, maybe a Bible. Gather for a discussion of logistics, some final words of inspiration, perhaps a prayer. Then walk into a variety store, sit down at the lunch counter, and request service. That was it. It was predictable and powerful. For those who experienced the sit-ins— whether participants, supporters, or critics—much of the wonder of the movement was that so many different people in so many different places were doing the same extraordinary thing.

Once seated at the lunch counter, the students' carefully scripted drama became far less predictable. The next move was in the hands of others. The students waited on their stools, uncertain of what was to come next. Often it was the indignity of being ignored. Or perhaps the lights would be turned off, the lunch counter closed for the day. Sometimes a waitress or the manager would talk to them, plead with them to leave and take their cause somewhere else. Or the manager might threaten to call the police. If the students remained, the manager might follow through on his threat. When the police arrived, they brought their own script. They would require the manager to request in their presence that the students leave, only then arresting the students, marching them to a paddy wagon, and taking them off to jail.

The first arrests of the sit-in movement took place in Raleigh on February 12. In the coming weeks, hundreds of protesters would be arrested, tried, and convicted on various charges—trespass, disorderly conduct, breach of the peace, loitering. As the protests moved farther south, the number of arrests increased. In the Deep South, protesters were subject to harsh reprisals. City officials in Montgomery, Alabama, responded with what one sit-in protester described as an immediate "brutal and wide-sweeping campaign of official verbal abuse, new laws, investigations, police and court action." The number facing criminal charges for civil rights protests soon reached into the thousands. When arrested, some refused to pay bail, electing instead to sit in jail until their trials; when convicted, some chose jail sentences over paying a fine.[7]

But there were other possible outcomes to a sit-in protest. The next move might come not from a store manager or police officer, but from the crowds of white boys and men prowling behind their backs, with their Confederate flags, some wearing the white robes of the Ku Klux Klan. It might be a relentless barrage of jeers or taunts. It might be a drink dumped on a head or a hot cigarette butt dropped down the back of a shirt. It might be getting yanked from a stool, thrown to the ground, and viciously beaten.

The sit-ins provided a drama with a familiar opening act, but whose ending varied day to day and place to place. Each community had its own sit-in story. The students could never be quite sure what to expect. And this made the sit-ins particularly newsworthy. Journalists from across the country arrived to cover the protests. It was compelling theater—exciting, inspiring, and, at times, appalling.

By the end of the spring, the movement reached across the entire South. According to one estimate, fifty thousand protesters took part in the sit-in movement. The Greensboro protest "started a brush fire," wrote one contemporary observer, "which in the brief period of two months has assumed the proportions of an unquenchable conflagration."[8]

Four unknown students in Greensboro had set in motion events that would move a nation. Their quiet, bold act ignited the pent-up hopes and frustrations of young African Americans. A new chapter in the struggle for racial equality began, one that was more openly defiant, more participatory, and, in many ways, more successful than any that had come before.

This book tells the story of the lunch counter sit-in movement of 1960, the events it set in motion, and what it achieved. In telling that story, I advance two arguments. First, I argue that the sit-ins cannot be fully understood without careful attention to the law—a point that historians of the civil rights movement have generally missed. Behind the now-iconic scenes of African American college students sitting in quiet defiance at whites-only lunch counters lies a series of underappreciated legal dilemmas—about the meaning of constitutional equality, the capacity of legal institutions to remedy different forms of injustice, and the relationship between legal reform and social change. At the time of the protests, some participants and many observers recognized the central importance of these legal issues. They remained at the center of debates over the sit-ins in the years immediately following, as the courts faced waves of appeals of protester convictions and as Congress considered a federal prohibition on racial discrimination by businesses that serve the public, including lunch counters and other eating establishments. Yet they have been largely overlooked in subsequent historical accounts. To understand the emergence and development of the sit-in movement, its reverberations throughout the nation in the years following, its achievements, and its failures, law must be at the heart of the story.[9]

Second, I argue that the national debate the sit-in protests generated about the constitutionality of racial discrimination in "public accommodations"—the legal term for privately owned and operated businesses that serve the general public—provides an illuminating case study of constitutional development in modern America. Although the students initiated the sit-ins with little conscious intention of making a formal claim of constitutional reconstruction, their actions sparked a debate on the scope of the constitutional meaning of equality that took place in the streets, in newspapers, in the offices of mayors, governors, and businessmen, in the courts, and in Congress. The courts, the traditional focal point for accounts of constitutional disputes, play a central role in this story, but judges were ultimately just one among many groups of influential actors. One of my goals for this book is to invite a broader understanding of how Americans have contested and constructed the meaning of their Constitution.

The lunch counter sit-ins stand apart from other major protest campaigns of the civil rights era in large part because they raised uniquely difficult and contested legal questions. As a general matter, the civil rights movement engaged the law in two basic ways. One was for activists to demand a change to established law. Laws and government policies that discriminated against African Americans defined southern society. Litigation challenges to segregation in public schools and to policies disenfranchising African American voters were aimed at removing flagrantly discriminatory laws from the books.

The other was for civil rights activists to demand that government enforce existing law. After the Supreme Court's breakthrough 1954 ruling in *Brown v. Board of Education* striking down state-mandated segregation in schools, the goal of most of the major protest campaigns of the civil rights era was to force southern officials to follow federal law or to pressure the federal government to step in and enforce its own law. The battles for desegregated education were largely efforts to get localities to comply with *Brown*. The 1961 Freedom Rides were designed to test a 1960 Supreme Court ruling declaring racial discrimination in interstate transportation facilities illegal. Their success, according to one of the organizers, depended "upon the racists of the South to create a crisis, so that the federal government would be compelled to enforce federal law."[10]

The sit-in movement was different. The legal history of the sit-ins does not fit comfortably in either the legal-change or legal-enforcement model. Some at the time understood what the students were doing as a challenge to existing law, either Jim Crow laws or the use of state authority to protect racial discrimination at lunch counters. Some saw it as an effort to enforce existing law, namely, the constitutional requirements of *Brown*. And some saw the protests as an effort to simply avoid these legal issues altogether and to remake racial practices through an appeal to morality rather than law. All these understandings could coexist because no one could state with much confidence what the law actually was when it came to the sit-ins. This pervasive uncertainty regarding the most basic question—*What is the law?*—set the sit-ins apart from the other major protest campaigns of the civil rights era.

By 1960 most southern states had either removed segregation statutes from the books or no longer enforced these laws. Most of the privately owned lunch counters the students targeted were not compelled to discriminate by law. But they were also not required not to discriminate by law. Outside the South, many states and localities had civil rights laws that prohibited racial discrimination in eating establishments and other public accommodations. Courts throughout the nation generally recognized a common-law right to service in places that provided lodging and in certain forms of public transportation, but they did not extend this right to service in retail or eating establishments. When sit-in protesters were arrested, southern officials charged them not with violating segregation policy, but with some race-neutral criminal violation, such as disturbing the peace, disorderly conduct, or trespass. The key question then—the question to which there simply was no clear answer—was whether a private citizen who operated an eating facility, subject to no legal requirement to segregate, could make racially discriminatory choices of whom to serve.[11]

The Supreme Court in the 1940s and 1950s launched two doctrinal revolutions involving its interpretation of the Fourteenth Amendment—the amendment to the Constitution ratified directly after the Civil War that prohibits states from depriving individuals of "life, liberty, or property, without due process of law" or denying them "the equal protection of the laws." One doctrinal revolution centered on the *scope* of the amendment's application. This involved a reconsideration of the limits of the Fourteenth Amendment's "state action" requirement. In its narrowest form, the state action doctrine is quite straightforward: The Fourteenth Amendment restricts government, not private individuals. The Supreme Court's seminal articulation of the state action doctrine, the *Civil Rights Cases* of 1883, outlined the basic public-private dichotomy on which the doctrine was based. The Fourteenth Amendment does not protect against "the wrongful acts of individuals, unsupported by State authority in the shape of laws, customs, or judicial or executive proceedings," the Court explained. "The wrongful act of an individual is simply a private wrong. . . ." The Court never abandoned this basic principle. Yet beginning in the 1940s, the Court steadily expanded the definition of state action to incorporate more and more activity that it had previously confined to the private sphere, thereby expanding the reach of the Fourteenth Amendment.[12]

The other, more famous Fourteenth Amendment revolution of the period involved the *meaning* of the equal protection requirement. The focal point of this line of cases was *Brown* and the Court's rejection of the *Plessy v. Ferguson* doctrine under which state-sanctioned segregation had been deemed to satisfy the equal protection requirement as long as equal facilities were available. If the facility at issue was publicly owned and operated, the law was clear. After *Brown* and decisions that soon followed extending *Brown*'s mandate to public beaches, golf courses, buses, and other publicly controlled facilities, segregation in government-operated facilities violated the constitutional requirement of equal protection. Similarly, if state or local law required the private lunch counter to segregate, the same reasoning applied: the law constitutes state action, the Fourteenth Amendment applies, and the segregation policy is unconstitutional.[13]

In the aftermath of *Brown*, these two lines of evolving equal protection doctrine—one centered on the scope of the equal protection clause, the other on its meaning—appeared to be converging. The Supreme Court not only reinterpreted the equal protection clause to prohibit state-sanctioned segregation; it also gradually expanded the reach of the clause into the private sphere. A business that opened its doors to all but refused to allow blacks to sit at the lunch counter seemed to mark the exact spot where these two lines of doctrine collided.

As a matter of constitutional law, the difficult situation arose when the owner of a public accommodation that was not required by state law either to segregate or not to segregate chose to discriminate. Could one claim that the discrimination policy of this "private" actor itself constituted an equal protection violation? The claim in this case would be based on the argument that a public accommodation that opens its doors to all customers and provides a basic service to its community, even if technically private, in effect functions as a state actor.[14]

Another legal wrinkle was the possibility of a constitutional challenge not to the owner's discriminatory choice, but to the involvement of the state in enforcing that choice. Even if there were no constitutional limitation to a private business owner's choice of whom to serve, there could be a constitutional problem when the owner, faced with an African American who refused to leave the establishment after being denied service, called the police. Although the police were acting under a trespassing or disorderly conduct statute—laws that were racially "neutral," in that the text of the statute made no reference to race—and although they were enforcing a private choice, the arrest and subsequent prosecution were obviously actions of the state. Were southern states denying African Americans equal protection of the laws by enforcing the discriminatory policies of private business owners? The critical precedent here was the 1948 case *Shelley v. Kraemer*, in which the Supreme Court held that judicial enforcement of private contractual agreements to refuse to sell property to African Americans violated the equal protection clause.[15]

At the heart of these constitutional questions is a dilemma basic to the entire premise of the state action doctrine: in modern society there is no unproblematic, neutral manner by which the line between the public and private spheres can be drawn. A group of legal scholars known as the legal realists had been insisting on this point since the early twentieth century, as they sought to break down the legal and conceptual barriers that limited the reach of the economic regulation. The public-private distinction on which the state action doctrine relies is not a fact. It is a decision. It is a legal construct. In practically any situation that might arise as a site of significant social contestation, state involvement of some sort can be located. State action might be found in state support or encouragement of private choice; the involvement of police or the courts in enforcing private decisions; licensing or regulatory schemes; the existence of durable customs that can be traced to prior or ongoing state action; the recognition that nominally private action is serving a particularly public function or affecting a public interest; or the acknowledgment that when the state has the capacity to act, the absence of state involvement is itself a choice—is itself a form of state "action." The inherent instability of the public-private distinction, amplified in the middle decades of the twentieth century by shifting judicial interpretations of the state action doctrine, meant that both sides of the contest over racial discrimination at lunch counters felt they had strong claims that the Constitution was behind their cause.[16]

Finally, there is the question of whether the federal courts or Congress should lead this particular constitutional transformation. Even if one believed that racial discrimination in this realm of public life violated the Constitution, was this a constitutional violation for which the courts could or should provide relief, or was the appropriate remedy for this found elsewhere, perhaps in the form of congressional action? If one concluded that this particular form of discrimination was constitutionally permissible, there remained the question of whether it should still be made illegal—legislatures, whether local, state, or federal, can protect rights beyond what the Constitution requires—because it violated basic principles of morality or it was unwise as a matter of policy.

This tangled web of legal questions gave the history of the sit-ins a distinctive trajectory. Although attacking racial discrimination at lunch counters and other public accommodations was integral to the civil rights movement of the 1960s, this particular facet of Jim Crow was not a central concern for racial justice groups prior to 1960—in part because civil rights lawyers saw other targets as more open to legal challenge. The student protesters thus aimed their energies at a target that was in certain ways a fresh one, its vulnerabilities uncertain. Yet because the legal issues were so fluid, the civil rights lawyers overcame their initial skepticism and joined the struggle. This is not to say the students always welcomed the lawyers when they arrived on the scene.

They were concerned that the lawyers sought to take over their movement by transforming their protests into a litigation campaign.

The contested legal issues also contributed to divisions among defenders of segregation. Those who opposed the students' claims differed on the strength of their commitment to segregation, on the lengths they were willing to go to protect segregation, and the role that the police and courts should play in this struggle. Southern officials generally wanted students arrested and prosecuted for their protest actions. Lunch counter operators were not anxious to send potential paying customers to jail and often hesitated to take this step.

At the Supreme Court, the justices struggled with the legal issues raised by the sit-ins. They were hesitant to give the civil rights movement another sweeping *Brown*-like constitutional victory—at least not on this particular constitutional claim. The state action issue that the sit-in challenge raised, according to one legal commentator, was the "most crucial" question that the Court faced in the early 1960s, and its resolution "may have more far-reaching implications and greater consequences than even" *Brown*. The justices overturned protester convictions in the sit-in cases, but they did so on narrow grounds, concluding that there was insufficient evidence to support a conviction or that there was direct state encouragement of or involvement in the lunch counter manager's decision to discriminate. It is one of the most extraordinary aspects of the legal history of the sit-ins that the Court never definitively answered the constitutional question raised by the sit-in protests.[17]

As a matter of law, the ultimate victory of the sit-in movement came not from the Supreme Court but from Congress, and it came more than four years after the sit-ins first captured the nation's attention. Title II of the Civil Rights Act of 1964 effectively outlawed racial discrimination in public accommodations across the nation. But between February 1, 1960, when the four students in Greensboro launched their first sit-in, and July 2, 1964, when President Lyndon B. Johnson signed into law the Civil Rights Act, the legal status of the students' claimed right to equal service remained an open question.

The sit-ins launched a national debate over the legality and morality of discrimination in public accommodations. "The whole Nation has to face the issue," Justice William O. Douglas wrote in 1964. "Congress is conscientiously considering it; some municipalities have had to make it their first order of concern; law enforcement officials are deeply implicated, North as well as South; the question is at the root of demonstrations, unrest, riots, and violence in various areas. The issue . . .

consumes the public attention." This book explains how a diverse collection of people, from college students and lunch counter managers to Supreme Court justices and members of Congress, struggled to come to terms with this issue.[18]

Why have historical accounts of the sit-ins missed the critical legal issues involved? Two reasons stand out. First, the students themselves made a self-conscious effort to define their actions as an alternative to traditional civil rights reform, as an alternative to litigation and lawyers. Historical accounts have generally embraced this perspective, leading to a focus on dynamics of social protest mobilization and organization rather than legal issues. This book will show, however, that the students' own anti-legalistic posture influenced their expectations about the law and the distinctive legal issues raised by racial discrimination in public accommodations.

Second, the legal history of the sit-ins lacks the dramatic courtroom victory that traditionally marks the triumphant endpoint of legal narratives. Unlike the powerful narrative arc of the history behind *Brown* or Clarence Gideon's fight for a right to a lawyer, the constitutional claim of the sit-in protesters never had its breakthrough moment in the Supreme Court. The passage of the Civil Rights Act was a dramatic and climactic moment, to be sure, but one that historians have generally connected to more proximate events, such as the dramatic 1963 protest campaign that Martin Luther King Jr. led in Birmingham, Alabama, rather than the student lunch counter protest movement that made headlines years earlier. Our historical understanding of the sit-ins thus has been detached from the legal context that shaped the movement and the legal debates that the movement sparked.

By insisting that the sit-in movement cannot be understood without careful attention to the distinctive legal issues involved in lunch counter discrimination, this book offers a fresh approach to this familiar but misunderstood historical episode. The law loomed large in the minds of movement participants, their opponents, and the many others—including judges, political figures, and the press—who played a role in the history of the sit-ins. Law should therefore have a central place in our historical reconstructions of these events. A full account of the sit-in movement requires a recognition of the ways that ordinary citizens with little knowledge or interest in the intricacies of constitutional doctrine were nonetheless moved by their assumptions about what the law required, what it allowed, and what it prohibited—

what scholars have called "legal consciousness." This book considers how various groups assessed the costs and benefits of relying on legal institutions. It also examines the nuances of equal protection doctrine as it stood in the early 1960s, for this was the terrain on which lawyers and judges struggled to make sense of the students' defiant challenge to the racial status quo. My goal in this book is to place in the foreground the legal issues that historical accounts of the sit-ins have too often relegated to the distant background.[19]

In *The Sit-Ins*, I strive to write a legal history in which the experiences, actions, and commitments of everyday people as they struggle to make sense of and improve the world around them blend, as seamlessly as possible, with formal legal change. My account seeks to capture the ways in which social action external to established legal institutions affects (or fails to affect) the path of the law as well as the ways in which formal legal norms translate into lived experience.[20]

Telling this story requires that I draw upon a variety of approaches to legal history. Narrowing my focus along certain dimensions—a single legal claim, charted over a five-year period—allows me to expand my cast of characters and institutional settings. Each of the following chapters revolves around a distinctly situated group of people who played a role in the legal history of the sit-ins: the student protesters, civil rights lawyers, movement sympathizers, civil rights opponents (a group that included white business owners, southern state officials, racist demagogues, and libertarian ideologues), the justices of the U.S. Supreme Court, and federal lawmakers who played a role in the passage of the Civil Rights Act of 1964. Each group confronted the constitutional claim that emerged from the sit-in protests. Members of each group were guided not only by their visions of the way the world should be, but also by their understanding of the tools they had at their disposal.

I consider not only how the claim fared in different contexts and different institutional settings, but also how it translated from one setting to another. I give careful attention to the ordering of rights claims: the way in which one institution treated a constitutional right often affected how other institutions subsequently evaluated the claim. One of the most valuable insights offered by recent scholarship on constitutional development outside the courts (what scholars sometimes label "popular constitutionalism") has been to emphasize the ways in which constitutional meaning emerges from the interaction of groups and institutions situated in distinct social contexts and responding to different institutional responsibilities—between, for example, movement activists and lawyers, courts and the political branches. It is at these points of intersection that we can see the crucial moments of recognition, the flow of alternative constitutional norms between society and its courts, the reconciliation of the formal language of the law and evolving social norms. The sit-in protests offer a rich case study to examine the ways in which constitutional claims took shape and were transformed as they moved into and through the legal system. The legal history of the sit-ins puts on display what one legal historian has described as "the movement of consciousness, arguments, and doctrine throughout the process of law creation."[21]

By giving proper attention to the distinctive organizational and institutional demands of these different groups, we can better understand the legal history of the sit-ins. We can better understand, for example, how student activists, civil rights lawyers, and liberal Supreme Court justices could all agree on the fundamental wrongness of racial discrimination at lunch counters, but could arrive at very different conclusions as to the proper remedy for this wrong. Or why southern business operators and student protesters shared a belief that the issue was best resolved outside of the courts, while southern politicians and civil rights lawyers shared a belief that the issue should be resolved in the courts. Attention to institutional sensibilities also illuminates the awkward dance between the Supreme Court and Congress that resulted in the passage and judicial approval of the Civil Rights Act.

It is to the young men and women who ignited this constitutional debate that we now turn.

ONE

The Students

We want the world to know that we no longer accept the inferior position of second-class citizenship. We are willing to go to jail, be ridiculed, spat upon and even suffer physical violence to obtain First Class Citizenship.

—STUDENT NEWSLETTER, BARBER-SCOTIA COLLEGE,

CONCORD, NORTH CAROLINA, FEBRUARY 1960[1]

As the lunch counter demonstrations spread across the South in early 1960, drawing in thousands of students and capturing the nation's attention, everyone—blacks, whites, supporters, opponents, the students themselves—struggled to figure out what was happening. Why had college students suddenly emerged as the protagonists of the nation's civil rights struggle? Why had they taken up this bold sit-in tactic? Why, of all the daily injustices that African Americans suffered in the South, did they focus on lunch counters? What was it about these particular protests that allowed them to catch on across the South like they did?

This chapter considers these questions from the perspective of the African American students who took part in the lunch counter protests in the winter and spring of 1960. When the students explained why they had been moved to action and what they hoped to achieve, one theme dominated: the sit-ins were about dignity. They spoke of the indignities of being refused service at a downtown lunch counter or cafeteria. They described the sense of pride they felt when they walked into one of these establishments, sat down, and refused to leave until served.

Even efforts to embarrass and demean them—whites dumping food on their heads, knocking them off their stools, kicking them on the floor; police officers marching them out of the stores and into police stations; judges telling them they were criminals—became, in the eyes of the students, new opportunities to display and demand recognition of their inalienable dignity. "I will not accept a back seat," announced one student leader following his first sit-in. "I will not accept being cast aside. I will not accept being ignored because I am a Negro."[2]

It is tempting to leave it here, with the sit-ins as a parable of resilient human dignity. Generations of subjugation and humiliation created a reservoir of frustration that eventually overflowed, expressed in an act of youthful resistance so simple and humane that it thrust before the eyes of a reluctant nation an object lesson in the vicious delusions of white supremacy.

Yet while this parable dominates American popular memory of the sit-ins—which we celebrate at commemorative events, watch in documentaries, and read about in everything from works of historical scholarship to picture books for children—it is limited as an explanation for this transformative chapter in American history. To explain why the sit-ins occurred when they did and achieved what they did requires situating the students' timeless claim of human dignity into its particular historical moment. We need to consider why thousands of young men and women shook loose the routines of their lives, why the protests took place at this time, and why, of all the indignities Jim Crow exacted, the students targeted this particular form of racial subordination. Economic and political factors—including the post–World War II growth of the African American middle class and explosion of American consumer culture—played key roles, as did the inspiring examples of anti-colonialism movements overseas and protests against segregation at home. To these, I add a factor that largely has been overlooked in histories of the sit-ins: the legal landscape of America in 1960.

Assumptions about what the law required, what it allowed, its capacity to uproot unjust practices, and the role of lawyers and courts in social change efforts all played a powerful role in defining how the students understood their situation. Although it was a moral sensibility—a belief that this form of racial discrimination was simply wrong—rather than any desire to make a legal claim that moved them to action, most of these young activists seemed to assume that the law was somehow on their side. They were demanding "rights which are already legally and morally ours," explained the leaders of the Atlanta student movement. Their actions were animated by the belief that the racial discrimination they suffered on a daily basis at these lunch counters was just as much a violation of their fundamental rights as discrimination in schools or voting or the many other realms of public life into which Jim Crow had extended its reach.[3]

As this chapter will detail, the sit-ins took shape at an opportune moment in the legal battle against Jim Crow. Legal breakthroughs such as the Supreme Court victory in *Brown v. Board of Education* had raised expectations for change. These expectations had dissolved into frustration as court-centered implementation failed to move a defiant white South to desegregate its schools. In launching the sit-in movement, the students offered an alternative to the litigation and lobbying campaigns that had promised so much but delivered so little.

The legal situation in 1960 also shaped the students' choice of target. One of the reasons racial discrimination at lunch counters was such an inviting and powerful objective for the sit-ins was the fact that, unlike schools or the polls, established civil rights organizations had largely avoided direct challenges to this particular facet of Jim Crow. Civil rights lawyers recognized the distinctively difficult legal dilemmas raised by privately operated businesses that served the public and thus focused their energies elsewhere. The relative neglect of this issue by others served the student movement well. Few of the students appreciated the concerns about constitutional doctrine that steered civil rights organizations away from the challenging discriminatory lunch counter service in the South. What they knew was that this was an offensive practice and no one seemed to be doing anything about it. Among the students themselves and among outside sympathizers, the sit-ins resonated in large part because it was clear that this was the students' protest, that it was not being orchestrated by faraway civil rights strategists or radical ideologues.

The students turned legal dilemmas into social movement opportunities. The atmosphere of frustrated expectations and legal uncertainty surrounding the sit-in protests proved critical to their achievements.

The Sit-Ins Begin

Precursors

As the sit-in movement spread across the South, many were left wondering: Where did this all come from? Everyone seemed to have an explanation. The students tended to emphasize the spontaneous elements of the sit-ins. The protests, they insisted over and over again, were nothing more than a necessary, commonsense response to this particular racial injustice. They were tired of the indignities of segregation, and no one seemed to be doing anything that actually changed their lives, so they acted. Leaders of civil rights organizations emphasized connections between the 1960 sit-ins and earlier protest campaigns—campaigns in which their organizations had more conspicuous roles. Segregationist opponents insisted that the students were actually controlled by "outside" groups intent on instigating racial unrest (perhaps not just outside the South, some insinuated, or just bluntly stated, but outside the United States).

Putting aside baseless claims that foreign Communists were behind the sit-ins, each of these seemingly contradictory explanations contain seeds of truth. The sit-in movement was a break from the past, a bold and largely unplanned venture into uncharted waters. Yet at the same time, established civil rights organizations played critical roles in the movement, and previous protest efforts, including earlier sit-ins, also contributed to the 1960 movement. A movement this decentralized, built upon thousands of individual and small-group decisions, was the child of many parents. It was spontaneous and independent. It was also a product of a complex network of communication between protest communities and the result of years of careful organization and planning. In its many locations and over its half-year life span, the sit-in movement was all these things.[4]

The two decades preceding the Greensboro sit-ins saw sporadic sit-in protests at lunch counters and restaurants. In the 1940s, the Congress of Racial Equality (CORE), a newly formed interracial organization committed to nonviolent protest, led restaurant sit-ins in Chicago; delegates at a Congress of Industrial Organizations meeting in Columbus, Ohio, sat in at a segregated restaurant; and African American federal employees in Washington, DC, sat in at segregated eating establishments. In the 1950s, CORE organized sit-ins in cities in the North as well as the Upper South. In 1959, CORE reached deeper into the South when it organized a series of sit-ins in Miami in conjunction with a workshop it held in the city.[5]

Another precursor to the Greensboro sit-ins was a protest campaign in the late 1950s that began in Oklahoma City and spread to cities across the Midwest. In 1958, members of the Oklahoma City NAACP Youth Council—led by Clara Luper, a high school teacher and the group's adviser—organized a series of lunch counter sit-in protests. Luper took a group of black children, ages seven to fifteen, into a downtown Oklahoma City drugstore, where, after being refused service, they sat until closing time. After several days of protests, the store's corporate management decided to desegregate lunch counters at its nearly forty stores in Oklahoma, Missouri, Kansas, and Iowa. When members of the NAACP Youth Council in Wichita, Kansas, heard about Oklahoma City, they began their own lunch counter sit-in. From there, sit-in protests and boycotts spread to several other cities in Oklahoma and Kansas.[6]

Although some scholars have insisted that these sit-ins, not the ones that took place in Greensboro in February 1960, mark the true beginning of the sit-in movement, it is important to recognize the limitations of the earlier protests. The press gave little coverage to these events. Victories could be frustratingly uneven. Lunch counters that activists thought they had desegregated would sometimes revert back to racial exclusion. The NAACP national office made no effort to publicize the actions of their youth branches. In fact, NAACP officials chastised Luper for organizing the protest and urged her to stop.[7]

The significance of these scattered, occasionally effective protests took on a new meaning after February 1960. Once it became clear that the sit-in movement was something to be embraced, the NAACP leaders discovered a new appreciation for what their Youth Councils in the Midwest had been doing in the preceding years, and they sought to link the Greensboro protests to the earlier sit-ins. The leader of the Durham NAACP Youth Council would later claim to have talked to the Greensboro Four (each of whom had connections to the NAACP through the Youth Councils) about earlier sit-in protests in nearby Durham. CORE founder James Farmer claimed that a CORE pamphlet that described early sit-in protests inspired the Greensboro Four to act.[8]

Despite these after-the-fact efforts, there was little evidence that these early protests had made much of an impression, if any, on those who initiated the 1960 sit-ins. The Greensboro Four, according to a person who interviewed them in the midst of the sit-in movement, had "heard vaguely of scattered protests such as the sit-in demonstration in Oklahoma in 1958, but their knowledge of this was hazy." In the many interviews they gave and statements they made in the winter and spring of 1960, they never mentioned earlier sit-ins. The influence the precursor sit-ins had on the student sit-in movement of 1960 was not as their model or inspiration, but as a piece of recent history that in February 1960 suddenly became a precious commodity among established civil rights activists struggling to claim a piece of credit for this new movement.[9]

Greensboro

When Ezell Blair, Franklin McCain, Joseph McNeil, and David Richmond walked into the Greensboro Woolworth on the afternoon of February 1, 1960, their demonstration could very well have followed the pattern of these earlier sit-ins. They could have gotten some local attention. They could have convinced a local restaurant operator to stop discriminating. Maybe, as in Oklahoma, they could have even inspired others to follow. But this time, to everyone's surprise, including the four freshman who started it all, things turned out quite differently.

From the first afternoon sitting at the Woolworth lunch counter, the Greensboro Four knew what they wanted. They wanted to be served while seated at the counter, just like any other paying customers. They wanted to demonstrate—to themselves, to their classmates, to their parents, to the whites who defended segregation—the severity of the injustice of racial discrimination and their commitment to doing something about it. Beyond this, as they were the first to admit, they had no elaborate plan of action. In the end, their February 1 sit-in is best described, in the words of historian Clayborne Carson, as "a simple, impulsive act of defiance."[10]

As more protesters joined the sit-ins in Greensboro, the demands of organizing and negotiation forced themselves upon the students. Thus began an often uneasy dance between the inspired spontaneity that brought the movement to life and the inescapable demands for strategy and guidance. Three days into the protest, the head of the Greensboro NAACP, George Simkins—who had no experience with and assumed the national NAACP office had little interest in this kind of protest—contacted CORE for help. Two CORE field secretaries headed to the South to conduct workshops in nonviolent protests, while others organized pickets of Woolworth and Kress stores in the North. CORE was the first of the national civil rights organizations to take decisive action in support of the students.[11]

As the Greensboro sit-ins gained strength, the opposition mobilized. On the fifth day of the sit-ins, with protesters numbering in the hundreds, the local Ku Klux Klan arrived in downtown Greensboro, joining forces with what one reporter described as "young white toughs with ducktail haircuts." "There were loud rebel yells, catcalls and clapping by white teen-agers along with shouts of 'tear him to pieces' and loud profanity." When these "toughs" paraded around waving Confederate flags, black students responded by waving American flags. As the tension rose, student spokespersons emphasized the need to maintain the decorum that they felt was integral to the protest. "We don't expect violence," one explained, "but if it comes we will meet it with passive resistance. This is a Christian movement." The police were there in force, with over thirty plainclothes and uniformed officers on the scene. Officers escorted a number of white men and women who were verbally abusing the protesters out of the store and arrested three white men— one for drunkenness, one particularly vocal person for disorderly conduct, and one who tried to set fire to a protester's coat for assault.[12]

That night, student leaders found themselves in a two-and-a-half-hour meeting with representatives from the local Woolworth and Kress stores and administrators from the area colleges (who were generally sympathetic toward the students' cause but not their tactics). The store managers agreed to a two-week study period to investigate whether local custom would allow for an integrated seating policy, but only if the students halted their sit-ins. When the student leaders shared their proposal at a meeting of about fourteen hundred students (which they did "without conviction," complained the chancellor of the Greensboro branch of the University of North Carolina, who was leading the negotiations), it was unanimously rejected. The sit-ins continued.[13]

The next day was Saturday, and the sit-in protesters were waiting outside the Woolworth when it opened. Soon some six hundred people—integrationists, segregationists, newspaper reporters, and curious onlookers—crammed into the eating area. Around midday someone called the store to say there was a bomb in the basement. The police emptied the store, but they found no bomb. "The Negro students set up a wild round of cheering as the announcement of closing was made and carried their leaders out on their shoulders," reported the local newspaper. They moved on to the nearby Kress store, which promptly shut down. Then they marched back to campus, chanting, "It's all over" and "We whipped Woolworth." Police blockaded the street behind them to prevent the white counter-protesters from following. The mayor issued a statement that praised the students for being "orderly and courteous," asserted that "peace and good order will be preserved throughout our city," and called on students and business operators to find a "just and honorable resolution of this problem." That night the students held another mass meeting. This time, they agreed to a two-week sit-in moratorium, for the purpose of "negotiation and study." When the Woolworth and Kress stores reopened on Monday, they kept their lunch counters closed. The first stage of the Greensboro sit-ins had come to a close.[14]

The Spark Catches

By this point, just a week after the Greensboro Four made their fateful decision to sit at the Woolworth lunch counter, the protests, which had gained the attention of the local and national press, inspired college students in other North Carolina cities to start their own sit-ins. On February 8, students in Durham and Winston-Salem started protests at their local lunch counters. In the following days, students in Charlotte, Raleigh, Fayetteville, Elizabeth City, High Point, and Concord joined what quickly became a statewide movement.

This first wave of North Carolina sit-ins followed the Greensboro model. They often started with a bold, spontaneous act. The Winston-Salem sit-ins began when Carl Matthews, an African American graduate of the Winston-Salem Teachers College who worked at a local factory, sat down at the lunch counter of the Kress store in the middle of the lunch rush. He asked for service and was refused. A waitress eventually gave him a glass of water. Matthews sat and smoked. In the middle of the afternoon, six other African Americans, several of whom were students at the Teachers College, joined him. In Raleigh, protests were sparked by a local radio announcer who confidently predicted that area college students would not follow Greensboro's lead. Intent on proving him wrong, the following morning a group of students went downtown and the Raleigh movement began.[15]

As in Greensboro, white counter-protesters flocked to the sit-ins, and with them came sporadic acts of violence and threats of more serious retribution. White youths threw eggs at black students seated at the Woolworth lunch counter in Raleigh. The protesters "gave no reaction either to this or to jeers and catcalls thrown at them," a reporter noted. Bomb threats became a common tactic for disrupting sit-ins. After a bomb threat shut down a Durham Woolworth store where some forty students (including four white students from Duke University) were engaged in a sit-in, protesters turned their attention to other segregated lunch counters in the downtown area, closing them down too.[16]

These early North Carolina protests also displayed important variations from the Greensboro template. In High Point, high school rather than college students initiated the sit-ins, and they received close guidance from adult civil rights leaders. Before their first sit-in, they had reached out to a supportive local NAACP official. For their first day of sit-ins, the students had impressive leadership: Fred Shuttlesworth, the firebrand Birmingham-based civil rights activist who happened to be visiting North Carolina when the sit-ins broke out, and Douglas Moore, a North Carolina civil rights leader. (After participating in the first High Point sit-in, Shuttlesworth called Ella Baker, executive director of the Southern Christian Leadership Conference (SCLC), in Atlanta and asked her to pass on a message to his close friend Martin Luther King Jr. "You must tell Martin that we must get with this," he said. The sit-ins "can shake up the world.") The High Point protests also ran into some new obstacles. The day after sit-in protests led to a shutdown of two variety store lunch counters, a local merchant paid off a group of white high school students to arrive early and occupy all the lunch counter stools at the Woolworth so the black protesters had nowhere to sit. When they came back the next day, the store had converted its lunch counter into a display counter and each stool was adorned with a box of Valentine chocolates. The students converted their sit-in to a stand-in and stood vigil over the chocolates through the morning. When large numbers of whites and black adults arrived, curious to see this unusual demonstration, the manager took police advice and shut down the entire store.[17]

On February 10, Hampton, Virginia, became the first city outside North Carolina to become a target of sit-in protests. The next day, sit-ins spread to two more Virginia cities, Norfolk and Portsmouth. Meanwhile, sit-ins broke out in new cities in North Carolina: Salisbury on February 16; Shelby on the eighteenth; Henderson on the twenty-fifth; Chapel Hill on the twenty-eighth.[18]

The first student arrests of the movement occurred on February 12. For several days, students had been targeting a Woolworth store at a shopping center outside Raleigh. After they once again forced the manager to shut down his lunch counter, the protesters gathered on a sidewalk outside the store to decide their next move. The manager of the shopping center informed police, who were already on the scene, that he wanted to bring trespassing charges against the students, and forty-one students were arrested. The students secured a lawyer, who promptly denounced the sidewalk arrests as a violation of the students' First Amendment rights and vowed to take the case to the U.S. Supreme Court if necessary. The students took their lawyer's advice to put a hold on protests at the shopping center pending the outcome of their court cases. They were convicted and fined $10 each, but state courts quickly overturned their convictions.[19]

On the same day of the mass arrest in Raleigh, lunch counter protests spread deeper into the South. Students in Deland organized the movement's first Florida sit-in. In a widely reported event, about a hundred demonstrators sat in at two lunch counters in Rock Hill, South Carolina. The Rock Hill protest attracted the attention of white youths, "mostly teen-aged boys with duck-tail haircuts," according to the *New York Times* reporter on the scene. Some of these "angry whites," the reporter added, "appeared to be juvenile delinquents." One of the delinquents knocked a black protester from his stool; another threw an egg at a demonstrator. Someone threw a bottle of ammonia into a store, setting off fumes that stung the eyes of the demonstrators inside. Bomb threats then cleared everyone out of both the targeted stores. The *New York Times* put the Rock Hill protest on its front page—another first for the sit-in movement.[20]

On February 13, students in Nashville joined the sit-in movement. In fact, Nashville students had been planning a protest campaign targeting downtown lunch counters for months. ("In an orderly and logical world," wrote one historian, "the great wave of student sit-ins that washed across the South early in 1960 should have flowed outward from Nashville.") Reverend James Lawson, an African American divinity student at Vanderbilt University, led preparations. Lawson was the project's director for the Nashville Christian Leadership Council, an affiliate of Martin Luther King Jr.'s Southern Christian Leadership Conference. A devoted follower of the nonviolent principles espoused by Mahatma Gandhi, Lawson had served a prison sentence for his refusal to report for the draft during the Korean War and then spent three years in India as a Christian missionary. In 1958 he began leading workshops in Nashville on nonviolent protest techniques, and in late 1959 he helped organize small-scale test sit-ins of local lunch counters, with the goal of confirming targets for sit-in protests that would begin after the holidays.[21]

When the Greensboro protests began on February 1, students in Nashville had yet to follow through on their plans. Lawson called a meeting to discuss whether the students in Nashville were ready to act. Older blacks who attended the meeting urged the students to delay, concerned that they needed time to line up a lawyer and raise money to have on hand for bail if the students were arrested. Another week passed before the Nashville protests began.[22]

Over a hundred students, including about ten whites, joined the first Nashville sit-ins. The protests were carefully organized, orderly, and relatively uneventful. Five days later, the next round of sit-ins brought out some two hundred students. Two days later, an estimated 350 students targeted four downtown variety stores. Each of the stores closed when the demonstrators appeared. Police were present throughout but made no arrests. Then another week passed before the next round of protests. This time students targeted five downtown stores. A young reporter named David Halberstam (who would go on to become one of the most prominent journalists of his generation) wrote the following account:

The scene was Woolworth's, and it was an almost unbelievable study in hate. The police were outside the store at the request of the management. Inside were almost 350 people, all watching the counter like spectators at a boxing match. To the side of the counter, on the stairs leading to the mezzanine, was a press gallery of reporters and photographers. At the counter were the Negroes, not talking to each other, just sitting quietly and looking straight ahead. Behind them were the punks.

According to Antoinette Brown, a student from New York who took part in the Nashville sit-ins, it felt "inevitable" that the situation would explode. "There is going to be bloodshed. I can feel it everywhere." "The slow build up of hate was somehow worse than the actual violence," Halberstam wrote. "The violence came quickly enough, however." For more than an hour, the assaults against the demonstrators escalated—taunting, spitting, hitting, first slaps, then blows; then banging the demonstrators' heads against the counter and dropping hot cigarette butts down the backs of their shirts. White boys dragged three of the black male protesters from their stools and started beating them. "The three Negroes did not fight back, but stumbled and ran out of the store; the whites, their faces red with anger, screamed at them to stop and fight, to please goddam stop and fight. None of the other Negroes at the counter ever looked around. It was over in a minute." At this point, the police stepped in, arresting eighty-one sit-in protesters (but no whites) on charges of disorderly conduct.[23]

By the end of March, just two months after the first sit-ins in Greensboro, the student protest movement had spread to eleven states and sixty-five cities in the South. Students from over forty colleges and universities had taken part in the movement. In the words of a writer for the *Chicago Defender*, the sit-ins "ripped through Dixie with the speed of a rocket and the contagion of the old plague."[24]

What Moved the Students?

What explains this remarkable explosion of protest activity? To answer this question requires first considering why this generation of young African Americans was so ready to act. Although moved by the raw indignities of life in a segregated society, students who took part in the sit-in movement were also inspired by recent breakthroughs in the long struggle for racial justice. Events of the 1950s had created within the ranks of African American college students a combustible blend of heightened expectation for racial progress and continued frustration with the intransigent reality of life in the Jim Crow South.

"Plain Optimistic"

Reasons for optimism were not hard to find. The students who took part in the sit-ins were born at a time when major strides were being made to break down some of the harshest inequities of white supremacy. World War II marked a turning point in American racial politics. As the nation mobilized against Nazi Germany, calls for the nation to live up to its own egalitarian ideals gained new resonance. African American soldiers returned from the battlefields of Europe and Asia less willing to accept second-class citizenship. The war also accelerated the demographic transformation of the Great Migration, and the growing population of African Americans in the urban North created a powerful voting bloc courted by both major political parties. In 1944 the Supreme Court struck down all-white party primaries. Since the Democratic Party dominated southern politics, the Democratic primary was often the only election that mattered. The demise of the white primary thus led to significant growth in the black vote in the South.[25]

In the years after WWII, American segregation became a geopolitical liability as the United States vied with the Soviet Union for the loyalties of peoples in Africa and Asia. Jackie Robinson broke Major League Baseball's color line in 1947. The following year, President Harry S. Truman ordered the desegregation of the military, and the Supreme Court ruled that courts could no longer enforce racially restrictive covenants in property deeds. The Court followed with 1950 rulings striking down segregation in graduate and professional schools and then, in 1954, came the Court's historic ruling in *Brown v. Board of Education*, declaring state-mandated segregation of public education unconstitutional. Three years later, Congress, for the first time since Reconstruction, passed a civil rights law. Although compromises and concessions watered it down to the point where everyone knew the law would accomplish little, it was a start. At the time of the sit-ins, Congress was considering another civil rights bill.[26]

Although much of the progress on civil rights issues in the 1950s came in the form of federal institutions that imposed their will on resistant southern states and localities, this was not always the case, particularly in the states of the Upper South. In the years preceding the sit-ins, in response to growing African American political influence, the Greensboro city council desegregated the city's police force, bus station, airport, and public libraries (although the council also shut down a municipal golf course rather than integrating under court order and sold a public swimming pool to a private party to avoid integrating it). Winston-Salem had desegregated most public facilities, and there were African Americans in its police and fire departments. Nashville adopted a gradual school desegregation plan and integrated its buses. At the time of the sit-ins, African Americans served on the Nashville police force, city council, and board of education.[27]

These breakthroughs signaled promising fissures in the historical acceptance of white supremacy by white-controlled institutions. The students who joined the sit-ins, observed one journalist, were "the first generation of American Negroes to grow up with the assumption, 'Segregation is dead.'" They grew up in a world in which expectations had been raised, in which new possibilities for a more equal and just society seemed within reach.[28]

Alongside these legal developments, recent displays of African American activism loomed large in the consciousness of the sit-in protesters. Knowing that whites in positions of power were condemning racial discrimination generated a sense that change was possible, even imminent; knowing that fellow blacks were standing up against racial injustice inspired them to do the same. The students who took part in the sit-ins often spoke of being inspired by acts of heroism by African Americans whom they had read and heard about.

The Montgomery bus boycott, which had taken place a few years earlier, was an inspiration for many of the students who were involved in the sit-ins. John Lewis, who would become one of the student leaders of the Nashville movement (and who would eventually have a long career as a member of Congress), was fifteen years old and living in a sharecropping community outside of Montgomery when the bus boycott began. "We didn't have television, but I kept up with what was going on, on radio, in newspaper, everything," he recalled. "In the papers that we got in the public school system in the library, I read *everything* about what was happening there, and it was really one of the most exciting, one of the most moving things to me to see just a few miles away the black folks of Montgomery stickin' together, refusing to ride segregated buses, walking the streets. It was a moving movement." When Martin Luther King Jr.—who as a young minister rose to national prominence because of his leadership of the bus boycott—came to Greensboro in 1958, he gave a sermon that "brought tears to my eyes," recalled one of the Greensboro Four. King "is a genuine hero for Negro students," noted one contemporary observer.[29]

Students in the sit-in movement also spoke of being inspired by school integration efforts in Little Rock, Arkansas, in 1957, which became a national drama when President Dwight D. Eisenhower deployed federal troops to enforce a school desegregation order. In the shadow of armed soldiers, nine black boys and girls walked into the newly integrated school while surrounded by taunting, threatening crowds of whites. The events in Little Rock made a powerful impression on the generation of black students who, three years later, would join the sit-in movement. About the same age as the Little Rock Nine, these students saw in Little Rock a demonstration of the power of young people taking a leading role in the struggle for racial justice. The Greensboro Four spoke of being inspired by the scenes of young people shaking the nation's conscience by the simple act of walking through a schoolhouse door.[30]

Students also cited anti-colonial campaigns in Africa as a source of inspiration. "Even the most unintellectual of these students are conscious of the African independence movement and at least vaguely moved by it," one reporter found. "Their heroes tend to be African," noted another. When student protest leaders wrote an open letter to President Eisenhower in April 1960, they described "the Africa struggle" as "a concern of all mankind." More established civil rights leaders encouraged the students to recognize their connection to freedom struggles elsewhere. King declared to a gathering of student leaders: "All peoples deprived of dignity and freedom are on the march on every continent throughout the world. The student sit-in movement represents just such an offensive in the history of the Negro peoples' struggle for freedom."[31]

For many students who in early 1960 were opening their eyes to the world around them, struggling to come to terms with their place in society, real change seemed possible. When reporters and social scientists talked to the students involved in the sit-ins, they were often struck by their sense of confidence in racial progress. "Optimistic, that's what I was, plain optimistic," recalled one young African American when describing how he felt upon first joining the sit-in movement. "I thought we'd demonstrate and then they'd fold up before us." The sit-in movement's early strongholds were in Greensboro, Nashville, and Tampa, relatively progressive southern cities in terms of racial politics, cities in which young blacks could believe old barriers were crumbling. This sense of optimism was a critical component in giving the students the confidence to act.[32]

Alongside this sense of hopefulness, however, was a sense of frustration, even disillusionment, with the state of race relations. This, too, was critical in moving the students. Of all the many ways of life in the Jim Crow South that frustrated the hopes of young blacks, none was more relevant and more personally felt than the lack of progress in the area of school desegregation.

Brown *and the Sit-Ins*

For the students who took part in the sit-in movement, the Supreme Court's 1954 school desegregation decision in *Brown v. Board of Education* embodied the mixture of hope and frustration that moved them to act.

Although the ordeal of actually desegregating public schools that followed would forever complicate *Brown*'s legacy, in 1954, when the Supreme Court first announced its decision, it appeared in the eyes of many Americans that the Court's ruling inaugurated a new day in American race relations. "The entire South will meet the test of the Supreme Court decision in the spirit of loyal, law-abiding citizens," Channing H. Tobias, chairman of the NAACP board of directors, confidently told a meeting of black leaders. There was a moment of opportunity in the year or so after the first *Brown* ruling—a moment that has largely been forgotten, swept away and overwhelmed by the defiant campaign to resist school desegregation that would soon take over the South. When the Court announced its ruling, and for a brief period following, white leaders across the South, while often expressing disapproval of the decision, mostly accepted it as the law of the land and resigned themselves to compliance. The first southern city to announce it would comply with the Court's ruling was the birthplace of the 1960 sit-in movement, Greensboro, North Carolina.[33]

Because of these heightened hopes, the minimal desegregation that resulted was all that much more disappointing, especially among younger African Americans. In the months and years that followed, as the courts approved limited, gradual—often so gradual as to be imperceptible—desegregation plans, and as President Eisenhower, himself a skeptic of legally mandated racial integration, refused to publicly endorse the Court's ruling, white opposition to *Brown* solidified and expanded. Early expressions of acceptance of *Brown*, in Greensboro and elsewhere, became embarrassments for southern political leaders, forgotten, repudiated, and replaced by various forms of resistance to desegregation. These ranged from open defiance of the Supreme Court, the "massive resistance" campaign waged by many southern states, to more subtle forms of resistance, such as the "middle-of-the-road" path embraced by North Carolina, where leaders determinedly searched for the minimal amount of desegregation that federal courts would accept. The result was stunning in its effectiveness. In the five states of the Deep South, there were 1.4 million black schoolchildren. Not one attended a racially mixed school in the years between 1954 and 1960. In the Upper South, the numbers were only marginally better, representing nothing more than token efforts at compliance. In three North Carolina cities where some of the first sit-ins took place—Charlotte, Greensboro, and Winston-Salem—only thirteen African American students were enrolled in previously all-white schools.[34]

When asked why they took part in the sit-ins, students often expressed frustration with the minimal progress that southern states had made toward desegregating their schools in the years since the Supreme Court issued *Brown*. The school desegregation decision was a topic of discussion in the Greensboro Four bull sessions that led up to their historical protest. "We are simply expressing what people everywhere believe, that the pace of desegregation and the securing of civil rights is ridiculously too slow," explained one student leader. "Not one Negro student in over a hundred interviewed had any vivid personal recollection of the day" *Brown* was decided, one journalist reported. "They all regard it as a failure." The generation of African American students who took part in the sit-ins had been told that racially segregated schools violated the Constitution, yet they continued to attend the same all-black schools. Students across the South felt "a profound impatience with the rate of change," noted Leslie Dunbar, executive director of the Southern Regional Council, which provided detailed reports on the sit-in movement. The primary reason for this impatience was "disillusion and disgust over the progress of school desegregation."[35]

At the time of the sit-ins, *Brown* was (as it remains today) a resonant if deeply conflicted symbol. The most significant Supreme Court decision of the twentieth century represented at once the power and the powerlessness of legal change to advance the cause of social justice. *Brown* "seemed so important" when it first came down, one sit-in leader explained. "It said to me that this democracy works and that things I knew were really wrong really were wrong. And so I waited for them to change. But then there was all this dodging and skuldugging and hiding and then the young Negroes got the idea that it wasn't going to happen—or at least it wasn't going to be done for us." *Brown* symbolized the possibility of change from the apex of the American legal order, which was no small thing, to be sure. But it also made painfully clear the frustrating reality that real change required more than proclamations from on high.[36]

The complicated attitude the students of the sit-in movement held toward *Brown*, equal parts inspiration and frustration, offers additional insights into a debate that has occupied historians and legal scholars in recent years over the relationship between *Brown* and the direct-action protests of the civil rights era. The long-held assumption—forcefully expressed in press accounts, popular histories, and legal scholarship—was that *Brown* catalyzed a wave of social protest. By declaring state-mandated segregated schools unconstitutional, the Supreme Court redefined the terms of the game, placing the law of the land behind the cause of racial equality and providing the crucial spark that would ignite the civil rights movement. *Brown* "fathered a social upheaval"; it "sired" the movement; it "initiated a social revolution." For advocates of this account, *Brown* served as a powerful example of the critical role of the courts in promoting social change.[37]

A recent generation of scholars has challenged this account. In his provocative 1991 book *The Hollow Hope*, political scientist Gerald Rosenberg argues that the social impact of *Brown* was minimal. Not only was there minimal desegregation of southern schools in the decade after the Court ruled, but the decision, he concludes, had little effect on the black protests of the late 1950s and 1960s. In a series of articles published in the 1990s and then in a major 2004 book, *From Jim Crow to Civil Rights*, legal historian Michael Klarman also sought to debunk the traditional, celebratory account of *Brown*, although his revisionist account recognizes that *Brown* was in fact deeply consequential. It was just that its consequences were found mostly in the actions of its opponents. *Brown*'s greatest effect on the course of the civil rights movement, Klarman argues, was indirect: it mobilized the white South to resist desegregation at all costs. The threat of integration, which *Brown* thrust into the consciousness of the white South, radicalized southern politics. This led to the bloody and highly publicized confrontations in Birmingham, Selma, and elsewhere, which in turn led to increased support in the North for civil rights and transformative national legislation such as the Civil Rights Act of 1964 and the Voting Rights Act of 1965. Klarman has labeled this the "backlash thesis."[38]

With regard to the possible linkage between *Brown* and the student sit-in movement, Rosenberg rejects any relevant connection. Klarman gives more sustained attention to the question and comes to a more qualified conclusion. He recognizes that "over the long term, *Brown* may have encouraged direct action by raising hopes and expectations, which litigation then proved incapable of fulfilling," but then he emphasizes the difficulties of "precisely measur[ing]" this connection. The six-year gap between *Brown* and the sit-ins "suggests that any such connection must be indirect and convoluted." "The outbreak of direct-action protest," he concludes, "can be explained independently of *Brown*."[39]

A closer look at the students who took part in the first wave of sit-ins in early 1960, however, shows that *Brown* and its aftermath were significant. The connection between the Supreme Court's proclamation and the student protests may have been "indirect and convoluted," as Klarman puts it, but this does not mean that *Brown* had no effects. To appreciate the influence of "top-down" law, we need to move beyond a model of judicial declarations either being followed or defied and recognize activists mobilizing around their own conceptions of their legal rights, which are influenced but not dictated by what judges have to say. Innovative recent work on the history of law and social movement mobilization has focused less on whether formal legal change produces social change and more on the ways in which law operates within different institutional and social settings.[40]

Thus, with regard to the sit-ins, the evidence suggests that the traditional claims that *Brown* served as some kind of unambiguous inspiration for the students is very much overblown. On this point, the revisionists are basically right. African Americans "did not need the Court's moral instruction to convince them that racial segregation was evil," Klarman notes. When discussing what moved them to take action, the students did not credit the Supreme Court or even Thurgood Marshall and the NAACP's litigation efforts.[41]

Yet *Brown* and other Supreme Court decisions nonetheless played a central role in the development of the sit-in movement. What *Brown* did was raise expectations for change that failed to materialize. This, in turn, fueled skepticism, even antagonism, toward litigation as a pathway to racial justice among the students who were on the front lines of the lunch counter sit-ins in the winter and spring of 1960. They distanced themselves from the NAACP's civil rights legal reform efforts, portraying civil rights lawyers as out of touch with their own concerns. One student complained that when someone asks the NAACP, " 'What can I do personally, right now?' they have no answer." "Many students regard the N.A.A.C.P. as stodgy and slow," a reporter found. "We are all dissatisfied with this slow legal maneuvering," explained one of the first wave of sit-in leaders. The anger and frustration that moved the students in early 1960 was aimed at not only the white defenders of Jim Crow, but also those who insisted the freedom struggle was best fought through formal channels of legal reform.[42]

No one captured this sentiment more powerfully than James Lawson. In his speech at the April meeting of student leaders in Raleigh, North Carolina, Lawson attacked the civil rights establishment. "Already many well-meaning and notable voices are seeking to define the problem in purely legal terms," he warned. "But if the students wanted a legal case, they had only to initiate a suit. But not a single city began in this fashion. . . . [T]he sit-in movement is not trying to create a legal battle." It is trying to address "that which is more than law"—"the habits of mind and emotion of both Negro and white." A failure to properly attend to these "inner attitudes and fears" had undermined efforts to desegregate schools, Lawson noted. He praised the sit-in movement as "a judgment upon middle-class conventional, half-way efforts to deal with radical social evil" and derided the NAACP as too focused on "fund-raising and court action rather than developing our greatest resource, a people no longer the victims of racial evil who can act in a disciplined manner to implement the [C]onstitution." "The legal redress, the civil-rights redress, are far too slow for the demands of our time," he explained. "The sit-in is a break with the accepted tradition of change, of legislation and the courts. It is the use of a dramatic act to gain redress."[43]

"None of the leaders I spoke to were interested in test cases," Michael Walzer (a Harvard graduate student who would go on to become one of the most prominent political theorists of his day) reported in an influential article covering the first weeks of the sit-ins. "That the legal work of the NAACP was important, everyone agreed; but this, I was told over and over again, was more important." The very identity of the first wave of sit-in protesters was shaped, in large part, by their opposition to court-focused approaches to civil rights.[44]

For the students, the courts were something to be avoided—not because they might lose in court, but because even if they won, they were skeptical that real change would follow. This was the ironic lesson that the great legal victory in *Brown*, which six years later had yet to produce significant results in southern schools, had taught the sit-in generation.

Generational Differences

When the Greensboro Four sat down at the Woolworth lunch counter on that fateful winter afternoon, the first person to respond was a black woman who worked in the kitchen. "You boys are getting yourselves into a lot of trouble," she told them. "You know you can't be served here." When they refused to leave, she called them "ignorant" and a "disgrace" to their race.[45]

The four young black men had little idea what to expect as they sat nervously on their stools. But the angry reception they received from this older black woman hardly surprised them. One of the themes of the bull sessions the Greensboro Four had as they talked themselves into walking downtown to the Woolworth was their frustration with the older generation of African Americans. Too many older blacks "have been complacent and fearful," Blair explained to a local reporter on the second day of their sit-ins. "It is time for someone to wake up and change the situation and we decided to start here." When two social scientists interviewed the Greensboro Four, they were struck by the frustration with, even animosity toward, what they saw as an apathetic or cowed older generation. One of the four, they noted, "was contemptuous of his grandmother's generation and their fearfulness. 'I began to see what those people were made of deep-down.' His tone of voice was bitter when making this statement."[46]

Much of the motivation for the protests emerged from frustration toward leaders within the African American community—with what the students saw as a too easy acceptance of Jim Crow by their parents and grandparents, and too strong a faith in painfully slow courtroom battles by established civil rights figures. Many participants saw the sit-ins as a way to send a message of impatience, even defiance, to their elders. "There can be no progress without struggle, and every struggle bears casualties," Blair declared, in reference to blacks who refused to support the student protests. The *Amsterdam News*, a New York–based black newspaper, reported that "where Negroes have stood or got in the way of the mushrooming movement, the Negro students and their leaders have not hesitated to lash out at them as they lashed out at whites who have barred their way."[47]

"Our adults are too worried about security to do anything," complained a student at North Carolina College. "They are too afraid of their jobs. We've got to do it. And we're not afraid." Some went so far as to describe Jim Crow as having "brainwashed" their parents into a state of "complacency" and fearfulness. They have had "subordination instilled" into their minds. "Mamma, I love you," an arrested protester told her mother when she came to bail her daughter out of jail. "But I am not free. And I'm not free because your generation didn't act. But I want my children to be free. That's why I'll stay in jail." The sit-in tactic captured the students' sense of frustration with their parents' generation and their approach to civil rights.[48]

These harsh judgments were, as student activists acknowledged in their more reflective moments, quite unfair. Their parents grew up in a world in which this kind of defiant protest could very well result in being lynched. "The elder Negro of the South learned all his life that he had a particular place in his society and that the white man had absolute control over him," explained student leader Edward B. King Jr. "Today's young Negro student has never had a chance to learn this fear. We have been raised in larger towns and cities, we have traveled more, and we have had more contact with the world. We Negro students have been so well educated that we cannot adjust to a Southern way of life that is wrong." Some recognized that their parents' hesitancy to embrace this kind of reform had much to do with their vulnerability to economic retaliation.[49]

On occasion, students offered a more sympathetic perspective on their relationship to their parents and their parents' generation, something approaching a sense of duty or responsibility. "My parents learned to live with segregation, to wait, to go to the back of the bus," explained a student involved in the Tallahassee sit-ins. "They saved and sacrificed on a little farm so as to send me here. In times of deep despair I would imagine I could feel the sweat of my father's and mother's hands on the coins in my pocket. I'd like to live long enough and be a part of whatever it takes to see them have a little dignity in their lives."[50]

Some of the students' criticism of their parents' generation was also simply inaccurate. Many older African Americans were dedicated to the struggle that these young men and women felt they had just discovered. Ezell Blair Sr., whose son so passionately criticized his parents' generation, was himself a bold and dedicated civil rights activist who supported his son's actions. And once the sit-in movement was under way, older blacks largely came out in support of the students. Indeed, the extent of their support—which ranged from moral encouragement to financial support to joining boycotts to sometimes even joining sit-in protests—repeatedly surprised the students and observers.[51]

But for all its unfairness and inaccuracies, this bluster and hyperbole about the conservatism and complacency of their parents served as an effective organizing tool for the students. Frustration with the perceived timidity, the acceptance of second-class citizenship, on the part of their parents' generation was a powerful tool for mobilizing the Greensboro Four and the thousands of students who followed in their footsteps.

"Tragic Inconveniences"—Why Lunch Counters?

In retrospect, lunch counter sit-ins seem such an obvious next step in the black freedom struggle. Yet before February 1960, lunch counters were hardly an obvious target. Why, then, did the students focus so much energy on this particular facet of Jim Crow America?

An African American student who wished to protest racial injustice in 1960 had plenty of targets to choose from. Through law and custom, in ways both oppressively comprehensive and capricious, white Americans had constructed a system of racial inequality that pervaded the nation. There were countless areas of racial oppression that the students might have targeted: Southern schools and public transportation were still largely segregated; African Americans still faced systematic disfranchisement throughout the South; the criminal justice system was notoriously biased against blacks. Practically any of these options would have given the students stronger, clearer legal justifications than an assault on privately owned lunch counters. These options would also have had the benefit of joining ongoing campaigns by established civil rights organizations. If the students had asked lawyers and civil rights leaders for guidance prior to initiating their protests, they would not have been advised to challenge segregation in privately owned lunch counters.[52]

Yet chain store lunch counters that refused to seat black customers were a particularly attractive target. Commentators have long emphasized the symbolic value of the protests. Here were students demanding equal service in this most American of institutions: the variety store lunch counter. They were seeking to join what historian Lizabeth Cohen has called the "Consumers' Republic," a republic that exploded in size and influence in the middle decades of the twentieth century and revolved around a conception of citizenship that included equal participation in the economic sphere. By 1960 Americans increasingly recognized participation in the consumer marketplace as on near-equal footing with participation in the political system and other basic legal rights. Activists of all sorts were focusing on the marketplace as a locus for social change activism.[53]

The symbolic value of lunch counters as a target for protests also stemmed from the particularities of this discriminatory practice. In the late 1950s, when James Lawson and the Nashville group were discussing where to focus their protests, a group of middle-class black women shared their experiences shopping downtown. They talked about the humiliation of separate bathrooms (or no restrooms at all) for blacks and the lack of respect from white employees. And they also talked about how they could go to a department store and be served at all the sales counters, but not at the lunch counter. Mothers said that having their children experience all this was particularly painful. Martin Luther King Jr. gave an eloquent summary of the "tragic inconveniences" of this particular form of racial oppression. "The answer" for why the students targeted lunch counters "lies in the fact that here the Negro has suffered indignities and injustices that cannot be justified or explained," he wrote. "Almost every Negro has experienced the tragic inconveniences of lunch counter segregation. He cannot understand why he is welcomed with open arms at most counters in the store, but is denied service at a certain counter because it happens to sell food and drink. In a real sense the 'sit-ins' represent more than a demand for service; they represent a demand for respect." "Like pouring salt into an open wound" was how one of the Greensboro Four would later describe the department stores' practice of embracing black customers throughout the store, but refusing them service at their lunch counter. It was "both injury and insult," southern writer James McBride Dabbs wrote in an account of the protests titled, appropriately enough, "Dime Stores and Dignity." "Sitting at a lunch counter may seem like a small thing to some," explained one participant, "but the right to do so is so inextricably bound up with the American idea of equality for all." It was the raw, personal experience of exclusion from department store lunch counters, not any specific legal claim, that pulled the student protesters toward this particular target.[54]

Alongside the symbolic and substantive importance of discrimination in the consumer marketplace generally and lunch counters in particular, a more prosaic factor played an equally important role in steering the students to this target: availability. As African American journalist Louis Lomax explained, the protesters "wanted to get into the fight and they chose the market place, the great center of American egalitarianism, not because it had any overwhelming significance for them but because it was there—accessible and segregated." Both before and after the sit-ins, racial discrimination in public accommodations ranked at the bottom when African Americans—young and old, self-described conservatives and liberals—were asked to rank the importance of different areas of racial discrimination. Just as the schools had been an attractive target of opportunity for the NAACP lawyers who devised the strategy that culminated in *Brown*, lunch counters were attractive targets for the students.[55]

Why Did the Protests Spread So Quickly?

Alongside the questions of why sit-ins and why lunch counters, another closely related question fascinated observers at the time and has intrigued social scientists ever since: Why did the sit-in movement spread as quickly and as far as it did? The factors discussed above—the attractiveness of the direct, dignity-based protest to the students, the particular indignities of lunch counter discrimination, the availability of this particular protest target—all played a role in pulling new groups of students into the movement. But a fuller analysis of why the sit-ins spread across the South in the winter and spring of 1960 points to at least three additional factors: the communication networks that spread news of the protests and supported protest mobilization; the replicability and accessibility of the sit-ins as a protest tactic; and the outside support that student protesters received. I consider the first two factors below; the third is the subject of a later chapter.

Networks

Key to the spread of the sit-in movement were communication networks—what social movement scholars call "channels of diffusion." The networks that played the most significant role in the diffusion of the sit-ins can be divided into four categories: the news media, colleges, churches, and movement organizations.

News media. The way most people learned of the protests was through radio and newspapers. When asked what moved them to act, one early protester answered simply, "Well, we read the papers." The sit-ins were a major news story across the South, particularly when the protests brought out the white counter-protests and sporadic episodes of violence. News accounts were not only an inspiration and a challenge to African American students in cities where protests had yet to happen; they also provided sometimes quite detailed operating instructions for those planning their own protests.[56]

Colleges. Much of the dispersion of information and peer-pressure dynamics that set in motion the protest movement came through the various communication networks that linked the black colleges and universities where most protesters were to be found. "Students, faculties and college presidents testified that after the Greensboro incident a strange fever swept across the campuses of the country's 120 Negro colleges," reported a journalist. "Within a week of Greensboro there was scarcely another topic of conversation on Negro campuses." Various explanations for how this fevered conversation spread from campus to campus have been offered. There is the "basketball thesis": the first wave of sit-ins occurred at schools that were in the same basketball conference, and competitive pressures between the schools might have inspired new protests. Some have suggested that dating patterns between the colleges might provide some of the connections. One study identified a correlation between the students involved in extracurricular campus activities and those who participated in protests, hypothesizing that the two might be connected based on the students' involvement in intercollegiate networks (although it likely had as much to do with their personalities).[57]

Churches. The sit-in movement also drew on existing organizational networks within the African American community, particularly the churches. Sociologist Aldon Morris—author of an influential study of the sit-ins as an episode in social movement mobilization—has insisted that the black church, not the black college campus, was the real heart of the sit-in movement. Morris demonstrated how in various communities the southern black church provided the essential tools for protest mobilization. It was a place where students met and organized. Activist church leaders regularly played key roles in organizing sit-in protests. And relationships among church leaders provided valuable communication networks that helped spread the reports that fueled the sit-in movement.[58]

Movement organizations. Most commentators at the time of the sit-ins reported what the students themselves proclaimed over and over: The students were acting on their own; they were not following the lead of adults or "outside" civil rights organizations. There is a good deal of truth to this characterization, particularly in the early weeks of the sit-ins. Yet the point should not be pushed too far. Adult activists were never far from the scene. In some places they played a minimal role in spreading and supporting the protests, but in other places their contributions were essential. Particularly important were the local chapters, youth councils, and college chapters of the NAACP; activists within the SCLC orbit, such as James Lawson in Nashville, also played key roles in certain locations. Although the role of established civil rights organizations was sporadic in the early weeks of the movement, it increased in significance as the movement progressed through the spring of 1960.[59]

In April 1960, student leaders would create their own civil rights organization, although here, too, they had important assistance from established organizations. SCLC executive director Ella Baker took the lead in organizing a conference for student activists. The "Youth Leadership Meeting" was held at Shaw University in Raleigh, North Carolina, on April 15–17. Baker assured the students that this was not a ploy by older civil rights activists to take over the student movement. "Adult Freedom Fighters will be present for counsel and guidance, but the meeting will be youth centered," she wrote in the call for participation. Baker worked tirelessly throughout the meeting and afterward to ensure that the students remained in control of the movement they had started. The students, she wrote in her summary of the meeting, "were intolerant of anything that smacked of manipulation or domination."[60]

The meeting was a success. It received national press coverage and brought together 142 student leaders (including ten whites) from eleven southern states plus the District of Columbia, representing over fifty different colleges and universities. Some sixty mostly white northern students also attended.[61]

The conference led to the creation of the Student Nonviolent Coordinating Committee (SNCC, pronounced "snick"), which would be based in Atlanta. SNCC was initially conceived of as a temporary organization that would help guide the local student protest movements that were already under way around the South. Its founders, many of whom were drawn from the Nashville group, created a decentralized organization, based on consensus building among smaller groups. It quickly became one of the civil rights movement's most important organizations.[62]

Tactics

The genius of the lunch counter sit-in was its simplicity. As a protest tactic, it was straightforward and easily replicated. The message the protesters sought to communicate was clear and powerful. It could be conveyed through nothing more than an image. A photograph of a group of well-dressed African American college students sitting unserved at a lunch counter said it all. A key strength of the movement was what sociologist Doug McAdam describes as the "accessibility" of the protest tactic. Unlike, say, a bus boycott, a sit-in could be launched by a small group; it could be used anywhere there was a segregated lunch counter.[63]

The tactic of the sit-in protests allowed for an immediate sense of accomplishment for many students. Many different outcomes could be seen as an achievement. Being part of this new defiant movement was an achievement. Simply creating student-run organizations that would strategize and coordinate sit-in protests might be cited as a "gain" for the movement. According to one observer, the sit-in "Workshop" not only trained students on the mechanism of a lunch counter protest, it also functioned as a "cohesive, morale-building mechanism which served to infuse an ideology into the Negro student participants."[64]

Joining a demonstration brought "a feeling of great release," explained Robert Moses, one of the legends of the black freedom struggle. A North Carolina student noted that in the Deep South, where "resistance to integration has only been entrenched" as a result of the sit-ins, "the best the Negroes can expect is a truce with honor, where students who've participated can hold up their heads in the knowledge they have flexed their muscles and lost no ground." For the most dedicated of freedom fighters, even enduring a beating was a victory. "This was an experience we needed," one participant said about the violence against sit-in protesters. As James Bevel, one of the leaders of the Nashville student movement, put it, "Maybe the Devil has got to come out of these people before we will have peace."[65]

Students also saw going to jail as a valuable experience, both for the individual protester and the larger movement. The students thus transformed the very response that segregationists saw as their greatest weapon against the protesters—the police officer, the paddy wagon, the jail cell—into a victory for the protesters. "These are members of a generation that talks constantly of 'the movement' and 'the struggle' and asks newcomers seriously, 'Have you been to jail?'" noted one journalist.[66]

And then there were the desegregation breakthroughs that the sit-in tactic produced. Changing a single person's mind could be a victory. When asked about what exactly they hoped to get out of their protests, a common answer was quite simple: they wanted the lunch counter operator, the person standing right in front of them, to let them sit down and be served. "We don't want brotherhood," one protester announced. "We just want a cup of coffee—sitting down." "All I want is to come in and place my order and be served and leave a tip if I feel like it," said another. One high school student was quite blunt in what he was after. "We don't care about eating here as such," he said. "We just want the right to come here." The "students have found something that is down to earth, has human appeal, and brings visible results," James Robinson, executive secretary of CORE, explained.[67]

Soon after the protests began, students began to see tangible results, as a growing number of restaurants desegregated in the face of the protests. At first the breakthroughs were small and uncertain. On March 7, a group of African Americans were served at what had been a whites-only lunch counter in Winston-Salem. The next morning all the stools in the lunch counter had been removed. That same day, in Salisbury, North Carolina, African American students were denied service at two drugstore lunch counters but then served at three others. The Southern Regional Council declared this "the first genuine victory of the movement." The first negotiated citywide lunch counter desegregation of the movement took place in San Antonio, Texas, on March 15, when local business leaders, working with local religious leaders, agreed to end their segregation policy before the protests actually hit their stores. Business owners in Galveston soon followed San Antonio's lead. By the end of the spring, lunch counters in eleven cities had begun to desegregate under pressure from sit-in protests.[68]

The most significant breakthrough of the spring was in Nashville. After an initial round of sit-ins, the students had called a pause to their protest to await the proposals of a committee appointed by the mayor. When the committee could do no better than propose that businesses desegregate a portion of their lunch counter for a ninety-day trial period, the students resumed their sit-ins, which were accompanied by a mass local boycott of downtown retail stores. (King praised the Nashville movement as "the best organized and most dedicated over the Southland today.") The turning point in Nashville came on April 19, when segregationists bombed the home of Z. Alexander Looby, an African American who was a member of the Nashville city council and a lawyer representing the students. (Looby and his wife escaped injury.) Later that day, nearly four thousand marched to city hall to confront Mayor Ben West about the escalating violence. When asked if he believed the lunch counters in Nashville should be desegregated, West, for the first time, publicly sided with the students, a concession that was, in the students' eyes, a crucial step toward an eventual breakthrough in Nashville. Following the mayor's dramatic pronouncement of support for the students, further negotiations between the store owners and protest leaders led to an agreement during the first week of May.[69]

The integration of Nashville's lunch counters was a carefully orchestrated affair. At 3 p.m. on May 10, after the lunch crowds had cleared, a group of African Americans, "carefully chosen, middle-class, well-dressed, well-mannered" and "on their best behavior," according to one news account, entered six downtown stores, sat down, and were served. "Negro patrons conducted themselves with dignity," an editorial in the *Chicago Tribune* approvingly noted. "Everything was serene." One reason for the prosaic nature of the event was that the agreement under which the lunch counters desegregated included a news blackout: local radio and television stations and newspapers did not publicize the event in advance. The other customers in the store were mostly plainclothes policemen. During the three-day interim period, the agreement was that blacks would only sit with other blacks and that no blacks would ask for service on the first Saturday of desegregated service (since this was the day "country people" tended to come into the city to shop). Although the event lacked the tense drama of the protests that had shaken the city in the previous months ("How much can you write about a mother and a child eating a hamburger?" complained one reporter), it did, for a moment at least, symbolize something of an achievement for a city whose citizens prided themselves on being better than their southern neighbors when it came to race relations. The breakthrough in Nashville made the front page of northern newspapers.[70]

The trickle of desegregation victories strengthened in the coming months. The summer of 1960 saw a number of new additions to the list of cities that had desegregated their lunch counters, as operators of targeted stores took advantage of the slowing or cessation of protests when school was not in session to make changes as inconspicuously as possible. In late June, lunch counters in several cities in northern Virginia ended their segregation policies after just two weeks of sit-in protests. On July 9, following a settlement between students and local business owners, lunch counters in Charlotte began serving blacks. Then, on July 25, "quietly and without incident," the Woolworth and Kress stores in Greensboro, the scene of the protests that six months earlier had set the sit-in movement in motion, served their first black customers at the lunch counter. The store managers made the decision, following the recommendation of the interracial committee the mayor had appointed. "The sky did not fall," the local paper noted. The *New York Times* found the event worthy of front-page coverage under the headline "Sit-Ins Victorious Where They Began."[71]

By midsummer, the Southern Regional Council issued a report identifying twenty-seven southern cities in which lunch counters desegregated in response to sit-ins. "No store in the South which has opened its lunch counters to Negroes has reported a loss of business," the widely publicized report noted. "Managers have reported business as usual or noted an increase. . . . Negroes have not congregated to demonstrate a victory. . . . White customers have observed the change calmly for the most part. . . ."[72]

Although these victories were more a steady trickle than the wave of reform the students were hoping for, and although they did not penetrate into the Deep South, they were generally understood to be an incredible achievement for a movement that seemingly sprang out of nowhere. "Buried in the reams of copy about the southern sit-ins," noted a CORE newsletter in April 1960, "is the fact that since the protest movement started, over 100 lunch counters and eating places in various parts of the south have started to serve everybody regardless of color." Victories over racial discrimination attracted attention, gave the protests an air of achievement, and pulled more and more people into the movement. After the Nashville breakthrough, Marion Barry, a leader of that city's student movement who had been appointed temporary chair of the newly formed SNCC, declared that the sit-in movement "demonstrates the rapidity which mass non-violent action can bring about social change." The movement offered students what Leslie Dunbar of the Southern Regional Council described as "the sweet experience of success." "You could put your hands on some changes," explained David Richmond, one of the Greensboro Four.[73]

Defining their goals in ways that could be actually realized in the near term empowered the students. Although restaurant operators generally resisted students' demands to desegregate, the most common response was to shut down the lunch counters temporarily in the face of the protests, an act that showed the students the power of their concerted actions. When the Greensboro protests led to the first lunch counter closing of the movement, cheers erupted from the students and, in a premature burst of enthusiasm, they started shouting, "It's all over." In the early weeks of the sit-in movement, a Woolworth in Hampton, Virginia, converted its lunch counter into a sales counter, and a McClellan dime store in Nashville removed all the stools from its lunch counter. When Nashville city officials and business leaders agreed to create an interracial committee to discuss the protesters' demands, students saw this as a significant victory—this was what they had been demanding. Merchants sometimes felt that students were too eager to declare success. In Raleigh, students announced they were calling off their protests at the local Kress store after they had been served coffee and donuts "indiscriminately" while standing at a lunch counter. The Kress store official explained that the store had not changed its policy, however. "They would just like to claim a victory," he explained. The possibility of these small-scale, tangible moments of accomplishment energized the sit-in movement in those critical opening months in the spring of 1960.[74]

Summer of 1960 and Beyond

When the spring term came to an end and many of the college students who were the leaders and the rank and file of the sit-in movement left campus, the lunch counter sit-in campaign, at least as a region-wide phenomenon, dissipated. Even before the end of the school year, there had been signs that the movement was slowing. The feverish excitement of those opening months was impossible to sustain. Much of the early energy had been channeled into more organized forms, such as coordinated boycotts and negotiations. As early as April, the *New York Times* was reporting that sit-in demonstrations had become "sporadic"; "more and more the conflict appears to have entered a cold war phase" in which "court and propaganda battles" took center stage. Leaders increasingly complained about students' declining interest in joining protests. When the term ended, support for demonstrations was increasingly difficult to maintain.[75]

With most college students scattered to hometowns and summer jobs, the work of the sit-ins was left to others. High school students took over the protests in some cities. In Rock Hill, South Carolina, a college student activist led a sit-in with a group of black children between the ages of ten and fourteen. In Knoxville, where a student movement had never really taken off, a group of black and white professionals (some of whom had opposed the student protest movement) formed a group they called the Associated Council for Full Citizenship and launched their own sit-ins. Their carefully orchestrated campaign was far more effective than the halting student protests that had preceded it, and in a matter of just over a month, they convinced Knoxville's merchants to provide service on a nondiscriminatory basis.[76]

By the summer of 1960, the sit-in movement had run its course, but the lunch counter sit-in, as a protest tactic, had not. It would remain one of the most powerful weapons of the larger civil rights movement for years to come.

The very success of the sit-in movement created new challenges for the students. Desegregating a lunch counter was a significant achievement. But everyone, integrationists and segregationists, recognized that this was but a step toward larger, more ambitious goals. The struggle for first-class citizenship was, as Ella Baker famously put it, "bigger than a hamburger." Some student activists turned their attention from lunch counters to other public accommodations and public facilities. In the Upper South, students turned their attention to suburban shopping centers and movie theaters. The Howard University students who had led successful sit-ins in northern Virginia targeted a segregated Maryland amusement park. NAACP Youth Councils began a summer "wade-in" campaign to desegregate public beaches along the East Coast. None of these efforts caught on in quite the way the lunch counter sit-ins had. According to one account, "A dwindling number of Negro students were sufficiently enthusiastic about these less immediate and electrifying actions."[77]

————

The students who organized and participated in the sit-in protests that spread across the South in the winter and spring of 1960 set in motion a cascade of events that would transform the civil rights movement and, eventually, remake civil rights law across the nation. They believed their actions were justified not only based on principles of morality and basic human decency, but also on the nation's foundational legal commitments. "As I sat," one student explained, "I could be speaking to the world and saying, in effect, 'I believe in the Declaration of Independence and the Constitution of the United States. Do you?'" The movement, according to student leaders who spoke to the Democratic Platform Committee at the party's national convention in July 1960, was intended to "affirm equality and brotherhood of all men, the tenets of American democracy as set forth in the Constitution, and the traditions of social justice which permeate our Judaic-Christian heritage." Their demonstrations were at once an effort at moral suasion— pleas to the hearts and minds of the white southerners, and beyond them to the nation at large—and a claim of their fundamental rights grounded in the United States Constitution.[78]

Theirs was what we might label an aspirational constitutional claim. It was a claim that drew upon one of the most foundational of constitutional principles—the right to equal protection of the law. But it was a claim that, at the time of the sit-ins, had never been squarely recognized in a court of law.

The key to understanding the students as constitutional claim-makers is to recognize that it did not matter that the courts had never recognized this kind of constitutional claim before. When the Greensboro Four launched their protests, and when thousands of young men and women across the South joined the sit-in movement, they did not even see themselves as making a formal "constitutional" claim—at least not one that required judicial recognition. In fact, the motivations for the first generation of sit-in protesters in the spring of 1960 pointed in the exact opposite direction: they wanted to make a case for equal treatment and respect, for first-class citizenship, that would not have to be settled in the courtroom. They did not see constitutional lawyers and judges as the arbiters of their claim. If their protests were turned into a formal legal issue, they feared they would lose control over them. Their claim would become a lawyers' cause. It would no longer be theirs. The very point of the protest was to create opportunities to *enact* their claim. By resisting the reduction of their efforts into a formal legal claim and by putting their faith into protest and negotiation, they might lose the leverage of a claim based on federal law, but they gained something that was, to them, considerably more valuable: they were able to maintain control over the course of their challenge.

To now turn the sit-ins into a formal legal claim—or worse, a legal claim whose legitimacy would depend on recognition in the courts—would seem to go against what the students and their supporters saw as the most innovative and valuable aspect of the protest. Yet this was precisely what the NAACP lawyers hoped to do.

TWO

The Lawyers

This situation has made all of us reassess ourselves.

—THURGOOD MARSHALL, MARCH 1960[1]

"There is a collision of two philosophies in the current efforts to end segregation in the South," warned Clarence Mitchell, director of the NAACP's Washington bureau. It was mid-April 1960 and Mitchell was explaining to NAACP executive secretary Roy Wilkins how the sit-in movement had transformed the landscape of civil rights reform. The students protesting at lunch counters across the South and the leaders of the nation's oldest and most influential civil rights organization were united in their commitment to ridding the nation of the stain of racial segregation. But they had quite different ideas about how this would be best accomplished.[2]

NAACP leaders did not oppose protest activity. They recognized the importance of publicity and economic pressure in creating the conditions necessary for racial progress. No one questioned the bravery of the students and the idealism that moved them. But as the first waves of sit-in protests spread across the South, awakening a generation of young African American activists, a cloud of unease and skepticism hung over the New York City headquarters of the NAACP and the NAACP Legal Defense Fund (LDF), the organization's legal arm. The NAACP's leaders believed that for all the attention gained and passions aroused, the protests risked being of limited actual effect because they were not a part of a strategized, coordinated reform agenda. They also worried that the bold actions of these students risked pushing their own work to the sidelines. No one felt these concerns more than the NAACP lawyers.[3]

To the lawyers who worked at the NAACP's national office and at LDF, the sit-in movement was not just a remarkable demonstration of dignified defiance. It was also a threat. The students who led and joined this new movement challenged, in ways both explicit and implicit, basic assumptions the lawyers held about the nature of civil rights reform. The civil rights lawyers sought to make sense of this dramatic departure from the litigation strategy they had famously pioneered over the previous decades. The lawyers knew how to take on Jim Crow in the courts. But now they struggled to define a role for themselves in this new rapidly unfolding drama.

This chapter examines the sit-ins from the perspective of the NAACP lawyers. I focus on lawyers in the national office (under the leadership of NAACP general counsel Robert L. Carter) and in LDF (under Thurgood Marshall), most of whom were initially skeptical toward the student movement—both of the strategy the students chose and of the legal merits of their claimed right. (In contrast, NAACP local branch leaders, some of whom were lawyers, generally supported the students from the start.) Yet Marshall and his colleagues soon came to reconsider their legal assessment and to see the sit-ins as an opportunity to revitalize their own work.[4]

By transforming the students' protest into a constitutional litigation campaign with the primary goal of winning test cases in federal court, these lawyers sought to remake the students' challenge into a more traditional civil rights claim, an approach they believed was the best way to ensure lasting reform. This chapter shows the first of several efforts to translate the students' constitutional claim into a new form and a new language. What began as a dramatic public act of nonviolent sacrifice and solidarity also became, in the hands of these skilled lawyers, an ambitious legal argument, one designed to persuade judges to reassess the meaning of the Constitution.

Civil Rights Lawyering, January 1960

Frustration. If there was one word to describe the atmosphere in the New York City offices of LDF, this was it. Before the explosion of the sit-in movement, Thurgood Marshall and his fellow LDF lawyers were frustrated—at how effective the obstructionist tactics of the defenders of school segregation were proving, even after the victory in *Brown v. Board of Education* in 1954; at the failure of the African American community to rally around the implementation battle; and at the inability for clear legal victories to translate into racial change.

Just a few years earlier, the atmosphere among the LDF lawyers had been hopeful, even celebratory. *Brown* marked a dramatic culmination of a litigation campaign decades in the making. Having persuaded a unanimous Court to abandon over half a century of contrary precedent and to reinterpret the Fourteenth Amendment's equal protection clause to prohibit states from requiring racial segregation in public schools, the lawyers felt a new day was dawning. They had not only won over the Supreme Court; they had also gained the support of presidential administrations from both major political parties—Truman's Justice Department filed an amicus curiae ("friend of the court") brief supporting LDF's position when *Brown* was first argued before the Supreme Court in 1952; Eisenhower's Justice Department did the same when the case was reargued the following year. Although there was the expected outcry from whites in the Deep South, in the rest of the nation reaction to the opinion tended to fall within a spectrum that ran from grudging acceptance to celebration. The ruling was an "inevitability," wrote the editors of *Life*. The Court had simply "kept pace with educational and social progress." Under the title "Emancipation," a *Washington Post* editorial explained: "The decision will prove, we are sure—whatever transient difficulties it may create and whatever irritations it may arouse—a profoundly healthy and healing one. It will serve—and speedily—to close an ancient wound too long allowed to fester."[5]

The period immediately following *Brown* was filled with optimism for LDF lawyers. In September 1955, *Time* put Thurgood Marshall on its cover. The accompanying article described "the astounding progress of racial desegregation" that *Brown* had set in motion. And although Marshall did not get the immediate desegregation with strict timetables that he asked for in *Brown II*, the implementation decision the Supreme Court issued in 1955, he still believed the Court had given the lawyers the tools they needed to bring down Jim Crow schools. In a private conversation, he declared: "The more I think about it, I think it's a damned good decision! . . . [T]he laws have got to yield! They've got to yield to the Constitution." "We've got the other side licked," Marshall proclaimed in early 1956. "It's just a matter of time." In the aftermath of the *Brown* decisions, Marshall's optimism was more the rule than the exception among the decision's supporters.[6]

This hopefulness dissolved in following years as segregationists rallied behind a last-ditch defense of Jim Crow and as racist demagoguery came to define southern politics. The magnitude of the gathering storm of southern white resistance was clear by early 1956. In March, practically all southern members of Congress (including a number who had initially counseled moderation in response to *Brown*) put their names on a statement, soon to be known as the "Southern Manifesto," denouncing *Brown* as "a clear abuse of judicial power." The Southern Manifesto's goal, wrote *New York Times* reporter Anthony Lewis, was "to make defiance of the Supreme Court and the Constitution socially acceptable in the South—to give resistance to the law the approval of the Southern Establishment." In February 1956 a young black woman named Autherine Lucy, backed by a court order the LDF lawyers had secured, attempted to enroll at the University of Alabama. White mobs instigated several days of violence, and the university responded by suspending Lucy. After more rounds of legal challenges, Lucy decided she had had enough and chose to drop her challenge. The entire experience was "traumatizing" for the lawyers, LDF lawyer Jack Greenberg recalled. Thurgood Marshall wondered whether they should just stop pursuing desegregation cases in the Deep South. Even if the courts could be convinced to issue strong desegregation rulings, dedicated white resistance seemed an insuperable obstacle to implementation.[7]

Whites in the Deep South blocked any school desegregation in the years immediately following *Brown*; in the Upper South, the best that LDF achieved was token compliance. The segregationists won "the first round in the battle for compliance," conceded an African American congressman in the spring of 1957.[8]

To make matters worse, NAACP branches throughout the South were in a fight for their own survival. In an effort to run the civil rights organization out of business, southern state governments sought to publicize their membership lists, a transparent strategy to expose NAACP members to intimidation and retribution. They also prosecuted civil rights lawyers for supposed violations of legal ethics rules. Much of the time and effort of the LDF lawyers in the post-*Brown* period focused on defending their legal work from these challenges.[9]

By early 1960, much of the LDF lawyers' optimism that had accompanied the *Brown* victory had dissipated. "In light of the present status of the law, no speedy or immediate resolution of the school segregation problem can be forecast," Robert Carter informed NAACP members several weeks before the first Greensboro sit-in. The lawyers had come to accept that the current agenda would be dominated by stalling maneuvers and nominal integration efforts—"a lot of fast play around second base," as Marshall put it. School "integration is not even considered a serious possibility" in the Deep South, the *New York Times* reported in January 1960. "I consider the [school desegregation] lawsuits as a holding action," Marshall explained, in a statement that captured the dramatically chastened vision of the NAACP lawyers toward the ability of the federal courts to end Jim Crow. "The final solution will only be when the Negro takes his position in the community, voting and otherwise."[10]

So, in a sense, the sit-ins gave Marshall what he wanted. The students were certainly asserting their position in their community. The problem was that, from Marshall's perspective, the students were using the wrong tactics and they had latched on to the wrong issue.

The Lawyers Confront the Sit-Ins

"The students took everybody by surprise," Marshall confessed. The student protests sparked a moment of reevaluation for the lawyers in the NAACP's national offices. It was, in the words of an internal memorandum, "a period of soul-searching, of testing, of weighing in the balance." The new wave of protests threatened their work. It seemed to give strength to "the many ill-informed hints from outside that we may have outlived our usefulness." In a widely discussed *Harper's* article, African American journalist Louis Lomax declared publicly what many at the NAACP were discussing privately: The sit-ins were "proof" that the NAACP "was no longer the prime mover of the Negro's social revolt."[11]

NAACP leaders struggled to figure out the best approach to dealing with the new wave of protests. "Unless we have . . . control" over the sit-ins, worried Robert Carter, "we cannot gain too much concentrating on sit-ins except a 'me too' to" other civil rights organizations that were more in tune with the protesters, such as CORE and SCLC. In these internal discussions, NAACP program director James Farmer was particularly blunt in his assessment:

Doubtless the sit-ins will creep into every discussion, as they should, but we cannot appear to be overwhelmed by their impact. . . . I seriously doubt that we should publicly air our confusion and uncertainties on this subject. . . . In the meantime, I think we must maintain the posture of knowing precisely where we are going, while at the same time speeding up our efforts through "inner circle" discussions to find out where we really want to go.[12]

Although the lawyers sought to create out of the sit-ins a systematic challenge to public accommodations discrimination, they realized that, unlike school desegregation litigation, they had little control over the unfolding of this civil rights campaign. "The legal questions and sequence of cases were being determined by students and prosecutors," Jack Greenberg recalled. "It was nearly impossible to make a plan that we could follow closely." Marshall had a record of skepticism toward direct-action protest and civil disobedience. Furthermore, as a dedicated anti-communist, he (like many white liberals of the day) generally dismissed public protest actions as tactically ill-advised. Even if the protests had no direct linkages to leftist organizations, they were vulnerable to accusations of radical infiltration. The students, he believed, were simply heading in the wrong direction. At a time when he was struggling with the daunting challenge of convincing the South to obey the new law of the land as defined by *Brown*, Marshall feared tactics that involved breaking laws "would devastate and undermine the progress that had been made."[13]

Marshall's uncertainty, even antagonism, toward the sit-ins was more than a lawyer's skepticism toward social protest as a tool for legal change, however. Marshall also had reservations about whether, in demanding nondiscriminatory service at these lunch counters, the students were on the right side of the law. His reading of the relevant legal doctrine made him doubt that the students had a viable constitutional claim.

When the sit-in movement began, Marshall was in London, where he was helping to draft a new constitution for Kenya. Upon returning home and learning what was happening, he immediately called a staff meeting. As recalled by Derrick Bell, a young LDF lawyer, Marshall "stormed around the room proclaiming in a voice that could be heard across Columbus Circle that he did not care what anyone said, he was not going to represent a bunch of crazy colored students who violated the sacred property rights of white folks by going in their stores or lunch counters and refusing to leave when ordered to do so." (LDF attorney Constance Baker Motley, who also witnessed Marshall's performance, worried that her boss might have a stroke.) Recognizing the limitations of existing equal protection doctrine, Marshall emphasized that, as a legal matter, targeting privately owned lunch counters was a completely different situation than if the protests had taken place in publicly owned facilities. "I don't want any of you trying to defend so-called protestors who are really trespassing on private property—unless you can come up with some powerful arguments that I know you can't because they don't exist," he told his staff.[14]

At a time when the efforts of the civil rights lawyers aimed to highlight the importance of the rule of law in the face of southern state defiance of the Supreme Court's school desegregation decision, not to mention continued disregard of procedural protections for blacks in the criminal justice system and pervasive violations of the right to vote, the students' lunch counter protests seriously complicated matters. As a matter of morality and human decency, the question was as clear-cut as possible. As a matter of law, however, the lawyers recognized that in many cases the students' actions were not protected—at least not by existing judicial interpretations of the Fourteenth Amendment. If the students wanted to press this admittedly ambiguous area of constitutional law, then there were better ways to do so, perhaps by challenging public accommodations that had a more direct linkage to the state, such as segregated lunch counters in public buildings, or segregation in accommodations that leased their space from the state. A further complication arose from the fact that if the sit-ins were considered acts of civil disobedience, the students were actually breaking the wrong laws. As a matter of strategy as well as moral principle, it is one thing to refuse to obey an unjust law, such as a segregation statute, but it is quite another to break a law that is essentially neutral on its face, such as a trespassing statute, just because the effect of that law is to protect an unjust practice. Also, from a more pragmatic perspective, the lunch counter sit-ins took on what many considered a sacred cow of American law: property rights.[15]

Marshall quickly changed his tune. In fact, he probably never truly believed the students' legal claims were as weak as he made them out to be. Those who had been working with him had seen this kind of performance before. Before he was willing to commit to any legal strategy, Marshall liked to give his best possible case against it. He then relied on his staff to argue with him, to challenge him. It was a classic lawyer's tool: master your opponents' arguments so as to better diffuse them. The lawyers had their own version of the bull sessions that the Greensboro Four had in their dormitory at A&T. Like the students, they talked and argued, eventually convincing each other and themselves of what they needed to do. They knew they had to try to get out ahead of this issue. And the only way they could do this was to develop a legal strategy. LDF lawyers became leading proponents of the argument that the students had a claim based not only on the immorality of segregation in public accommodations, but also on its unconstitutionality. It was a strategy that was just as ambitious, just as much of a challenge to the legal status quo, as the strategy that NAACP lawyers put together thirty years earlier when they turned their attention to school desegregation.[16]

The evolving, still uncertain status of Fourteenth Amendment doctrine at this time allowed the LDF lawyers to make this tactically savvy about-face. When Marshall had dismissed the possibility that the students had a valid constitutional claim for equal service, he had offered a fair assessment of the existing precedent. And now, in defending this same constitutional claim, he was offering a reasonable advocate's assessment of the possibility of changing that precedent.[17]

In mid-March, Marshall and his staff convened a conference at Howard University of sixty-two civil rights lawyers to look at the legal issues behind the sit-ins. "Those boys and girls didn't check the law when they sat down on those stools," he told reporters. "Now we're going to have to check the law." Even before the lawyers met, Marshall had begun adopting a dramatically different perspective toward the sit-ins. Abandoning his initial skepticism, he now characterized them as "legal and right." When asked whether the NAACP intended to take the issue all the way to the Supreme Court, he responded, "We wouldn't bother with it unless we did." In the weeks leading up to the conference, he discussed the possibility of making a free expression argument on the students' behalf, and discussions with lawyers at the conference gave him a newfound faith in using the sit-ins as a vehicle for making an equal protection claim. After the three-day legal strategy meeting, Marshall declared, "We're pulling out all the stops. We're really in it." He promptly headed to North Carolina, where he assured NAACP members, "We are going to give to these young people the best legal defense available to them."[18]

Marshall offered two variations on the constitutional argument he would use on behalf of the students. One was more limited and context-specific: that the initial invitation into the department store effectively converted the private business into a public space in which the requirements of the equal protection clause applied. "Once a Negro, or any other law abiding person[,] has been admitted to a store to buy pins and needles," Marshall explained, "he has the right to buy everything in the store." This line of argument drew upon the constitutional reasoning expressed in *Marsh v. Alabama*, the 1946 decision in which the Supreme Court held that a privately owned company town that, for all intents and purposes, looked and acted like a regular town was subject to the restrictions of the First Amendment and therefore could not prohibit sidewalk solicitation. As the Court wrote in *Marsh*: "The more an owner, for his advantage, opens up his property for use by the public in general, the more do his rights become circumscribed by the statutory and constitutional rights of those who use it"—powerful language that LDF lawyers cited at every opportunity in their defense of the sit-in protesters. The basic question was whether a private business that purported to serve the general public was engaged in a public service of such an essential nature that the Constitution did not permit it to practice racial restrictions in its service policy.[19]

The other prong of Marshall's equal protection argument found clearer support in Supreme Court precedent, but it raised even more fundamental difficulties about the boundaries of the state action doctrine. It sought to extend the controversial and enigmatic precedent of *Shelley v. Kraemer*, in which the Court held unconstitutional judicial enforcement of racially restrictive covenants. Under this theory, it was not the business owner's choice to discriminate that violated the Fourteenth Amendment, but the introduction of the power of the state to enforce that private choice, in the form of the arrest and prosecution of protesters. Pervasive state involvement in sit-in prosecutions was obvious, Marshall told the NAACP meeting in North Carolina following the lawyers' strategy session, and the slew of arrests for participating in the sit-ins "once again" showed "the full strength of the state government, paid for by white and black taxes, arrayed against young people solely because of their race and color." The constitutional violation that flowed from this fact was clear, Marshall explained. Whether the state expresses its authority "when the police are called in to prevent the Negro being served" or by enforcing "a state law [that] prohibits the Negro from getting equal service," in either case, "the 14th amendment is violated."[20]

When it came to persuading federal judges, each of these lines of argument for extending the state action doctrine had its particular challenges. The *Marsh*-based argument raised difficult line-drawing questions. Judges who might be sympathetic to the students' claim still need to be convinced that the reasoning for their decision made sense when applied to analogous situations in other contexts. No one argued that all private businesses that served the public should fall under the full force of constitutional restrictions. Certain private businesses, however, did more than just serve the public. They provided highly valuable, perhaps even essential public services; people relied upon them; they played a government-like role in public life. The critical question was whether lunch counters—or, more generally, eating facilities—fell into this category.

The *Shelley*-based argument raised its own line-drawing problems. Sure, police and court involvement constituted the action of the government, and these actions must align with *Brown's* nondiscrimination requirement, but did this mean that courts had to inquire into the motivation of private actors who called on the police to enforce race-neutral laws, such as a trespass law, to ensure that government was not involved in racial discrimination? If the answer was yes, does the same reasoning apply to private actors who infringe on speech rights? What if a private club called on the police to remove someone who was unwelcome because of his skin color? What about a host of a dinner party in her home? "If a state could not enforce private discrimination in a restaurant by arresting trespassers, could it enforce it in private clubs? Or private homes?" asked a late February *New York Times* article previewing possible judicial approaches to the sit-ins. "If a Negro walked into a club that excluded Negroes from membership, and he refused to leave, could the club call the police to remove him? Or would that be unconstitutional?" The problem with walking down the *Shelley* path was that its logic risked exploding the distinction between the public and private realms that most lawyers, judges, and scholars assumed was essential to the proper functioning of constitutional rights.[21]

Marshall was fully aware of these challenges. As much as anyone in LDF, he kept insisting that they be taken seriously. Yet the enthusiasm with which the generally cautious civil rights leader took to these ambitious constitutional claims on behalf of the students reflected the powerful impact the sit-ins had on Marshall and others in the national office of the NAACP. "This situation," he admitted, "has made all of us reassess ourselves."[22]

Points of Division

The parameters of the lawyers' reassessment were limited, however. For Marshall and his colleagues, the sit-in movement broadened their horizons of viable constitutional argumentation, but it did not inspire a reconsideration of the role of the NAACP in the civil rights movement. The LDF lawyers came to the sit-ins with already formed ideas about the way in which civil rights reform should take place. They had the experience of *Brown*, which showed that carefully planned litigation could overturn even the most seemingly entrenched of constitutional interpretations—and the status of the constitutional issue at the heart of the sit-ins was far from well entrenched after two decades of Supreme Court decisions expanding the meaning of state action under the Fourteenth Amendment. They understood their litigation efforts as having played a critical role in securing victory for the Montgomery bus boycott. (LDF lawyers won a constitutional challenge to Montgomery's bus segregation policy at the Supreme Court at just the moment when the boycott appeared on the verge of crumbling. "All that walking for nothing!" was Thurgood Marshall's response after the Court issued its ruling. "They could just as well have waited while the bus case went up through the courts, without all the work and worry of the boycott.") With the students mobilizing themselves as an alternative to the NAACP's court-centered approach to racial progress, it was no surprise that when the NAACP lawyers arrived to offer their help and advice to the students, the lawyers and the students would have sharply different views about the situation.[23]

In the early stages of the sit-in movement, the lawyers and the students struggled to reconcile their different views on two tactical issues. One was over the relationship between the protests and the test cases the NAACP hoped to create. The other was a debate over the "jail, no bail" policy advocated by many of the students.

Protests and Test Cases

Although Thurgood Marshall and other NAACP lawyers publicly supported the protesters and represented them in court, they disappointed the students (or perhaps confirmed the students' distrust of the NAACP) when they suggested that since the sit-ins had made their point—and given the lawyers plenty of test cases with which to work—they should stop the protests. "There has been confusion about the purposes of these activities," explained a NAACP memorandum.

If the aim is to test the law, then the threshold question is what is gained by the large numbers of people being arrested and involved in appeals in the courts? The financial burden of furnishing bond to keep these people out of jail and the costs of appealing hundreds of such cases through the courts is enormous. . . . Whatever the merits of the mass action technique, when it requires that kind of financial outlay, its virtues must be closely examined. . . . [O]ne does not need hundreds of cases and appeals to test the validity of a particular law. One or two is usually sufficient.

The money that was being used to bail out arrested protesters, the memorandum noted, could be put to better use. The cost of representing the hundreds, soon thousands, of arrested students was starting to add up. This memorandum captures a fundamental divide between the NAACP's national leadership and the protesters. The NAACP assumed that the aim of the protests was to change the law. But on this point the students would take issue. This might be one of the aims of the protest, or it might be a beneficial secondary effect of the protest, but it was not their only purpose. The students certainly did not see themselves as simply providing test cases for lawyers.[24]

Thus, in their effort to justify their own involvement in the sit-ins, NAACP lawyers sought to redefine the goals of the protests. NAACP strategy memos on the sit-ins repeatedly referenced the importance of "ultimate success" in the sit-in battle. Activists must never forget the "main objective" of the protests, and they must always keep in mind the "long run" aims, none of which would be achieved without "a carefully planned and continuous attack." The NAACP assumed that the end goal of the protest was the judicial recognition of the constitutional rights of the protesters. "The only way we will be able to successfully break down the practices of segregation and discrimination and undermine the legal support of these practices through the law is by the process of having such laws and ordinances declared unconstitutional." "As far as [Marshall] was concerned," complained one student activist after a conversation with the legendary civil rights lawyer, "it was all going to be settled in the courtroom."[25]

Sometimes the students followed the counsel of the lawyers. This was what happened in Atlanta. Within days of the first Greensboro sit-ins, students at Atlanta's six black colleges were planning their own demonstrations. Yet over a month passed before anything happened, as student leaders followed the advice of older black community leaders to focus their energies on negotiation and litigation. After weeks of false starts, delays, and bickering among factions within the civil rights community, Atlanta's sit-in movement began on March 15. But here again, Atlanta's movement retained a distinctly lawyerly character. Rather than targeting national chain stores, student leaders followed the lawyers' advice that they focus their protests on publicly owned facilities or facilities that were involved in interstate transportation (and thus subject to federal nondiscrimination rules). Police responded to the coordinated sit-in demonstrations at cafeterias in the capitol, the country courthouse, city hall, and several bus terminals and train stations by arresting seventy-seven demonstrators and charging them under the state's new anti-trespassing law. The day after the mass arrests, at a meeting of fourteen hundred students, Donald Hollowell, one of the lawyers representing the arrested students, advised the students to stop their protests until they get a "final judgment" in the pending court cases. The students took his advice and called a halt to further sit-in demonstrations until the protesters had their trials. An organized lunch counter sit-in campaign would not return to Atlanta until the following fall. CORE's executive director lamented the Atlanta students' willingness to "transfer[] the action to the legal phase" of the reform project.[26]

Civil rights lawyers did not necessarily fail to appreciate the unique value of the student protests. They just felt that, at some point, their protests must give way to formal legal claims: protesters must eventually yield to lawyers.

The "Jail, No Bail" Debate

The divergent agendas of the students and the lawyers were even more starkly reflected in the debate over how the arrested students should deal with the legal system—whether they should pay bail and thereby avoid spending time in jail while their cases were being heard and whether they should choose a jail term rather than paying a fine after conviction. The civil rights lawyers felt the students should plead not guilty to charges of disorderly conduct or trespass, pay bail, and appeal the conviction. They were being unjustly prosecuted, and there was a clear legal remedy for this. But the students had another option: although they would plead not guilty, they would then refuse bail and remain in jail as a way of drawing further attention to the injustice of the situation. "Let us not fear going to jail," declared Martin Luther King Jr. in a February 1960 speech to student protesters in Durham, North Carolina. "If the officials threaten to arrest us for standing up for our rights, we must answer by saying that we are willing and prepared to fill up the jails of the South. Maybe it will take this willingness to stay in jail to arouse the dozing conscience of our nation." "When groups of people are willing to sit in jail," explained CORE leader James Robinson, who, like King, was a dedicated proponent of this tactic, "their very presence there does put pressure on the community to consider searchingly how much they really want to impose segregation—to consider how thoroughly persons must reject segregation in order to willingly accept jail in preference to failing to make an attack on the system."[27]

"Jail, no bail" became a new mantra for the student movement. The students envisioned filling up the jails with protesters and thereby elevating their moral challenge to the southern system of racial oppression. At the meeting of student activists in Raleigh, North Carolina, in April 1960, after listening to King encourage the students to "consider training a group of volunteers who willingly go to jail rather than pay bail or fines," the students issued a statement urging protesters to do just that. The announcement of this recommendation was met with overwhelming enthusiasm from those in attendance. Inspired by King's speech, on April 21 Greensboro students refused to leave a lunch counter and were arrested—the only arrest of the Greensboro lunch counter sit-in campaign. This "jail, no bail" approach, its advocates believed, would help solidify the black community, mobilize public opinion, and weaken opposition "by showing that a threat of arrest cannot deter us." "As this movement grows," noted Robinson, "it is conceivable that refusal to pay bail and fines may be essential to its success."[28]

Sitting in jail when given an opportunity to walk free "is a strange concept to a lawyer who is concerned about getting his client out of jail as soon as possible," Robinson explained. Next to the commitment and bravery required for a black youth (or white integrationist) to choose to remain in a southern jail, the NAACP's counter-arguments were uninspiring in their practicality. According to the lawyers, the "jail, no bail" tactic—and its correlative "prison, no fine" and "no appeal" tactics—was, at best, unnecessarily risky; at worst, it was counterproductive to the movement's goals. By accepting their convictions and serving out their sentences, not only did the students earn a criminal record, but, more significantly for the NAACP, they gave up an opportunity to challenge the legal rules that made Jim Crow possible. Again, the divide over what the sit-ins were trying to accomplish was made stark. "If the objective is to dramatize the illegalities and to disrupt the social order," a NAACP memorandum explained, then there was really no role for the lawyers: "the people who participate should refuse legal help and engage in this activity only with the idea of staying in jail." But this was not the best path, for it failed to appreciate the "long run" goals of the movement, which were best served by following "the Association's basic policy and philosophy." The students must always "know exactly what their rights are"—a requirement that NAACP officials could facilitate. "The NAACP firmly believes that every citizen has the constitutional right to enjoy on the same basis as any other citizen the facilities of any public place, business, or any other profit enterprise which offers its services to the public. To obtain these rights we must carry on a carefully planned and continuous attack."[29]

To achieve these ends, the students must not get caught up in symbolic gestures that, in the eyes of the lawyers, did nothing to advance the cause of civil rights. "It is the firm belief of the NAACP that you should plead *not guilty* to the charges and accept bail," the national office explained to the students. "We realize that remaining in jail has moral and ethical implications not to be discounted, yet there is a grave danger that the individual, by his failure, neglect, or refusal to right a criminal charge levied against him and through accepting a jail sentence in lieu thereof, will *defeat* his main purpose and thus render ineffectual our overall legal attack on this spiteful, vicious system." Upon arrest, student leaders should "immediately contact their NAACP lawyers and follow the advice of counsel. In this way we will be better able to direct our efforts toward our main objective, that of crushing an outmoded system, and thus also avoid stigmatizing our youth with criminal records, the efficacy of which is extremely doubtful."[30]

Like their call for the students to stop protesting and allowing the lawyers to take over, the NAACP's attack on the "jail, no bail" strategy disappointed many of the protesters and served to widen the gap between the students and the lawyers. John Lewis recalled hearing Marshall counseling the students to stay out of jail and allow the NAACP to challenge the legality of their arrests. "It was clear to me that evening," the Nashville student activist later wrote, "that Thurgood Marshall, along with so many of his generation, just did not understand the essence of what we, the younger blacks of America, were doing."[31]

"A Turbulent but Workable Marriage"

Despite the divide between the students and the lawyers when it came to their visions of civil rights activism, as the sit-in movement unfolded throughout the spring of 1960, the two groups settled into a functional alliance. "In something so enormous as the task of ending racial segregation," Clarence Mitchell concluded in his April 1960 report to Roy Wilkins, "there is a great deal of room for many workers and ideas." "We know that shock troops are necessary," Wilkins would later explain. "We also know that solid basic legal moves are necessary if there is to be a foundation for other action." The NAACP lawyers laid essential groundwork for the students, he insisted. "Once the legal status and constitutional rights were established, the battle to enjoy them follows as night the day."[32]

Recognizing the sit-ins as both a threat and an opportunity for the NAACP, the leaders in the organization's national office went on the offensive. In late February, Wilkins announced, "Negro college students in their fights have the 100 per cent backing of the NAACP," and he praised the sit-ins as "legitimate expressions of citizens in a democracy." NAACP leaders swept aside their initial skepticism and launched a public relations campaign in which they insisted the NAACP was a key force behind the sit-ins. "We need to amplify our public image," a staff memorandum explained, "from the NAACP as purely a 'legal' agency to the NAACP as a multi-weapon action organization." At every opportunity, the NAACP publicized that its branches had been behind sit-in efforts that predated Greensboro and played up the association's role in the new wave of sit-ins. As one NAACP report explained, the wave of sit-ins "marked the continuation of similar activity which started in Wichita and Oklahoma City in 1958. . . . In both cities, the victories were won by NAACP youth councils composed of high school and elementary youth." The memorandum also noted a February 1959 "sitdown" in St. Louis, in which the NAACP represented the arrested students and was able to integrate a previously segregated restaurant. Publicity material highlighted the fact that several of the Greensboro Four had been members of NAACP youth chapters and that the NAACP youth secretary "kept in close touch with the situation." (What the NAACP did not mention was that when the Greensboro Four had made an effort to reach out to their national office before they began their protest, they received no response.)[33]

NAACP leaders also emphasized the connections between their achievements in the Supreme Court and the current burst of protests, arguing that NAACP courtroom victories "made inevitable the aggressive expressions of discontent with the status quo which resulted in the sit-ins, boycotts and mass Negro protest against social injustice. . . ." "If the Supreme Court had not signaled the end of separate schools in its 1954 decision," wrote LDF president Allan Knight Chalmers in a letter to the *New York Times*, "today's young people might not have had the confidence for their broad assault against segregation."[34]

On March 16, the NAACP declared a new "racial self-defense policy," the centerpiece of which was a national boycott, organized by local chapters, of all chain stores that operated segregated lunch counters in the South. "We always have used persuasion through various means of political and economic pressure," Wilkins explained, "but now we are going to use it much more intensively than in the past because the membership has become restless over the slow pace of the civil rights proceedings."[35]

At the start of the sit-ins, the students benefited from having the NAACP focused on issues other than lunch counters. Now, with the movement under way, they benefited from having respected LDF lawyers proclaiming the students' cause constitutionally justified. Once Marshall became convinced that the students had a viable constitutional claim, he and his colleagues declared at every turn that the students' cause was justified as a matter of law. It was, in sociologist Aldon Morris's apt description, "a turbulent but workable marriage." These statements further entrenched the idea, already assumed among many civil rights sympathizers, that lunch counters were a logical next step in the battle to realize the full meaning of the Fourteenth Amendment. Even for those students who feared that the civil rights lawyers might co-opt their cause, being told that they had the law—and ultimately the Supreme Court—behind them surely did not hurt.

The NAACP's embrace of the student movement also had tangible benefits. Funding was essential to the continued survival of the sit-in movement. For all the attention and controversy over the "jail, no bail" protest tactic, not all arrested protesters were interested in sitting in jail. Many thankfully accepted the legal and financial assistance the NAACP offered. "The N.A.A.C.P. continues to have the loyalty of most students, who admit that after they dash ahead they often have to ask the N.A.A.C.P. for legal help," explained one journalist after spending time with the protesters. As legal historian Tomiko Brown-Nagin writes, "Activists, clever and restless, modulated their attitudes toward civil rights lawyers and court-centered activities as circumstances dictated." The NAACP was the best positioned among the civil rights organizations to assume the role of financially supporting the student movement. The organization made an effort to tone down potential friction with the students. By the summer of 1960, NAACP lawyers estimated that they were participating in the legal defense of between 1,500 and 1,750 protesters, all at considerable expense.[36]

This was a relationship in which each side needed the other. Moreover, those who supported the larger civil rights agenda needed the relationship to work. "Instead of saying, as so many have, that the sit-ins represent a new strategy, would it not be more reasonable to regard them as opening up a new front?" asked Leslie Dunbar of the Southern Regional Council. "Instead of announcing that the sit-ins mean a downgrading of the courtroom struggle, would it not be more reasonable to recognize that litigation is not an effective means for desegregating lunch counters, and that sit-ins are not an effective means for desegregating schools?"[37]

Even CORE's James Robinson, a frequent critic of civil rights lawyers, accepted the value of an effective alliance of lawyers and activists. In a memorandum prepared for a meeting of civil rights groups in June 1960, he noted that the involvement of civil rights lawyers in the sit-in movement has led to some "confusion." It "has left the movement somewhere between the usual legal method and the nonviolent direct action procedure." "Both techniques should be used," Robinson urged, "but I believe that they should be consciously used, and never confused." Pointing to the Atlanta example, where he saw student deference to legal advice as having stymied protest mobilization, he expressed concern that civil rights leaders should not allow "the legal method" to displace direct action. "The two methods are supplementary, not contradictory," Robinson insisted. On this point, CORE and the NAACP agreed. "This job requires youth and enthusiasm," Wilkins explained in a letter to NAACP local branch officers. "It also requires age and experience. It requires praying and preaching. It also requires legal activity in court. It requires both old and the new."[38]

———

Unified by the recognition of their common enemy of Jim Crow, bolstered by the contagious atmosphere of excitement and possibility surrounding the students in the early months of the movement, both students and lawyers generally sought to tamp down potential flashpoints of ideological division. The NAACP publicly supported the protesters and offered legal and financial assistance when the students were arrested. The national office issued instructions for local NAACP branches on recommended tactics to best prepare the legal challenge, and LDF lawyers worked with local lawyers and traveled to the South to teach the students about their constitutional rights and how they could most effectively contribute to a legal attack on segregated public accommodations. LDF lawyers represented arrested students in court or they assisted local lawyers. Enough students allowed the lawyers to appeal their convictions, setting in motion the first step in a constitutional challenge to segregated public accommodations. Both the students and the lawyers advanced the cause of racial equality as best they knew how.[39]

THREE

The Sympathizers

It seems clear that this "lunch-counter movement" will become a historic milestone in the American Negro's efforts to win the rights of citizenship which are guaranteed him by the Constitution.

—EDITORIAL, *COMMONWEAL*, APRIL 1960[1]

In April 1960, at the height of the lunch counter sit-in movement, *Time* magazine ran a story entitled "The Sympathizers." It noted that "while police clamped down on demonstrations in the South, sympathy demonstrations by white students spread over campuses in the North." The story described meetings at northern colleges, fund-raising efforts, letter-writing campaigns, and boycotts of chain stores that were the targets of sit-in protests in the South. It even told of a white sociology professor at Mac-Murray College in Illinois who accompanied ten of his students to Montgomery, Alabama, where they all were arrested after attempting to eat with African American students at a segregated restaurant.[2]

As the *Time* article indicates, the sit-in story involved not just heroic acts of protest by African American college students in the South, but also the remarkable level of support those students received. To be sure, plenty of people, in the South as well as the North, denounced the students for breaking laws or for undermining fundamental rights to private property and association. Yet considering the bold act of defiance that was at the heart of the protests, the sit-ins generated significant levels of approval from across the nation. Sympathetic observers were moved by the drama of the sit-in movement as it played out on the front pages of their daily newspapers, in popular periodicals, on the evening news, and in television specials. The powerful imagery generated by the movement—the well-dressed young men and women sitting at counters, asking for nothing more than a cup of coffee, and getting ignored or attacked or thrown in jail for their efforts—produced many sympathizers. They thrust the issue of racial discrimination in public accommodations into the national spotlight. Defenders of Jim Crow, whose aggressive and confident mobilization against the Supreme Court's *Brown* ruling had yielded impressive concessions and delays in the realm of school desegregation, now found themselves on the defensive again. As the sit-ins spread across the South, more and more people asked why African Americans should be forced to suffer such indignities when they asked for nothing more than to spend their earnings on equal terms with white Americans. The sit-ins, Martin Luther King Jr. observed, "impart[ed] light and heat to distant satellites."[3]

This chapter considers the people who supported the sit-in movement. It has two goals. One is to explain why the protests gained such substantial support from such varied sources, and to consider the different ways this support was expressed. Sympathizers were critical to the success of the sit-in movement. They urged boycotts, which put the power of profits behind the moral message of the protests, creating further pressure on local businesses and national chain stores to rethink their discriminatory policies. Their public expressions of sympathy bolstered the protesters and helped draw reinforcements to their ranks. Their financial support provided a critical lifeline for the movement as the number of students arrested rose into the thousands.

The chapter's other goal is to explain the key role that sympathizers played in transforming the legal significance of the sit-ins. Just as civil rights lawyers translated the students' bold claims for dignity and equality into the language of judicial doctrine, outside sympathizers translated these same claims into the language of "popular constitutionalism"—the rich blend of legal norms, moral sensibilities, and public policy with which the American people contest, and sometimes remake, the meaning of the Constitution. By considering how an eclectic cast of characters, from the president of the United States to ordinary citizens, understood the sit-ins, this chapter charts how an aspirational constitutional claim—a claim, that is, without solid footing as a matter of court-defined constitutional law—took shape in the crucible of public discourse. The formation and strengthening of the right to nondiscriminatory access to public accommodations as a matter of constitutional principle in the years following the sit-ins would increase pressure on formal legal actors to respond.

Constitutional Change Outside the Courts

Before turning to the public response to the sit-ins, this idea of "popular constitutionalism" merits further consideration. As developed by a recent generation of legal scholars, the concept derives from a quite simple premise: engaging with the Constitution—making claims based on it and, ultimately giving meaning to its words—is not, never has been, and should not be the left to lawyers and judges alone. The American people also play a role in shaping and reshaping the Constitution's meaning. They do so through acts of popular engagement, such as protests and social movement mobilization. They also do so through their elected representatives (scholars sometimes distinguish these variants as executive or legislative constitutionalism). The courts obviously affect these extrajudicial constitutional debates. Indeed, over the course of American history, judges have played an ever-increasing role in shaping how people outside the courts understand the meaning of the Constitution. But judicial constitutionalism (which I will also refer to as constitutional doctrine or constitutional law) has never comprised the entirety of our constitutional tradition.[4]

The key to appreciating the dynamics of popular constitutionalism is to recognize that the validity of a given constitutional claim cannot be assessed simply by looking to what the courts have said on the matter. Just because the justices of the Supreme Court never agreed that racial discrimination by a private business that served the general public violated the Constitution does not mean that this kind of discrimination does not violate the Constitution. The American people and their elected officials (who take the same oath to "support and defend the Constitution" that judges do) also play a role in giving meaning to the nation's founding document. This approach recognizes what Americans have recognized since the founding: that the Constitution is the fundamental law of "We the People," not some obscure legal document that can only be interpreted by judges.

The sit-ins offer a powerful case study of the dynamics of popular constitutionalism. The protests had the effect of transforming an issue of private choice and local policy into one of constitutional principle. As detailed in the previous chapter, this dynamic of translation can be seen in the legal arguments that civil rights lawyers developed to try to convince judges of the constitutional merits of the students' claim. But unlike the struggle for school desegregation, in which litigation was the primary mechanism by which the constitutional claim was advanced and then recognized in the *Brown* ruling, the sit-ins followed a different course, one in which the courts played only a supporting role. The constitutional claim at the heart of the sit-ins was expressed, in the first instance at least, not in the form of a lawyer's argument, but in the form of a public act of protest. What would prove to be the most critical deliberation over the merits of this claim took place not in a private room of Supreme Court justices, but in public debate. And the most consequential act of recognition of this constitutional claim came not in the form of a judicial opinion, but in the form of an emerging public consensus, eventually captured and enforced through an act of Congress in the landmark Civil Rights Act of 1964.

To explain how this dynamic of popular constitutionalism operated in the context of the sit-ins, I break down my examination of the public response to the demonstrations into three steps in what may be considered the *constitutionalization* of the sit-in movement. These three steps show how the actions of the sit-in protesters—who were motivated less by a conscious desire to reinterpret the Constitution than by a volatile mix of frustration, a demand for dignity, and an intoxicating sense of empowerment that the protests provided—became, in effect, a claim on the meaning of the equal protection clause of the Fourteenth Amendment.

The first step was a *salience* shift. The sit-in movement elevated the importance of racial discrimination in public accommodations as a public policy issue. A marginal issue on the civil rights agenda of movement leaders and public officials became a matter of intense debate throughout the nation.

Second, there was growing *support* for the claimed right for which the students were advocating. The sit-ins changed minds. Public figures who had previously expressed no opinion on the question of racial discrimination in public accommodations now denounced the practice as immoral and un-American. People whose initial response to the protests was to defend a business owner's right to discriminate in the choice of customers now moderated and, in some cases, reconsidered their positions.

The third step, and the one that moved the issue from a pressing concern of public policy into the realm of constitutional principle, was a shift in the *framing* of the issue. With increasing frequency in the months and years following the Greensboro sit-ins, those who supported the claimed right to the nondiscriminatory treatment that the students demanded treated the claim as one based not only in wisdom or utility or morality, but also in the Constitution. Sympathizers sometimes did this explicitly, through direct reference to the Constitution or to constitutional doctrine. Sometimes they did it more by implication, linking the claimed right to nondiscriminatory service at lunch counters to other rights that were unquestionably grounded in the Constitution, such as the right against state-mandated segregation in schools or the right to vote. Thus, regardless of the intentions of the protesters themselves, we see emerging from the sit-ins a rights claim that growing numbers of Americans saw not only as important, not only as just or moral, but as based in the nation's fundamental law.

Attention to the dynamics of popular constitutionalism should not marginalize the role courts have always played in the development of new constitutional norms. To say that the courts have been generally less important to constitutional development than is commonly assumed is not to say that the courts have been unimportant. To the contrary, from the beginning of the Republic, the courts, particularly the Supreme Court, have been uniquely influential interpreters of the Constitution. By the early 1960s, constitutional doctrine—that is, what the courts said about the meaning of the Constitution—cast a long shadow over any efforts for those outside the courts to assert a claim on the meaning of the Constitution.

The story of the sit-ins powerfully demonstrates how the status of the students' claimed right as a matter of judicial constitutional understanding affected each step in the development of their claimed right as a matter of extrajudicial constitutional understanding. Doctrine helped set the terms of debate. The marginalization of public accommodations discrimination as a major civil rights issue prior to 1960 was in part a product of the recognition of civil rights lawyers and activists that judges were resistant to apply constitutional equal protection requirements to private businesses. The dramatic increase in the salience of and support for the students' claim was bolstered by the sense that this judicial resistance was weakening, that the relevant constitutional doctrine seemed to be moving toward possible recognition of the students' claim. The uncertain nature of the law, as defined by the courts, helped open the door to the robust, generative dynamics of popular constitutional development that took place in response to the sit-ins.

As a result of the sit-in protests, and the ways in which sympathizers across the nation responded to them, the issue of racial discrimination in public accommodations was transformed. Out of the process of social movement mobilization and political contestation, a viable, and to a growing number of Americans, persuasive, claim on the meaning of the constitutional principle of equal protection took shape.

The Sit-Ins Transform the Civil Rights Agenda

The student sit-in movement reshaped the national civil rights debate. The flood of public support for the students and their cause elevated the issue of segregation in public accommodations to the top of the reform agenda for civil rights activists and their allies in the nation's courts and legislatures. From the spring of 1960 through the passage of the 1964 Civil Rights Act, segregation at lunch counters, restaurants, hotels, and other businesses that served the public resided alongside school desegregation and voting rights as the most urgent policy reforms of the civil rights struggle.

Prior to the sit-ins, most civil rights organizations included the problem of discrimination in public accommodations as part of their reform programs, but it was rarely a top priority. It had not always been that way, however. African Americans had a long tradition of resisting discrimination in the public sphere in all its forms, including segregation in facilities that were privately operated but ostensibly open to the general public, and some of the most significant political and legal battles following the Civil War involved this issue. In 1875 Congress passed the last major national policy initiative of the Reconstruction era, a law designed to ensure "the full and equal enjoyment . . . of inns, public conveyances on land and water, theaters, and other places of public amusement." The Supreme Court struck down most of the law as beyond the power of Congress to enact in the *Civil Rights Cases* of 1883 (the decision defining the state action limitation on the Fourteenth Amendment that civil rights lawyers confronted when defending sit-in protests almost a century later). The ruling limited federal but not state authority, and northern states responded by passing their own public accommodations laws, although they were only fitfully enforced in the following decades. As the racial egalitarian impulse of Reconstruction receded in the late nineteenth century, replaced by a hardening of the color line and formalization of white supremacy in law and practice, public accommodations discrimination became less of a priority for racial justice activists. Their efforts were aimed at what they saw as more elemental concerns, such as protection against violence, the right to vote, equal access to basic public services (including schools), and economic opportunity. By the mid-twentieth century, civil rights activists were giving increased attention to racial discrimination in public accommodations in the North (this often involved enforcing laws that had been on the books since the nineteenth century). But prior to 1960, the major civil rights organizations did not see privately owned public accommodations, particularly those in the South, as a viable target for their limited resources.[5]

The marginalization of public accommodations discrimination on the national civil rights agenda could be partially explained by the particularities of racial justice activism in the 1950s. CORE, the organization best suited in terms of temperament and interest to organize a frontal challenge to discrimination in public accommodations, had been severely diminished as a civil rights force in the 1950s, one of the many victims of McCarthy-era repression of political radicalism. Martin Luther King Jr. and the Southern Christian Leadership Conference (SCLC), the organization that King and a group of black ministers created in 1957 to build on the success of the Montgomery bus boycott, were still searching for an agenda in 1960. Most of their work at the time was centered on voting rights. The NAACP national office was concerned with implementing *Brown* in the courts and passing voting rights protections in Congress. Its leaders showed little interest in leading a charge against this particular form of racial subordination. The fact that NAACP and LDF lawyers thought the students' constitutional claim a long shot in court only reinforced the relative lack of interest in public accommodations discrimination on the part of the NAACP's central office. A combination of tactical differences and a reading of the legal landscape thus steered the dominant civil rights organization of the day toward voting and school desegregation litigation, leaving public accommodations a largely unoccupied field for civil rights activity.[6]

The sit-ins, and the public support they received among influential public figures and organizations, changed all this. The protests drew national attention to the high value placed on equal access to public accommodations by those who faced systematic exclusion. The sit-ins refuted, in the most powerful way imaginable, segregationist arguments that this form of discrimination concerned "merely" social relations, that discrimination at a place such as a lunch counter simply reflected social norms, accepted and acceptable by whites and blacks alike. By putting their physical safety on the line, by risking arrest and accepting jail time—all in the name of being served a cup of coffee—

the protests displayed the deep commitment of many in the African American community to knocking down this particularly offensive Jim Crow practice. "The lunch counter sit-down protests have brought to my attention in sharp focus an injustice that I formerly thought of, when at all, only vaguely," confessed one white southerner. In a way that could not be captured by a petition to representative government or by a court challenge, the sit-ins expressed, in uniquely powerful terms, a sense of sacrifice and deep personal commitment to a cause, which had the effect of heightening the importance of public accommodations in the national dialogue on civil rights.[7]

"Water Over the Dam": African Americans in the South

Among those who were most powerfully affected by this salience-raising dynamic of the sit-in movement were adult African Americans in the South. As a group, they were of course intimately acquainted with the harsh indignities of racial discrimination at lunch counters, restaurants, hotels, and countless other private businesses that served the public. The student demonstrations taught them nothing on this count. But what the sit-ins did was to push this particular facet of Jim Crow further up the priority list for many older African Americans. In a world of limited time and money and willingness to absorb the costs of segregationist retribution for civil rights activism, black southerners needed to choose their battles. The students persuaded many older blacks that lunch counter discrimination was a battle worth fighting, and fighting now.

As described in the first chapter, early sit-in protesters consciously framed their protests as an alternative to the perceived complacency or fearfulness of their parents' generation or to the legalistic reforms that adult activists favored. This portrait of the older generation had kernels of truth in it, but the reality was that attitudes within the larger black community about the sit-in movement were considerably more complex. Although many older African Americans criticized the sit-ins as rash and perhaps counterproductive, most adult blacks supported the students in one way or another. As one black businessman in Atlanta explained, "If these students had consulted me, I'd have advised against it. Demonstrations can breed mobs, and boycotts can cut both ways. But that's water over the dam. The youngsters have made their decision, and you've got to be proud of the way they've handled themselves. Whatever happens from now on, I'll back them up all the way."[8]

After listening to some the strong criticisms that sit-in leaders expressed toward older blacks, reporters who arrived on the scene were often surprised at the extent of the older generation's support for the students and their protests. Accounts from the major sit-in locations —Durham, Greensboro, Nashville, among others—repeatedly emphasized the unity of the black community behind the demonstrations. "The zeal of the students rubbed off on their elders," noted one black reporter. "In a great upswelling of moral indignation, church groups, politicians, and political figures climbed on the sit-in bandwagon." A Nashville student explained how the sit-ins had transformed the perspective of older African Americans. "The older Negro looked only to the courts for help. While this community, at first, felt the sit-in was too radical and kept its hands off, once we got into it and they saw how we felt they supported us wholeheartedly. It is no longer just a student movement. It is a community movement." Journalist Ben Bagdikian recounted listening to a white cabdriver in Birmingham confidently declaring how "this whole integration business" had no support from "old niggers in town." "See that old nigger at the stand on the corner?" he asked. "I asked him about it and he said he wanted no part of it." When Bagdikian later asked the man the cabdriver had pointed out what he thought about the student movement, he gave the reporter "a long, hard look" before saying, "I'm with them. The only way our people can move ahead is to stick together."[9]

Adult African Americans in the South translated these expressions of encouragement and sympathy into tangible support in a number of ways. They could contribute money to funds for legal assistance and bail. They could help with transportation to demonstrations. The way most sympathetic southern blacks expressed their solidarity with the sit-in protesters was through joining boycotts of department stores with segregated lunch counters. The relatively low-risk decision to refuse to patronize a store brought many older blacks into the movement. Even those who remained critical or agnostic toward the sit-in protests could express their opposition to racial discrimination in this way. The boycott, explained the Savannah branch of the NAACP in a letter to city business leaders, "is a manifestation of the kind of sacrifices Negroes are willing to make for full freedom."[10]

"We Walk So They May Sit": Northerners

Just as financial support and boycotts offered a way for older African Americans in the South to support the sit-in movement—to show that they agreed with the students that this was indeed a battle worth placing at the forefront of the black freedom struggle—these same actions offered a way for people outside the South to support the students and their effort to draw attention to the issue of lunch counter discrimination.

One of the notable aspects of the sit-in movement was the opportunities it offered for effective, engaged support by those who were not actually protesting at segregated lunch counters. In contrast, for example, to the struggle to desegregate public schools or protect voting rights, in which there were relatively limited ways in which civil rights supporters outside the South could translate their beliefs into supportive action, the campaign to desegregate privately operated lunch counters offered many opportunities for sympathetic actions. In addition to contributing money for legal expenses and bail money for arrested protesters or even going to a southern city to join a demonstration, the sympathetic northerner could boycott northern branches of stores that practiced racial discrimination in the South. Soon after the start of the southern movement, sympathy protests broke out across the North.

As in the South, college campuses were hotbeds of civil rights activity. "The 'quiet generation' of American college students is getting noisy about the student lunchroom demonstrations," reported the *Washington Post*. The protests "released waves of dammed-up energy that flowed to every section of the country," declared a black journalist. "Northern students trooped from cloistered campuses and set up picket lines. Strong feelings were displayed by students who had been dubbed 'beat' or 'cool.'" CORE's executive director attributed the awakening of the college generation to the sit-ins offering students "something that is down to earth, has human appeal, and brings visible results." "Northern students have wanted to speak out for integration for some time," a white Columbia University student explained. "Now, the lunch counter sit-ins have given us the awaited opportunity to act." By mid-April 1960, sympathy demonstrations had been organized on over thirty college campuses in thirteen different states outside the South.[11]

Additional organizational support and encouragement for northern sympathizers came from national student organizations, CORE, and the NAACP. In cities across the country, blacks and whites picketed chain stores whose southern branches maintained segregated lunch counters. By mid-April, sympathy picketing had taken place in thirty states outside the South. Picketers carried signs such as: "Do Not Patronize F.W. Woolworth Until They Provide Equal Service to All People in All Parts of the Country"; and "We Walk So They May Sit."[12]

The sit-ins thrust the goal of desegregating public accommodations to the forefront of the civil rights movement. The resonant images of lunch counter demonstrations, the commitment and bravery put on display by college students asking for nothing more than to be served a meal, the many opportunities for sympathizers to align themselves with the students' efforts—all of these factors help explain why the actions and words of African American college students were so effective in changing the direction of the national discourse on civil rights. Between the first sit-ins in February 1960 and July 1964, when President Johnson signed the Civil Rights Act, segregation in public accommodations was arguably *the* central issue on the national civil rights agenda. The resolution of the constitutional issues involved in the sit-ins, one legal scholar wrote, would be more significant than the *Brown* decision. "The whole Nation has to face the issue; . . . [it] consumes the public attention," wrote Supreme Court Justice William O. Douglas in the spring of 1964. "No question preoccupies the country more than this one."[13]

Changing Minds

The sit-in movement not only drew attention to the issue of racial discrimination in public accommodations; it also persuaded many to support the students' goal of securing the right to nondiscriminatory service in public accommodations. The protests sparked a period of "national soul-searching," one commentator wrote. "By the end of the first month," noted an approving observer, "the sit-ins had made firm their roots in popular support."[14]

From the beginning of the sit-in movement, prominent public figures and politicians expressed their support for the students. In a May 1960 memorandum assessing the achievements of the sit-in movement, the NAACP compiled an impressive list of national figures who had gone on record as supporting the students' cause; it included President Eisenhower, Vice President Richard Nixon, and Senators Hubert Humphrey and Stuart Symington. Eleanor Roosevelt declared the protests "simply wonderful"; New York governor Nelson A. Rockefeller described them as "exciting and wonderful." Retired African American baseball star Jackie Robinson was an early and vocal supporter of the protests. U.S. senator and presidential candidate John F. Kennedy praised the sit-ins. He said, "It is in the American tradition to stand up for one's rights— even if the new way to stand up for one's rights is to sit down," and he called for "equal access to the voting booth, to the schoolroom, to jobs, to housing and to public facilities, including lunch rooms." Both the Republican and Democratic Party platforms in 1960 included language supporting the protests. Arguing before the Supreme Court in a 1960 case unrelated to the sit-in movement but raising analogous constitutional claims, President Eisenhower's solicitor general argued that the Constitution protected against racially discriminatory treatment in all public accommodations.[15]

The California Assembly passed a resolution praising the sit-in demonstrators. The student councils of the YMCA and YWCA issued a supportive statement, as did numerous national religious organizations and teachers unions. *Ebony* ran an article in its June issue with pictures of President Eisenhower, Democratic National Committee chairman Paul Butler, Florida governor LeRoy Collins, Atlanta mayor William Hartsfield, and Eleanor Roosevelt, each accompanied by their supportive words about the sit-ins. Ross R. Barnett, the arch-segregationist governor of Mississippi, was so exercised about what he saw as the "distorted and unfair treatment" of the sit-ins by the national media that he tried to get his fellow southern governors to join him in demanding an opportunity on all major media outlets to present "the *other* side of the story—*our* side—to the American public."[16]

Why such support for the sit-ins? Different aspects of the protests appealed to different groups. Sympathizers saw in the movement what they wanted to see. Some praised the sit-ins for offering a more confrontational, assertive alternative to litigation. Others praised them for offering a more concessionary, less confrontational alternative to litigation. Some insisted that they should not be seen as an alternative at all, that they were complementary to litigation campaigns—the protests could be used to revitalize litigation, and litigation was essential to the ultimate success of the sit-ins.

Demonstrating the Power of Direct Action

The sit-ins responded to the desire many Americans felt for a new path forward on the race question, one centered on sacrifice and moral suasion rather than adversarial litigation and court orders. The students were far from alone in their frustration with the NAACP and litigation-based reform strategies. By 1960, with the NAACP's school desegregation campaign largely stalled, many civil rights proponents were eager to embrace alternative approaches to bringing down Jim Crow. The NAACP had always had its critics on the left, and the slow progress of the implementation of *Brown* strengthened their voices. Those who viewed the NAACP as elitist and overly cautious embraced the sit-in movement as a way to attack the NAACP and its commitment to litigation and lobbying as the primary tools of racial change. In his widely discussed *Harper's* article, African American journalist Louis Lomax praised the students for displacing the "Negro leadership class"—most notably the NAACP—as "the prime mover of the Negro's social revolt." He lauded the students' accomplishments:

The demonstrators have shifted the desegregation battle from the courtroom to the market place, and have shifted the main issue to one of individual dignity, rather than civil rights. Not that civil rights are unimportant—but, as these students believe, once the dignity of the Negro individual is admitted, the debate over his right to vote, attend public schools, or hold a job for which he is qualified becomes academic.

Howard Zinn, a young professor at Spelman College (who would go on to fame as a leftist historian and activist), approvingly noted that the sit-ins "cracked the wall of legalism in the structure of the desegregation strategy."[17]

For Martin Luther King Jr., the sit-ins demonstrated that the tactics of nonviolent direct-action protest could actually work. King described the sit-ins as "definitely following the same philosophy and techniques as the Montgomery bus boycotts" and suggested that they had provided "the answer to how we can meet delaying tactics that come through litigation." In his commencement address at Lincoln University in June 1961, King, in describing the value of nonviolent protest, posed the rhetorical question, "Does this bring results?" His first piece of evidence to demonstrate the efficacy of "creative protest" was the sit-ins: "In less than a year, lunch counters have been integrated in more than 142 cities of the Deep South, and this was done without a single court suit."[18]

King and his fellow leaders of SCLC shared Lomax's and Zinn's critique of what they saw as the NAACP's excessive commitment to litigation. The sit-ins created a flashpoint in the already tense relationship between SCLC and the NAACP. King saw in the student movement confirmation of his own commitment to direct-action protest and tactics based on moral persuasion—as well as further corroboration of his skepticism toward the NAACP. King and his inner circle were scathing in their private criticism of the NAACP's tactics in dealing with the sit-ins. King accused the NAACP of trying to "sabotage our humble efforts." Stanley Levison, one of King's closest advisers, wrote to King that the students "are demonstrating the bankruptcy of the policy of relying upon the courts and legislation to achieve real results." Levison attacked Thurgood Marshall for "saying that the first stage of demonstrations should be ended and a new one in the courts now [is] to be developed." The leaders of the NAACP "want to give a tranquilizer or pacifier to the whole movement and send the people back to their ordinary preoccupations. More and more they are revealing themselves as gradualists in reality while they pretend to be uncompromising and firm." If the NAACP failed to adopt new policies, Levison concluded, its "influence will sharply diminish and the true forces of struggle will move into effective leadership." While King and his allies would have embraced the student movement regardless, tensions with the NAACP sharpened their enthusiasm for the students' cause as well as their skepticism toward litigation-centered reform efforts.[19]

"Laws Will Not Solve Our Problems"

Not only those who might be considered to the left of the NAACP used the sit-ins to launch a critique of the NAACP and its approach to civil rights. Also taking this approach were some civil rights moderates— people who generally supported the antidiscrimination goals of the civil rights movement but counseled tactical caution in achieving these goals. Although some moderates criticized the protests as unnecessarily confrontational and disruptive, others praised the students for turning attention from litigation to moral persuasion and negotiation. Whereas King, Lawson, and Lomax felt the sit-ins showed that litigation-centered strategies were too slow, too cautious, and too reliant on elite leadership, moderates used the protests as an opportunity to criticize litigation as unnecessarily divisive. They argued that the backlash against *Brown* and the failure to desegregate southern schools showed the limits of court victories that face widespread social opposition. Judicial proclamations were limited in their ability to change hearts and minds. Protests—at least certain kinds of protests—may be more effective at changing views. "The sit-ins were, without question, productive of the most change," noted Ralph McGill, editor of the *Atlanta Constitution*. "No argument in a court of law could have dramatized the immorality and irrationality of such a custom as did the sit-ins. . . . Not even the Supreme Court decision on the schools in 1954 had done this. . . . The central moral problem was enlarged." "The approach in Christian charity and love of neighbor, is the only answer," explained Father Ernest L. Unterkoefler of Richmond, Virginia, in a radio discussion of the sit-ins. "Laws will not solve our problems."[20]

Leaders of the Southern Regional Council, a prominent voice of southern liberalism and a strong supporter of the sit-ins, shared this skepticism toward litigation and top-down legal change. SRC president James McBride Dabbs celebrated the protests as "a new heroism, a non-violent heroism, a creative heroism." By "appeal[ing] to conscience and self-interest instead of law," the students brought a desperately needed fresh approach to the problem of racial discrimination, one SRC report explained. "They have argued on the basis of moral right and supported that argument with economic pressure. By their action they have given the South an excellent opportunity to settle one facet of a broad problem by negotiation and good will instead of court order." It was in the best interest of both the students and southern whites to avoid "a new rash of time and money-consuming law suits." If law enforcement remained neutral in the confrontation, everyone could stay out of the courts, and the controversy could be resolved "through mediation and opinion leadership." Such a resolution, working through "economic pressures and civic sense of responsibility," "would quite likely be a better settlement than one hammered out through litigation in already over-burdened courts." "No one ever speaks of the 'school desegregation movement,'" noted SRC leader Leslie Dunbar. "Almost from the beginning the sit-ins have been referred to as a 'movement.'"[21]

An SRC report written in early April provides a fascinating portrait of the racial moderate attitude toward the student movement. The report divided the sit-ins into three "aspects." The first, described as the "essential nature" of the protest, had nothing to do with law or state power; it was simply "an appeal of one segment of the citizenry to another." This was the protest from the perspective of the student demonstrators. But this approach could be sustained only so long as southern whites refused to call on the police. Once this happened, the protest was transformed: "The issue now is no longer between citizens, but has become a struggle between Negro citizens and state power." This then opened the door for the third and final "aspect" of the sit-ins, when the civil rights lawyers arrived, offering "a systematic program of legal defense of the demonstrators." The goal of this line of attack was to "seek a re-definition of the legal duties and rights of property owners in the conduct of their business." Although the sit-ins "began as an issue of community relations," they "may well end as a question of legal rights and privileges." From the perspective of the lawyers at the NAACP, this move from protest to litigation was an inevitable and productive development; it was how real change happened. From the perspective of the SRC and many racial moderates in this period, still reeling from the segregationist onslaught that *Brown* awakened, the move, if perhaps inevitable, came with real costs. The larger movement would benefit from more time and effort spent struggling on the community level, without the intervention of the courts.[22]

By aligning itself with the students and their protest tactics, by insisting that litigation be just one tool—a tool to be relied upon only when others failed—the SRC saw in the sit-ins an opportunity to justify its particular role in the rapidly changing campaign against Jim Crow. The SRC took up an active supporting role for the student movement, researching developments across the South, providing information to newspapers, and offering to mediate negotiations in various southern cities.[23]

Moderate white southerners echoed, generally in more qualified form, the SRC position. Newspapers editors in the Upper South published editorials supporting the students' cause (if not necessarily their tactics). "Negro patrons occupying seats at the lunch counter have a position which demands consideration," wrote the *Greensboro Daily News*—and then insisted that this issue would only be resolved through "petition and negotiation" and not "a sit-down strike." When Greensboro students wrote a strongly worded open letter to North Carolina's attorney general for his statements encouraging the use of the state trespassing law against protesters, the newspaper chastised the students for their "hot-headedness" and failure to show "good will." Yet the paper also lamented the arrests of students in Raleigh, lashed out at the law-and-order proclamations of the state attorney general, and asserted that "the only sensible course is to find some way to serve all those customers who want to be served." The *Winston-Salem Sentinel* urged local lunch counters to desegregate. "Such a move," the editors explained, "would tell the Negro citizens that the white community is receptive to reasonable requests for removing racial discrimination."[24]

Various white southern politicians—most of whom relied on African American votes to hold on to their offices—also expressed some degree of support for the students. The mayor of Greensboro cautiously praised the students for remaining "orderly and courteous" and called upon business leaders to reach a "just and honorable resolution of this problem." The Nashville mayor's expression of support for the students when confronted by thousands of protesters at city hall was a turning point in that city's sit-in movement. After Winston-Salem's first student arrests in late February, its mayor appeared to come out in support of the students, announcing that the only two options the stores had were to "keep the counters closed, or they can open and feed everyone." The most widely noted expression of approval of the students' cause from a white southern politician was Florida governor LeRoy Collins's March 20 speech, covered live on radio and television, in which he denounced the practice of segregated lunch counters and announced the creation of a state commission to look into the issue. According to one account, "more than any other public figure, [Governor Collins] has succeeded in provoking discussion of segregation as a moral question."[25]

White religious leaders in cities across the Upper South publicly called for an end to lunch counter discrimination. From its office in High Point, North Carolina, the southeastern regional office of the American Friends Service Committee—a Quaker organization long dedicated to advancing social justice through nonviolence—issued a statement condemning racial discrimination and praising the students for showing the effectiveness of nonviolent methods. In late March, a Richmond-based leader of the Southern Presbyterian Church praised the students' cause (while questioning their choice of methods) and called for an end to racial discrimination.[26]

Communism and the Sit-Ins

One tactic defenders of segregation frequently relied upon was to dismiss local civil rights activists as puppets of "outside" operators, with these nefarious outsiders assumed to be linked to the Communist Party. This was a standard line of attack by the white South against the NAACP after *Brown*; it was no surprise when defenders of Jim Crow used it to attack the sit-ins. Segregationist die-hards attempted to link the movement to national civil rights organizations (CORE being a popular target), to Communists, or to unidentified "left-wing" organizers. "These youngster are catspaws of . . . an organized effort projected from outside sources," declared the editors of the *Nashville Banner* after Nashville's first sit-ins. Georgia's governor denounced the statement of principles Atlanta students released prior to their sit-ins as "a left-wing statement" that "obviously . . . was not written by students." These kinds of claims received an unexpected endorsement when ex-president Harry S. Truman questioned whether Communists were somehow behind the sit-ins.[27]

These attacks struck only glancing blows to the sit-in movement. The students proudly and insistently emphasized the homegrown nature of their movement. The sit-ins "are not part of a plan and were undertaken independently," one student leader explained in the early weeks of the movement. "We did not consult with groups or individuals at the other schools. There is no organization behind us." (The widely published Associated Press story noted that this same student leader had recently testified before the House Committee on Un-American Activities about his work refuting Communist "anti-American propaganda.") After a white northerner joined a picket line in Charlotte, North Carolina, leaders of the local student movement quickly issued a statement explaining that the person was just a reporter and that the "students keep themselves free from all groups which are considered 'outsiders.'" When a CORE field secretary arrived in Charlotte, the students sought to separate themselves from the organization and its perceived radicalism. "This movement has no intention of reconstructing social history, nor economic factors in Charlotte," the student leadership declared. "All we want to do is sit down and eat when we are tired."[28]

Ironically, the students had considerable "outside" help in their effort to emphasize the indigenous, youth-led nature of their movement. The SRC urged the use of the label "sit-in" rather than "sit-down," to emphasize the novelty of the tactic and to distinguish the student protest from the factory "sit-down" strikes of labor activists in the 1930s and from the radical connotations that accompanied the label. NAACP executive director Roy Wilkins played up the independence of the students in an attempt to protect them from accusations that they might be under Communist influence. "Remember, these students want to run their own show; they don't want any advice from Moscow," he explained. The NAACP also worked to keep Communists away from the sit-ins. A memorandum from the national office to NAACP local branches warned: "Other elements, including Communists and related groups, undoubtedly will try to 'muscle in.' . . . Every reasonable and firm effort should be used to prevent such an intrusion." "The movement has been spontaneous and contagious," reported the SRC in its report on the opening weeks of the sit-ins; "it has been carried out by students." The mainstream press largely embraced this portrayal, emphasizing that the sit-in movement was a grassroots, locally produced, student-led campaign. By the second month of the sit-in movement, the SRC believed these efforts by the students and their supporters had been successful: "The protests spread by their own momentum, spurred no doubt by a natural spirit of emulation, and this fact was by mid-March generally recognized by public opinion."[29]

Framing a Constitutional Claim

From the earliest lunch counter sit-ins of the 1960 movement, participants and observers described the fundamental issue at stake—the right to racially nondiscriminatory access to public accommodations—as not only a matter of right and wrong, not only a matter of dollars and cents, but as a matter of constitutional principle. This was not necessarily the dominant reading of the sit-ins. Students involved in the protests more often spoke about their actions in moral or religious rather than constitutional terms. Sympathizers frequently praised protesters for shifting the terms of the struggle—from changing laws to changing hearts and minds. Yet alongside and entwined with the dominant moral and religious frames was a constitutional one: the idea that the right that the students were claiming by sitting at lunch counters across the South was grounded in the Constitution's requirement that all people receive equal protection of the laws.

With their frequent references to the issue as one of first-class versus second-class citizenship, student protesters often implied that they believed a constitutional principle was at stake. Sometimes they explicitly declared their actions as justified under the Constitution. But the promotion and widespread acceptance of the idea that the students were claiming a right grounded in the Constitution was not primarily the work of the protesters themselves. It was the work of sympathetic commentators, civil rights lawyers, legal scholars, government officials, elected representatives, and judges. Within the overlapping realms of public discourse and judicial decision making in which constitutional norms are formed and transformed, influential figures regularly embraced the idea that the racial discrimination at lunch counters was a question of constitutional rights.

Those who stood opposed to the students' cause also played a key role in the constitutionalization of the right the sit-in protesters demanded. From the beginning of the sit-in movement, defenders of segregation confidently proclaimed that the Constitution was on their side. Their constitutional argument had two components. One was their reading of the Fourteenth Amendment. The Constitution, they insisted, made a sharp distinction between publicly operated facilities (such as schools or public beaches) and privately owned public accommodations. Even if the equal protection clause prohibited racial discrimination in relation to the former (a grudging concession for many segregationists), they argued it did not apply to the latter. The other constitutional claim segregationists advanced was to insist that store owners had constitutional rights to liberty, property, and freedom of association that deserved protection against efforts to force them to serve all races on equal terms.[30]

These arguments demanded a response by civil rights proponents. For all the efforts of students and their allies to shift the discussion from the realm of law to morality, they could not leave unanswered segregationists' claims that the Constitution either said nothing about this particular form of racial discrimination, or that it affirmatively protected a proprietor's right to discriminate. Civil rights lawyers, in public statements and courtroom arguments on behalf of arrested protesters, led the charge in pressing the argument that the Constitution forbid lunch counter discrimination or, at minimum, state enforcement of this form of discrimination.

But it was not just civil rights lawyers who transformed the protests into claims of constitutional reconstruction. The historical moment in which the sit-ins took place ensured that the protests would be understood as raising not just a moral or legal claim but a constitutional one. Most importantly, the experience of *Brown v. Board of Education* and the national struggle over the meaning of the Constitution's principle of equal protection that followed encouraged many Americans, in what seemed an almost instinctive move, to see the sit-ins as a constitutional issue. The six-year experience with school desegregation allowed for this intuitive transformation of the sit-ins into a constitutional issue to which the logic of *Brown*'s desegregation principle seemed to apply. "The Negroes now confront us with the Constitution in one hand and the Bible in the other," wrote a white southern minister. Many assumed that, like school desegregation, the public accommodations question would need to be resolved at the Supreme Court. Following the first mass arrest of protesters in Raleigh, North Carolina, the local paper wrote, "The picket line now extends from the dime stores to the United States Supreme Court and beyond that to national and world opinion." "The true answer," explained Jacob Javits, a liberal Republican U.S. senator from New York, "is the rule of equal opportunity under the constitution and support for the mandates of the courts upholding civil rights by all levels of government."[31]

In explaining *Brown*'s role in defining the issues of concern and the terms of debate for the sit-ins, particularly relevant are the rulings that followed *Brown* in which the Court, in terse, unsigned "per curiam" decisions, extended the constitutional prohibition of segregation to public parks, auditoriums, golf courses, beaches, and buses. "Looked at en masse," wrote one legal scholar, these rulings "seem collectively to stand for the general principle that publicly ordained racial segregation is inconsistent with the demands of the equal protection clause." By the time of the sit-ins, the Court's refutation of the "separate but equal" principle had moved beyond schools into all areas of public life that fell under direct state control. The question for many civil rights supporters, then, was whether this trend would eventually encompass restaurants and hotels and other public accommodations whose purpose was to serve the general public. As the sit-ins spread across the South, conservative *New York Times* columnist Arthur Krock apprehensively wrote, "The grounds of the 1954 ruling [in *Brown*] are so broad that the court might find room for a decision that, regardless of damaged private-property values, police protection could not be given the discriminatory lunch rooms when the sit-in protests were peacefully registered."[32]

These developments convinced many observers that the principle animating *Brown* applied to public accommodations. A generation of shifts in constitutional doctrine by the Supreme Court had destabilized any comfortable assumptions about the reach of the constitutional prohibition of racial discrimination, thereby giving an opening in the public discourse in which the claim embodied by the students in their sit-in protests could be understood as a viable challenge to existing understandings of the limits of the equal protection clause—that is, a challenge to traditional conceptions of state action.

The application of the *Brown* principle to public accommodations was commonplace in the months and years following the sit-ins. One of the most influential proponents of this position was Martin Luther King Jr., who urged the student protesters to see the sit-ins as the logical extension of the school segregation struggle. He echoed the famous words of Chief Justice Earl Warren's *Brown* opinion when he told the students that "separate facilities, *whether in eating places or public schools*, are inherently unequal." During his appearance on NBC's news show *Meet the Press* in March 1960, King was asked whether there was a risk of inconsistency in denouncing white segregationist defiance of the law while urging sit-in protesters "to break the local laws." King responded that "the law of the land is a law which calls for integration." In *Brown*, he explained, the Court "made it palpably clear that separate facilities are inherently unequal. So that in breaking local laws we are really seeking to dignify the law and to affirm the real and positive meaning of the law of the land." When one of his interviewers challenged King, noting that "there have been court decisions saying that a storekeeper can select his customers," King pushed his constitutional argument further, insisting that *Brown* meant "that segregation is wrong even in lunch counters and public places because that decision said in substance that segregation generates a feeling of inferiority within the segregated and, thereby, it breaches the equal protection clause of the Fourteenth Amendment." He added hopefully, "I'm sure that if we follow this through in this area the same thing will follow." Similarly, when civil rights activist Bayard Rustin commissioned a fund-raising advertisement to run in the *New York Times* in late March 1960 under the title "Heed Their Rising Voices," it called attention to the "thousands of Southern Negro students [who] are engaged in widespread non-violent demonstrations in positive affirmation of the right to live in human dignity as guaranteed by the U.S. Constitution and the Bill of Rights."[33]

While such statements by leading civil rights advocates are best understood as claims for a reformed vision of justice bolstered by an aspirational claim on the Constitution, the striking point is that the implication of these kinds of statements—that the Fourteenth Amendment protected the students' actions—echoed throughout the discussions of the sit-ins. And they often came from unexpected quarters.

Consider the words of President Eisenhower soon after the sit-ins spread across the South. Eisenhower was generally not recognized as a friend to the cause of racial justice. His refusal to publicly support the *Brown* decision had frustrated civil rights proponents. Yet when faced with the sit-in movement, he seemed to assume the students had the Constitution on their side. Responding to a question about the protests at a press conference, he noted that "we have a responsibility in helping to enforce or seeing that the constitutional rights guaranteed are not violated," before wavering and claiming uncertainty about the constitutional status of these protests. A few moments later, when pressed again on the issue, the president seemed to have more confidence, noting that "demonstrations, if orderly and seeking to support the rights of equality, were constitutional" and that "my own understanding is that when an establishment is, belongs to the public, opened under public charter and so on, that equal rights are involved." When again pressed for his views on the sit-in movement later in the spring, he went on something of a ramble. "We here can talk and believe in the ideals that have been set up for us by the Constitution, and certainly we have a responsibility in helping to enforce or seeing that the constitutional rights guaranteed are not violated," he explained. But he then confessed that "when it comes to sit-ins, I am just not enough of a lawyer to say just exactly what they do mean—what they mean in the constitutional or legal terms. . . . I would say for that question, you ought to go to the Attorney General. I am just not that much of a lawyer." The president's public comments highlight the fact that the constitutional claims raised by the sit-ins were, at minimum, viable in public discourse. The students had effectively destabilized any certainty that the *Brown* decision did not logically entail the desegregation of restaurants. Even a president notoriously reluctant to endorse *Brown* was inclined to not only express support for the students but to view the issue as implicating basic constitutional principles.[34]

The assumption that the lunch counter sit-ins involved a valid constitutional claim was also encouraged by the fact that students did not just target privately operated public accommodations. Sometimes on advice of counsel (as in Atlanta), sometimes with little apparent strategic forethought, students sat-in at government-operated facilities, such as courthouse cafeterias or public libraries, where existing judicial doctrine unquestionably protected their claimed right to nondiscriminatory treatment. Lawyers versed in the state action doctrine recognized a sit-in at a courthouse cafeteria and a sit-in at a Woolworth lunch counter as raising distinct legal claims. To protesters and most observers, however, the distinction was less clear.

For example, in response to then-senator Kennedy's expression of support for the sit-ins during the 1960 presidential campaign, Eugene Patterson, editor of the *Atlanta Constitution*, chided Kennedy for the imprecision of his remarks. Kennedy had expressed approval of sit-ins at "public facilities, including lunchrooms." Patterson asked, "What does he mean 'public'? Publicly owned? Or privately owned, open to the public. He didn't say. Nobody asked him. The point is rather important. There is an element of deception in the uncritical question: Are you for or against sit-in? The intelligent response must be: What kind of sit-in?"[35]

Strategic civil rights lawyers saw an opportunity in this "deception." In Portsmouth, Virginia, sit-ins took place at the same time lawyers pursued a lawsuit to desegregate the city's library. A federal judge ordered the library desegregated, but also took the opportunity to warn that "the day there is a sitdown strike in the Portsmouth Public Library somebody is going to account for it." Len Holt, the CORE-affiliated lawyer who won the library case, responded with his own statement declaring the lunch counter sit-ins a justified claim for a constitutional right. Here we can see how the simultaneous challenge to segregation in public facilities, such as a library, and in privately owned public accommodations, such as a lunch counter, provided opportunities for civil rights activists to reframe the legal issues in a way that strengthened the claimed right in the latter category. As the actions of this segregationist judge demonstrated, the post-*Brown* line of cases clearly established a constitutional right to nondiscriminatory service in state-operated facilities. By aligning the claimed right to nondiscriminatory service in a public accommodation with the right in a public facility, as Holt did, he reinforced the controversial, aspirational lunch counter constitutional claim.[36]

Whether knowingly or not, sit-in movement participants worked an incredibly powerful trick: by juxtaposing an aspirational constitutional claim alongside judicially recognized constitutional claims, they leveraged the latter to strengthen the former. Lawyers are always advancing their arguments by way of analogy: A is like B; the law treats A in a certain way; therefore the law should treat B the same. The sit-in movement offered, in effect, the same kind of argument by analogy. Movement activists took what was, as a matter of constitutional doctrine, a significant gap between two quite different legal claims and reframed it, as a matter of public discourse, into the same basic issue.

This trend toward constitutionalizing the racial discrimination in public accommodations only strengthened in the following years. In February 1963 President Kennedy gave an address in which he said: "No act is more contrary to the spirit of our democracy and Constitution—or more rightfully resented by a Negro citizen who seeks only equal treatment—than the barring of that citizen from restaurants, hotels, theaters, recreational areas and other public accommodations and facilities." Later that spring, in announcing his support for federal civil rights legislation, Kennedy declared the "right to be served in facilities which are open to the public" to be an "elemental right," comparable to education and voting. "We are confronted primarily with a moral issue," he went on to say. "It is as old as the scriptures and is as clear as the American Constitution." The public accommodations provision of the proposed civil rights bill would protect "the basic constitutional rights of an individual to be treated as a free and equal human being," he asserted the following month.[37]

During the debate over the public accommodations provision of what would become the Civil Rights Act of 1964, many in Congress, in the Kennedy administration, and in the press assumed that the Fourteenth Amendment provided Congress with the necessary power to desegregate public accommodations. The law "has a simple purpose," explained Senator Hubert Humphrey on the floor of the Senate. "That purpose is to give fellow citizens—Negroes—the same rights and opportunities that white people take for granted. This is no more than what was preached by the prophets, and by Christ Himself. It is no more than what our Constitution guarantees." Upon signing the Civil Rights Act into law, President Lyndon Johnson said of the "unequal treatment" that the law targeted: "Our Constitution, the foundation of our Republic, forbids it. The principles of our freedom forbid it. Morality forbids it. And the law I will sign tonight forbids it."[38]

As a claim pressed upon national opinion and the political branches of government, the students' actions offered, in effect, a persuasive reinterpretation of the scope of the equal protection of the law. By protesting at privately owned lunch counters, at municipal pools, in bus terminals, in the libraries, and in other publicly owned places, and by arguing that segregation in all these places raised the same fundamental concerns about dignity and citizenship, the protesters were making a case to the larger society that the principle of equal protection entailed a government responsibility to stand on the side of those combating the most egregious manifestations of Jim Crow, regardless of whether existing constitutional doctrine delineated these acts as "private" or not.

At a time when many felt frustrated with the direction of the civil rights struggle, the sit-ins responded to a wide array of hopes and desires. For those who demanded direct-action protest rather than lobbying, litigation, or deal making, the sit-ins showed a new path forward. For those who favored negotiation over litigation, the students' tactics presented a powerful contrast to the school desegregation litigation that had shown frustratingly little progress since the breakthrough decision in *Brown*. For those who believed African Americans should push for reform through demonstrating their economic power, the sit-ins, in combination with boycotts, were just what was needed. For those who sought to separate the youth movement from the established civil rights organization, the sit-ins offered a kind of spontaneity and local initiative that was lacking in the more carefully calculated protests of SCLC and the NAACP.

The uncertain nature of the constitutional claim inherent in the sit-in protests bolstered the case for those who championed the students' cause. It allowed for the promulgation of the argument that the claim for nondiscriminatory service was the next logical step toward completing the constitutional process begun in *Brown*. As a matter of legal doctrine, this was contestable. As a matter of public discussion over civil rights in the wake of *Brown* and in the optimistic atmosphere encompassing the sit-ins, it resonated. What might appear to be a relatively narrow question of constitutional doctrine thus helped to define the spectrum of choices available to activists, businessmen, local officials, and lawyers as they all struggled to come to terms with the consequences of the sit-in protests.

The sit-in movement, and the supportive responses it received, offers a case study of the development of constitutional principles in the distinctive realm of extrajudicial constitutional contestation. Because of the sit-ins, a right to nondiscriminatory access to lunch counters and hotels, regardless of whether they were publicly or privately owned, now had a place, alongside school desegregation and voting rights, as a central goal of the civil rights movement. The sit-ins show how the transformation of public values and priorities can transform a constitutional norm. They show how public expectations about the Constitution can be shaped not only by signals from authoritative constitutional interpreters, such as courts, but also by transformative acts of social protest.

FOUR

The Opponents

You know and I know that desegregation is coming—but not tomorrow.

—HOTEL MANAGER, SOUTH CAROLINA, FEBRUARY 1960[1]

To understand the constitutional challenge posed by the sit-ins, we also need to consider the claims of those who opposed the students' cause. Just as the distinctive legal status of racial discrimination in public accommodations in 1960 America shaped the protesters' actions, so did it affect how white southern opponents of the civil rights movement understood their options when faced with the sit-ins. The story of the sit-in movement, and the legal challenge it placed before the nation, cannot be fully told without attending to the varied commitments of those opposed to the students' claim, whether they understood their position as defending the prerogatives of white supremacy, questioning the viability or constitutionality of civil rights remedies, or simply placing other priorities— such as running a profitable lunch counter—ahead of racial equality.

One of my goals in this chapter is to demonstrate the diversity of interests and tactics contained within a group that too often has been lumped into the monolithic category of "segregationists." Those opposed to the goals and tactics of the sit-in movement were hardly a unified front. Lunch counter operators complained about being caught in a battle they were not sure they wanted to fight. The police were frustrated by their limited authority to shut down the demonstrations, which they saw as a significant threat to public order; they often were reduced to unhappy spectators of the drama of the sit-in protest. Local political leaders often tried to stay above the fray, striving to play the role of the honest broker between the competing groups. State-level political leaders tended to be more committed to segregation than their local counterparts, more aggressive in denouncing the sit-ins as threats to public order, and more insistent that store operators call on the police. But their authority, much like that of the police, was constrained by the particular legal architecture of private racial discrimination in the post-*Brown* period. Then there were the most dedicated defenders of Jim Crow, whom I term segregationist "ideologues." This group launched a constitutional counter-offensive in which they proclaimed that private business operators had a legally protected "right to discriminate." Recent scholarship has given greater attention to divisions among segregationists, resulting in more complex and richer historical accounts. This chapter places the sit-in movement squarely within this new narrative of the civil rights era.[2]

These divisions among southern whites were particularly consequential in the sit-in movement because of the distinctive legal issues involved. For other episodes in the civil rights struggle, law operated to minimize these divisions. This was the case with the backlash against *Brown v. Board of Education*, for example. State leaders who led the opposition against *Brown* effectively neutralized divisions on school desegregation among white southerners by a legal maneuver: they removed power from localities and consolidated authority to the state level, where the segregationist cause could be more carefully strategized and managed. Ultimately a relatively small number of leaders—leaders who saw political advantage in defending segregation—controlled the white South's stand against school desegregation. This kind of legal option was unavailable when it came to the sit-ins. The sit-ins targeted not state institutions but thousands of private businesses. These businesses decided whom to serve; they decided whether to press charges against sit-in protesters. The legal factor that made the constitutional claim of the sit-in protesters such a challenge to existing equal protection doctrine in the courts—the fact that these were private businesses—also made mobilizing in opposition to the sit-ins much more difficult.[3]

Another way in which legal factors amplified divisions among white southerners was what might be described as a misalignment between incentives and authority. Those who most wanted to use the law to crack down on the students—police, state-level officials—were often unable to do so. Those who least wanted to use the law—store managers—were the ones who needed to start the legal process. The legal dynamics of racial discrimination in public accommodations meant that the dividing lines among the diverse ranks of opponents to the sit-ins were highly consequential. These divisions ultimately benefited the sit-in protesters.

The Businessmen

C. L. "Curly" Harris, the manager of the Woolworth store in downtown Greensboro, was in his second-floor office when he learned what was taking place at his lunch counter on the afternoon of February 1, 1960. A waitress told him that four young African American men had requested service at the lunch counter. When refused, one declared, "We are going to sit here until we are served." "Let them sit there," Harris told the waitress. "Don't say anything else to them."[4]

The sit-ins did not catch Harris completely by surprise. Several years earlier, Harris had reached out to the regional Woolworth office in Atlanta to ask what he should do if faced with this kind of situation. The regional office supported the plan Harris proposed: do nothing. The best approach, they agreed, was to let the black patrons sit there until they got bored and left. Despite this preparation, when he saw this hypothetical situation actually happening in his store, Harris became nervous. He immediately left the store and went to the police station to, in his words, "find out what kind of action the police would offer." The police chief told him that he could have the students arrested for trespassing. Harris did not want to do this, however. He told the police chief that he would only take this step if there was violence in his store. "No service, no talk, no provocation, no arrests"—this was how Harris described his plan. "They can just sit there," Harris told reporters when the protests continued the next day. "It's nothing to me." The sit-ins continued, each day bringing more demonstrators than the last. Segregationist counter-demonstrators showed up. And growing numbers of newspaper reporters captured it all.[5]

Harris felt trapped. His store was in "the middle lane of a three-lane highway, in a 'no-win' situation." Why had his lunch counter been singled out when all the food establishments in the city had the same policy? Wasn't he a victim of "discrimination," he wondered. To keep his predominantly white clientele, he believed he needed to run a segregated lunch counter. This was local custom, and he was not going to challenge it, certainly not on his own. Arrests had to be a last option.

Giving more attention to these protests, as arrests would surely do, would be bad for business. It would scare away white customers, and it would alienate black customers, who contributed a sizable portion of his store's revenue. Harris felt he was up against not only the lunch counter protesters, but also the growing numbers of news reporters and photographers. Harris tried, unsuccessfully, to prevent any photographs taken inside his store. (Looking back on these historic events, Harris would identify the press, rather than the student protesters, as his primary antagonists.) The police chief sent officers to keep an eye on the situation, but the police would not act unless Harris called on them to do so. Harris complained to anyone who would listen that city officials were doing nothing to help. They just left the targeted businesses to work out the issue on their own. The Woolworth national office did not offer much guidance either. Company policy, a spokesman explained, was "to abide by local custom." If a local branch believed changed custom allowed for changed policy, "we will of course go along with that."[6]

The situation took a dangerous turn on Saturday, February 6, when a tense face-off between hundreds of black protesters and white counter-protesters was broken up by a bomb threat, which gave the police an excuse to clear out the store. That evening the students consented to a moratorium on their protests while negotiations between the students and lunch counter operators continued. Harris agreed to keep the Woolworth lunch counter shut down during negotiations.

With African American college students having transformed his beloved Woolworth store into ground zero of the nation's civil rights movement, Harris sat down in late February to explain his situation in a seven-page handwritten letter to the North Carolina governor. His first order of business was to make sure that Governor Luther Hodges appreciated what kind of business he worked for: "Never in all the years with this company have I heard a statement received or given an order of an act that was unethical." He pointed out the considerable role of the Woolworth chain in North Carolina's economy and the valuable service the store provided by offering affordable, quality merchandise to the lower and middle class. With regard to the demands of the sit-ins, the dollars and cents simply did not add up, he insisted. Less than five percent of his sales were to African Americans. "To integrate our lunch dept. would mean the loss of white trade to gain very little colored trade." At the same time, the current situation was unsustainable: the protests were bleeding away his profits. As to his position regarding the rightness or wrongness of segregation, Harris was coy with the segregationist governor. "From a moral point of view . . . we won't argue from that. . . . The only basis for our stand is that we will not breach the custom—when other restaurants serve we would. . . . Actually we are fighting a battle for the white people who still want to eat with white people and it's costing us."[7]

Harris's approach to the issue was broadly representative of how most lunch counter operators confronted the sit-ins. They were businessmen first and foremost. They wanted to make a profit, and they viewed themselves as catering to their clients' preferences, not dictating them. After discussing the issue with managers of targeted stores in Durham, the Durham Mayor's Committee on Human Relations concluded that the managers "feel that the current demonstrations directed against them are unjustified, since they are unable to dictate or direct public opinion." They believed that protesters would do better to direct their "efforts toward educating the Community to the acceptance of de-segregation." According to a reporter for the *New York Times*, Nashville's store owners "do not view integrated lunch service to Negroes in terms of morality. They say it is just a matter of dollar and cents." Integrating their lunch counters would turn away the "country folk they have attracted to the city area at great effort." Noted a Nashville businessman: "Well, after all this fuss, if these rural people from out in the country think they're going to eat with Negroes, they may not come here to shop. They'll stay in their own towns and try some of these new shopping centers."[8]

The store managers faced a classic collective action problem: if others integrated, then a store manager would fall into line, thankful, in many cases, to simply have the controversy resolved; but no single store wanted to be the first to integrate. Harris made this point again and again. In Nashville, "business men have indicated their readiness to desegregate facilities," noted the *Times* reporter, "but they say they will do so only if their competitors agree."[9]

Store operators whose businesses were targeted by sit-in demonstrations felt they were targets of opportunity—even victims—in someone else's battle. His store was "not responsible for the customs in Greensboro," Harris explained, and therefore "the people of Greensboro and the City Council should have stepped in." Nashville store owners pleaded with their mayor to stop demonstrators from entering their stores. The store operators are "defenseless against this situation," complained one businessman. "We are being singled out as tyrants who are being unfair to Negroes, when our duty and that of all business firms is to do the best job they can for the majority, and whites comprise the majority of our trade." As a contributor to a chain store industry newsletter described the situation: "Until a higher judgment is reached, variety chain stores may continue to be helpless hostages of a conflict they did not create and are powerless to avert."[10]

Harris resented the lack of support he felt businessmen received. Greensboro public officials did nothing to help. When negotiations broke down, the mayor just called on local businesses to abandon their segregation policy. "For God's sake, do something!" Harris demanded of the mayor at one point. (Harris would later say that the entire controversy could have been removed if the city council had just passed a public accommodations ordinance.) The local press called on him to desegregate. He carefully calculated the costs of the protests to his business. At one point he talked with the regional Woolworth manager about retiring. In an interview almost twenty years later, Harris remained angry. "Wound up I lost one-third of my profits, and I lost one-third of my salary," he complained. "I resented it because I got no help from my company, I got no help from the city. I got no help from anybody."[11]

The lunch counter operators' general resistance to calling upon the police to deal with the sit-ins reflected their effort to maintain this posture of perceived neutrality. In his letter to the governor, Harris echoed the position that the governor and his attorney general had been energetically promoting regarding the state of the law. "As a legal issue," he wrote, "a firm has the right to choose its customers and to choose what it sells to them." But, he added, he chose not to "embarrass" the students by having them arrested. Harris was not necessarily opposed to any use of law enforcement to deal with the sit-ins. In his letter to the governor, he indicated that he would welcome police action to deal with "mob" situations. But he was not willing to rely upon the formal processes of law if he had to be the one to take the initiative. He did not want to carry this kind of direct responsibility for propping up what any decent Greensboro businessman knew to be a fading edifice of Jim Crow. His attitude toward the role of the courts in dealing with the protest was not particularly ideological. Nor was it motivated by his assessment of the legal options available to him, since he believed the law was on his side if he chose to call upon it. Rather, his position was pragmatic, economic, with perhaps a touch of humanity.[12]

Harris was not alone in his hesitancy to call the law in to deal with the sit-in protests. While many students were arrested, prosecuted, and often fined or sent to jail, the overwhelming majority of those who participated in the sit-ins were not. When faced with a group of protesters

who refused to leave, the most common response by restaurant operators was to shut down their lunch counters. In some instances, the operators tried more creative tactics, such as converting lunch counters
to sales counters and removing all the stools from the lunch counters.
During the first wave of protests in both Greensboro and Nashville,
for example, no students were arrested. Most business operators simply wanted the protests to go away. They wanted to make money, and
the sit-ins were preventing them from doing that. Sending potential
paying customers off to jail was not good business, a point that the
business owners regularly made when asked why they were unwilling
to call the police and have the protesters charged with trespassing on
private property. Many assumed (or hoped) the sit-ins were nothing
more than a college prank ("of the 'panty-raid' variety") that would
soon blow over.[13]

If there was an official policy of the white South, this was it: private
business owners were to bear the responsibility for calling upon the
law to maintain Jim Crow. This was a burden that, by the spring of
1960, many, perhaps most, lunch counter operators, regardless of their
personal beliefs on segregation, were not enthusiastic to shoulder.

The Police

The sit-ins frustrated the police. Franklin McCain, one of the Greensboro Four, recalled that a police officer learned what was happening
on the first day of their protest and came into the store. He "was pac-
ing the aisle . . . behind us, where we were seated, with his club in his
hand, just sort of knocking it in his hand, and just looking mean and
red and a little bit upset and a little bit disgusted. And you had the feeling that he didn't know what the hell to do. . . . [H]e doesn't know what
he can or what he cannot do."[14]

From the perspective of the police, the law that they were empowered to enforce was agnostic when it came to racial discrimination in
public accommodations. Although many southern states and localities still had segregation laws on the books, the police rarely tried to
enforce them. In light of *Brown* and subsequent Supreme Court rulings striking down government-compelled segregation beyond public
schools, even the most biased southern judge would have had trouble
in 1960 trying to enforce a law requiring racial discrimination in eating facilities. Although civil rights opponents sometimes referenced
segregation laws to threaten protesters, no sit-in protester was charged

with violating a segregation statute. Nor was there a legal requirement that lunch counters refrain from racial discrimination, as there were in many northern states and localities that were covered by public accommodations laws. The choice of whether to segregate or not was left to the business operators. Unless a protester created a public disturbance (and they carefully avoided behavior that would risk this), police had to follow their lead.[15]

As long as the situation remained orderly, the official policy of the police was to step in only when requested by the restaurant owners. During the first week of protests, as the movement spread across several North Carolina cities, police kept on eye on the protests but, as the Associated Press reported, "there was no violence or incidents that required their attention." "We will answer requests for service [from restaurant owners] as they come in," explained a Raleigh, North Carolina, police chief. "But we have no part of this unless there is a violation of the law." "We are not taking sides," explained the police chief of High Point, North Carolina, "but we cannot tolerate violations of laws. . . ." They watched and waited for something to happen that would require them to intervene.[16]

Just as the students arrived with carefully prepared scripts, so did the police. In Atlanta, for example, the police followed explicit guidelines that had been crafted to implement a new trespass law the state legislature passed in response to the sit-ins. They would wait until the establishment manager called upon them to make an arrest. Upon arriving, the officer would read the text of the new law, which made it a misdemeanor to remain in a place of business after being asked to leave. The officer then asked the manager to request the protesters to leave. Only then, after the police witnessed the students refusing the manager's request, did they step in and make their arrests. "You leave me no choice," declared the Atlanta police captain at the end of one of these artless performances. "I will have to arrest you."[17]

There were plentiful reports of flagrantly biased policing. Most police, like most white southerners, supported racial segregation and condemned the disruptive nature of the sit-in demonstrations. In Nashville, for example, the first round of disorderly conduct arrests included only sit-in protesters, not the segregationist counter-protesters who attacked the demonstrators. In the Deep South, racist, abusive policing was the norm. In Baton Rouge, the police arrested a group of protesters for disturbing the peace for simply requesting service at a whites-only lunch counter. ("How were they disturbing the peace?" the students' lawyer asked the arresting officer at the subsequent trial. "By sitting there," he answered.) For these police officers, the threat of disorder was enough to initiate arrests of protesters—a tactic that would produce convictions that were particularly vulnerable on appeal.[18]

Yet the kind of flagrant brutality that would surely have met the students had they attempted their sit-ins a generation earlier was not a viable option for the police in 1960. Growing black voting power, increased federal oversight of local policing practices, and more attention from the press—especially once the sit-ins became a major national news event—made violent police crackdowns on peaceful protests too costly to the defenders of segregation. Students even reported that some police were fair, unbiased, and, on occasion, grudgingly supportive of their efforts.[19]

In the end, the police seemed to want what the lunch counter operators wanted: someone in authority to do something. The sit-ins led to volatile confrontations, and the police felt helpless watching them unfold day after day. According to a report filed by a detective on the fourth day of the Greensboro sit-ins, "The situation will explode in my opinion if there isn't some decision or clear cut policy made. . . ." Even if they would have liked to have acted to end the protests, their legal authority limited their ability to do so. Unlike the store operators, they wanted to use the force of the law to diffuse these volatile situations. But short of a public disturbance, the operators held the authority to initiate the legal process. The misalignment of authority and incentives created a situation in which the protests would explode across the South.[20]

Local Leaders

White local leaders in urban areas of the Upper South and in major cities throughout the rest of the South had their own incentives to consider. They lived in communities where African Americans voted in significant numbers and where the growing black middle class held considerable economic sway, through both black-owned businesses and black patronage of white businesses. White political and economic leaders also sought to portray their communities as more progressive on racial issues, so as to better attract coveted economic investment from outside the South. As a result, local leaders usually searched for a conciliatory approach to the sit-ins. The primary goal of city officials, newspaper editors, and other influential figures in the local communities was to diffuse the explosive issue. Whether this meant desegregating lunch counters or keeping in place the segregation policy often was less important than that the issue be resolved. And they generally agreed that the best way to reach a resolution of the sit-in crisis was to limit the role of state authority and the legal process.

Some sided with the students' cause. "This is a matter for negotiation and conciliation and not legal action," urged the mayor of Miami. Greensboro's mayor echoed this sentiment. When his city appeared on the verge of major racial confrontation following the February 6 bomb scare that closed downtown lunch counters, he issued a statement asserting that "peace and good order are essential to the personal civil rights of anyone, white or colored." He then called on "the leadership of the Negro students and the business concerns involved to place the public interest above personal considerations, even to the extent of foregoing, for a while, individual rights and financial interest, if by doing so a peaceful solution can be evolved." Nashville's mayor eventually came out in support of the students during a dramatic confrontation with a mass student demonstration. Supportive statements of various local officials were key in the success of the sit-in campaign in northern Virginia, which did not begin until June but achieved a desegregation agreement in just two weeks.[21]

In Atlanta, Mayor William Hartsfield praised the statement that local student activists released prior to their sit-ins for expressing "the legitimate aspirations of young people throughout the nation" and "perform[ing] the constructive service of letting the white community know what others are thinking." At the same time, he tried to talk the students out of their protests. Once sit-ins began, he condemned them as a threat to public order. Demonstrations "carried on in excess . . . endanger the progress Atlanta has made in maintaining good racial relations," he warned, adding that "it is bad to hurt business and innocent merchants in your efforts to get what you are seeking." He rejected proposals for a biracial commission, arguing that the issue should be resolved in the courts and at the polls.[22]

Some local officials came out against the students from the start. Raleigh mayor W. G. Enloe threw his support squarely behind his business owners. "We are in sympathy with the merchants involved in that they must, to operate profitably, follow this custom over which we have no control," he said after the first day of his city's sit-ins. The protests were "destined to fail," and the students should call them off before they jeopardize "other more valuable relations long enjoyed between all races in our city." In the Deep South, this kind of sentiment was the norm among local officials. Tallahassee's mayor arrived on the scene of a sit-in, along with several police officers, and personally demanded that the students leave. When they refused, he directed that they be arrested.[23]

Whether they expressed their support for one side or the other, mayors urged negotiation and compromise as a way to deal with the issue and put an end to the protests. They were limited, however, in their authority to deal with the situation. Like many lunch counter operators, they, too, felt a sense of helplessness in the face of the sit-ins. They could not force the students to stop; they could not force the businesses to desegregate; and they could not force the counter-protesters to stay home. When faced with the pressure from demonstrators on the one side and their business community on the other, they often shifted responsibility (and blame) by creating committees of leading local citizens, usually including African American leaders, who were charged with studying and resolving the issue.[24]

Local newspapers provided critical support for the mayors. The press regularly praised their mayors for their approach to the sit-ins: pushing for negotiations rather than protests, counseling against criminal prosecutions of protesters, and perhaps expressing support for the students along the way. Like many southern mayors, moderate voices among southern newspaper editors expressed a desire for dealing with the issue of racial discrimination in public accommodations without resort to direct involvement of the law. "A private business, of course, has the legal right to serve or refuse any customer," noted the editors of the *Winston-Salem Sentinel*. "Unwanted customers can be arrested for trespass if they disobey an order to leave the premises." But this was beside the point, since "arrests for trespass are not the answer to the lunch counter protest." The best solution, the paper concluded, was for the lunch counters to voluntarily desegregate. The *Greensboro Daily News* agreed: "The spirit of the law is more important than the letter."[25]

The introduction of the law, in the form of police and criminal prosecutions, risked efforts of southern localities to control the course of change. "It was possible until the arrests of yesterday that the Negro protests might have petered out," the *Raleigh News & Observer* explained following the first arrest of the sit-in movement. "A few cups of coffee might have settled this matter in North Carolina. The price may be much greater in terms of Southern customs and Southern lawyers in the United States Supreme Court toward which this case is now clearly headed." Although North Carolina courts may hold that there are no constitutional impediments to private places of business that segregate, "it is not equally clear that the U.S. Supreme Court will reach the same conclusion," the *Greensboro Daily News* wrote. The paper noted that when it came to school desegregation, North Carolina did "what we reluctantly deemed necessary" to prevent "the courts from breathing down our necks." The sit-ins risked exploding this carefully calibrated response to *Brown*. "Now what is public and what is private about a commercial establishment will be a question for court decision, and that may stir up more racial snakes than it kills."[26]

For southern moderates—including mayors, newspaper editors, and other leaders of the white community—the fall of Jim Crow, a social transformation they recognized as inevitable, would be less traumatic, less controversial, and would entail less federal involvement (and other forms of "outside interference") if it was accomplished by private initiative, rather than legal mandates.

The Governors

State-level politicians tended to be quicker and harsher in their condemnation of the sit-in movement than their local counterparts. Whereas elected officials in cities in the Upper South often depended on the black vote, this was much less the case when it came to state-level politicians, many of whom were elected with aggressive prosegregationist platforms. In response to a statement of student leaders in Atlanta announcing their support for the sit-in movement and their intention "to use every legal and non-violent means at our disposal to secure full citizenship rights," Georgia governor Ernest Vandiver—who had come to office with promises of unwavering support for segregation and was elected on the strength of the rural vote (which held disproportionate sway over statewide elections in the South because of the severe malapportionment in electoral districts)—denounced the "left wing statement" that was "calculated to breed dissatisfaction, discontent, discord, and evil." Vandiver personally ordered the arrest of the Atlanta students who targeted the state capitol cafeteria and then issued a statement that described "these mass violations of State law and private property rights" as "subversive in character." When San Antonio merchants integrated eating facilities in response to sit-in demonstrations, Vandiver lamented their "abject surrender." Georgia's attorney general reiterated his public effort to draw attention to the legal tools available to lunch counter operators to prevent sit-in demonstrations—including Georgia's newly passed anti-trespassing law designed specifically to combat sit-in protests. Louisiana governor Earl K. Long attacked the sit-ins as being led by "some radical outfit." "If they want to do any real good," he added, "they should return to their native Africa—where colored men don't have any more privileges . . . as a good mule does in Louisiana."[27]

In South Carolina and Alabama, the first wave of sit-ins brought an immediate and often violent response by local white segregationists, which created the opening for a state-initiated crackdown on the protests. South Carolina governor Ernest Hollings insisted that the police had a responsibility to enforce breach-of-peace statutes against a gathering that posed a threat to public order. "They think they can violate any law, especially if they have a Bible in their hands: our law enforcement officers have their Bibles too," Hollings warned. Alabama governor John Patterson denounced the protesters for "provok[ing] whites" and for "spoiling for a fight."[28]

As the sit-ins spread across the South, southern state legislatures pushed new criminal trespass laws to deal with the protests. Southern legislators feared that existing trespass laws failed to adequately cover situations in which a customer was first invited into a store but subsequently asked to leave. On February 16, by a vote of 137–0, the Georgia legislature rushed through a bill making it a crime for a person to refuse to leave a private business establishment after being asked to do so by the manager. Virginia passed a similar law in on February 25, along with a prohibition on conspiracy to trespass. In April the Mississippi legislature passed a new breach-of-peace law. After a legislator expressed concerns that the new law went too far in limiting lawful assemblies, a defender of the bill responded, "You know what the bill's for. There's no need to talk about it." When the Senate unanimously passed the bill on April 27, one of its members noted that they needed to move quickly because "it may be needed in Biloxi this weekend," referring to the city where there was a "wade-in" campaign to desegregate local beaches. The editors of the Jackson *Clarion-Ledger* made no effort to obscure what the law was all about, referring to it as a "segregation" and an "anti-sit-down" bill. The headline in the *Jackson News* was only slightly more careful: "Tough Bill Signed to Deter Mixers." Louisiana passed its own harsher trespass and disorderly conduct laws in June.[29]

These new trespass laws law still required private initiative to set the legal process in motion, however. Police would only make an arrest after being contacted by the business manager and having the manager, in the presence of the police officer, indicate his refusal to serve the patron. State officials were "helpless" to enforce the law if store managers chose not to go through the necessary steps, complained the frustrated Georgia attorney general, Eugene Cook, after Atlanta merchants and protesters negotiated a desegregation agreement in early 1961.[30]

Although most southern governors took a hard line in denouncing the sit-ins, Florida governor LeRoy Collins was a prominent exception. He distinguished himself by openly supporting the sit-in cause (if still criticizing their tactics). Initially he had denounced the sit-ins as "illegal and dangerous" and had emphasized that Florida law allowed proprietors to refuse service to undesirable clients. But he soon changed his tune. "We've got the moral rights and we've got the principles of brotherhood that are involved in these issues," he declared in a televised address on March 20, 1960. The practice of excluding blacks from lunch counters while inviting them to all other sections of department stores was "unfair and morally wrong." In contrast with his fellow governors (but like many southern city mayors), Collins warned against turning to the courts to resolve the issue. Although "a merchant has the legal right to select the patrons he serves," he argued, "we are foolish if we just think about resolving this thing on a legal basis." "The essence of his stand," a reporter summarized, "has been that integration must come and that the South must accept it, but that it must be achieved gradually and with mutual consent, by negotiation rather than force."[31]

While not about to go as far as Governor Collins did in Florida, North Carolina governor Luther Hodges sought to distinguish his position on civil rights from the more defiant defenses of Jim Crow embraced by most of his fellow southern governors. North Carolina was going to follow a more considered, moderate approach to defending its racial practices. When the sit-ins began, he was careful to avoid any public statements supporting segregation in privately operated facilities. His private correspondences, however, made his sympathies clear. The sit-ins were "'gang' demonstration[s]" that "would do no one any good and would in fact harm those and as well as the community itself."[32]

Hodges's official position was to remain agnostic on the matter of lunch counter segregation, but to give a full-throated defense of the need to protect against lawlessness and disorder. However orderly the sit-ins might appear, he explained in his first official statement on the protests, they could, at any moment, "degenerate into a serious threat both to bi-racial good will and public order." He also accused civil rights activists of hypocrisy: "It is both illogical and dangerous for those who insist on meticulous obedience to the law as the courts interpret it, where segregation is banned, to resort themselves to un-lawful measures calculated to speed up acceptance of the philosophy of racial integration." This was not a question of free speech because this right did not extend to "trespass on private property." "Irrespective of either the legal or moral pronouncements which might be presented in support of one view or another . . . [d]isorder in connection with lunch counter demonstrations should stop—now."[33]

Yet absent some episode of violent confrontation—something the protesters sought to avoid if at all possible—the state had limited power to do anything about the demonstrations. The governor, explained his attorney general in a memorandum prepared in response to the sit-ins, lacked authority "to supplant or oust local law enforcement officials en-gaged in the proper discharge of their traditional criminal law enforce-ment responsibilities." Local police had to take the lead in dealing with the sit-ins. Short of declaring martial law in response to a breakdown of local law enforcement, the best the governor could do would be to use state highway patrol to support local police. Hodges thus was in some-thing of a bind. He had to wait for local law enforcement to act. But they, in turn, needed private businessmen to make the first move, to call the police to and press trespassing charges. But lunch counter op-erators in North Carolina were generally unwilling to do this. Hodges wanted to act; he wanted to show his constituents that he was taking a strong stand on the side of law and order in the face of these protests. But in this case, the most powerful man in the state was reduced to making public statements and engaging in a letter-writing campaign with private businessmen, pleading for them to do what he could not.[34]

Hodges lamented that the business owners' refusal to take a strong stand against the protests only heightened the explosive nature of the situation. As he put it in a letter to the president of Woolworth, to al-low a "jostling crowd to congregate, and then to close the facility or the store just before the situation physically explodes, and then to re-open the facility again in a few days and go through the same rou-tine" was a recipe for chaos. The best way to head off potential dis-order, Hodges insisted, was through private initiative on the part of the targeted businesses. "It is my belief that if your company and the other companies involved continue to follow the course you have up to now, the situation will worsen," he wrote to the Woolworth regional manager. Call in the police, Hodges urged in letters and phone calls with the lunch counter operators. "Stand on your legal rights to oper-ate as you choose." To resolve the situation, the owners must "confront this problem directly, frankly and courageously." They must be clear in their policy and call upon the law to enforce that policy. "We do have laws in North Carolina to enable the private owner to handle such situations," he explained to C. L. Harris. As Hodges's administrative assistant explained to one constituent, "It is the Governor's view that if the Negro citizens have a legal right to integrated service at lunch counters, the issue should be resolved in the courts."[35]

Hodges even went so far as to offer a draft statement for lunch counter chains, which he encouraged them to release to clarify their positions. He urged the businessmen to explain that when the sit-ins began, "we elected not to bring trespass charges in against any persons, notwithstanding the fact that in all of the states in question the laws have clearly given us this legal right." But the situation had to change: "It is now clearly evident that the situation has progressed to the point that reason and proper concern for recognized legal rights are receiving little or no consideration." The draft statement included an assertion that unless there is "an authoritative declaration of law [to the] contrary," the owners "have the legal right, as a private business, to elect to operate lunch counter facilities on a racially integrated basis or a racially segregated basis."[36]

From the perspective of Governor Hodges, the use of law enforcement and the courts was the best way to achieve his desired ends: to maintain order in North Carolina's communities, while also propping up segregationist racial practices that he believed a majority of his constituents wanted to continue. Segregationists were accustomed to relying on state courts to serve their interests, to protect property rights, and to protect social order. After *Brown* and subsequent decisions extending its reasoning to all government-operated facilities, segregationists saw their last best hope in barricading themselves behind the public-private divide. They started private white "segregation academies"; they shut down municipal swimming pools and golf courses. When the sit-ins arrived, they insisted that public accommodations were nothing like public schools, pools, and golf courses because they were privately operated. If this defense of segregation in public accommodations were to fail, whether by "an authoritative declaration of law" declaring such practices unconstitutional or by statute or by the voluntary adoption of new business practices, there was, in Hodges's view, clearly a right and a wrong way of going about it. The sit-ins were the wrong way. Since the students were not listening to his calls to stop their protests, he had to rely on the lunch counter operators to defend their private property rights by calling upon the law. But, to the North Carolina governor's frustration—a frustration shared by most of the southern governors—the lunch counter operators refused to do what he wanted them to do.

The Ideologues

For the most dedicated defenders of segregation, none of these approaches was satisfactory. These were the people who believed racial segregation was a cause worth fighting for, not because it was profitable or because it was a way to get elected to public office, but because it was right, because it protected certain basic principles that should not be negotiated away. For them, segregation was an ideological commitment. Too many business owners, they believed, placed profits ahead of southern principles. The same could be said of the mayors who were primarily interested in courting black votes and attracting northern business investment. The governors tended to be better—at least they denounced the demonstrators for the rabble-rousers they were and called on the law to protect property rights and crack down on these riots in the making—but for all their talk of protecting law and order, they tended to speak less forcefully about the values of segregation. What was needed, these ideological segregationists believed, was a clearer affirmative case for what they were defending.

Segregationist ideologues had two paths they could take. The blunter approach—the one that had roots going back to slavery and reflected the commitment on which white southerners had built Jim Crow in the first place—was simply to defend the principle of white supremacy and the value of separating the races. When white youths or the KKK showed up to heckle, threaten, and abuse sit-in demonstrators, this was the language they used. ("It is impossible to convey the tension, antagonism and open hatred pervading these conflict situations," one observer noted.) Letters to the editor of local newspapers were filled with fervent defenses of the values of segregation. Some public officials also condemned the protests in these terms.[37]

But this approach had its limits. Overt racist arguments were losing adherents in the South. Directly defending white supremacy was alienating to potential allies outside the South. These kinds of arguments further isolated the South and increased the risk of federal intervention. The fact that the most visible proponents of this position were what reporters tended to describe as white "juvenile delinquents" and KKK members did little to strengthen the standing of this position. In Raleigh a small, elderly white woman chastised white counter-protesters: "I'm as much a segregationist as you are, but I believe you should meet courtesy with courtesy." James Kilpatrick, the segregationist editor of the *Richmond News Leader*, had a similar reaction:

Here were the colored students, in coats, white shirts, ties, and one of them was reading Goethe and one was taking notes from a biology text. And here, on the sidewalk outside, was a gang of white boys come to heckle, a ragtail rabble, slack-jawed, black-jacketed, grinning fit to kill, and some of them, God save the mark, were waving the proud and honored flag of the Southern States in the last war fought by gentlemen. Eheu! It gives one pause.

What was needed was an affirmative case for the white South's cause that was not simply a defense of racial supremacy. This was where the ideologues turned to an alternative path for defending segregation: the U.S. Constitution.[38]

What about the "rights of property owners?" asked Atlanta restaurant owner Lester Maddox. In response to the Atlanta sit-in movement, Maddox formed Georgians Unwilling to Surrender, a group dedicated to protecting segregation. The newsletter for the Citizens' Council, a white supremacist group formed in response to *Brown*, published an editorial titled "Seditious Sit-Downs" that described the sit-in tactic as an effort to "take[] over a private business establishment." Sit-ins "violat[e] the basic civil rights of a majority of the people of the South." U.S. senator Herman Talmadge of Georgia condemned the sit-ins as "government by mob action." "The crime is trespass," he explained. "Even if the trespasser carries the Holy Writ and sings hymns it does not alleviate the seriousness of the crime. It is a subversion of the Constitution of the United States and the laws of the land." "It may be surprising to some people," Georgia's other senator, Richard Russell, lectured his colleagues, "to learn that [the Fourteenth Amendment] is supposed to protect the life, liberty, and property of white citizens equally with the Negro." To compromise on property rights at lunch counters would risk property rights elsewhere—"in a home, or an automobile, a television set, or a milk cow."[39]

Kilpatrick's embarrassment over being aligned with the "ragtail rabble" did not prevent him from insisting that the Constitution stood squarely on the side of the segregationists and chastising those who claimed otherwise. "The constitutional rights in this matter belong entirely to the restaurateur, the innkeeper, the store owner, and violent invasion of these those rights cannot be countenanced without jeopardy to the personal freedoms as precious to Negroes as they are dear to whites." The students had a right to exercise their free speech rights, Kilpatrick wrote. "They can complain to their hearts' content." But they had no right to trespass on private property. Such a "deliberate abuse of the rights of others is bound to lessen respect for the rights they seek themselves."[40]

By highlighting the rights of discriminating store operators, the ideologues were shifting the lines of defense for the segregationist cause in important ways. In place of arguments for white supremacy, they offered a more individualistic, anti-statist, liberty-based argument, which its proponents insisted was grounded in the text of the Constitution. "If there is a right to integrate, there is a right to segregate," Maddox insisted. The constitutional right to association includes "a freedom of choice to NOT associate." The constitutional argument that segregationists rallied around in the face of the sit-ins was an individual rights claim. Defenders of segregation claimed a "right to discriminate," grounded in various constitutional provisions. It was sometimes described as a right to "freedom of choice" or a property right, which traced to the due process clauses of the Fifth and Fourteenth Amendments. It was sometimes a right to associate, which sounded in First Amendment jurisprudence. Some even framed it as a right against "involuntary servitude" (the idea being that a requirement to serve someone was a form of forced labor), which was protected in the Thirteenth Amendment.[41]

The civil rights movement thus nurtured constitutional rights claims not only among proponents of the black freedom struggle, but also by those opposed to the cause. Opponents of antidiscrimination policy understood themselves to be fighting for the cause of freedom. This was a particular kind of freedom, one quite different from the egalitarian freedom vision that moved civil rights activists. But the vision of freedom motivating defenders of the right to discriminate also had deep roots in America's constitutional tradition. At different times and in different contexts, claimed rights to property, association, and freedom of choice have been used for much more admirable purposes. Those who resist policies designed to oppress vulnerable minorities, suppress political dissent, or force social conformity have often drawn sustenance—and sometimes achieved courtroom victories—from these principles. They have always been essential components of American democratic constitutionalism, available to individuals and groups who fear, for causes good and for causes bad, the constraining hand of government. Even the most well-intentioned regulations, such as a public accommodations law, impose a cost on personal liberty. The issue has never been whether there is, in some form, a right to discriminate. There surely is. The issue is in what circumstances government—including but not limited to courts—should recognize this right as a limit on its authority.

As segregationists shifted their rhetoric from unvarnished white supremacy toward defending the constitutional rights of individuals, a trend that the battle over the sit-ins accelerated, a new version of racial conservatism took shape. Alongside venerable arguments based on principles of states' rights and deference to majoritarian white supremacist traditions, a libertarian critique of antidiscrimination policy now became a basic element of the white South's legal case against civil rights. Although an occasional judge with strong libertarian or conservative leanings might express some sympathy for these kinds of claims, by the 1960s a claim of a constitutionally based right to discriminate had little to no chance of being accepted in a court. A judicial recognition of a broad right to discriminate would put at risk state and local public accommodations laws, many of which dated back to the nineteenth century and had been repeatedly upheld in court. Such a drastic doctrinal change would also raise the specter of a return to discredited decisions such as *Lochner v. New York*, the 1905 decision in which the Supreme Court struck down a maximum-work-hour regulation as a violation of the right for employers and employees to make contracts without unreasonable government interference. Simply put, few judges were interested in undermining the validity of long-standing public accommodations laws or reviving *Lochner*-style jurisprudence.[42]

Despite their weakness in the courtroom, claims of a right to discriminate provided a prominent and powerful language for opposing or limiting civil rights reform. They were an integral part of the public debate over the sit-ins. And they would continue to be heard in the coming years as the nation debated federal legislation that would outlaw racial discrimination in public accommodations.

The power of this right to discriminate argument was evident in the way it resonated, in some form, beyond the ranks of segregationist ideologues. Justice Hugo Black, usually a strong ally of civil rights causes, explained his opposition to the sit-ins to his colleagues and clerks by talking about a country store run by his "Pappy," who, Black insisted, had a right to control his property. Former president Harry S. Truman surprised many civil rights supporters when he denounced the sit-ins. "If anyone came into my store and tried to stop business, I'd throw him out," he declared in March 1960. "Private business has its own rights and can do what it wants. . . . The Negro should behave himself and show he's a good citizen." When the NAACP challenged Truman for his "attempt to smear the gallant young sit-in demonstrators," he refused to back down. "I would do just what I said I would do," he wrote in a telegram. He warned the NAACP that in supporting the sit-ins, "they are losing friends instead of making them." Truman repeated his accusations in the coming months.[43]

The debate sparked by the sit-ins operated as a pivot in American racial politics and law. Prior to this point, southern state and local government acted as the critical support mechanism for Jim Crow. The entire point of segregation laws was to compel private actors who might otherwise not practice racial segregation to do so. When legally mandated segregation was the rule throughout the South, segregationists rarely talked about discrimination as a personal right. Jim Crow was driven by an agenda of conformity. Hence, the right to discriminate only arrived on the scene when mandating discrimination by law was no longer an option. Now defenders of Jim Crow turned to the private sector as the last bastion of racial segregation. The freedom of choice that so threatened the architects of Jim Crow generations earlier was now the last bulwark in protecting some semblance of the racial status quo.[44]

The sit-ins steered segregationist ideologues toward their own distinctive—and distinctly effective—version of what is sometimes called "rights talk." The right to discriminate was not the kind of right that courts tended to take all that seriously. But it was a right that was effective for those who were searching for a viable way to express their opposition to the sit-in movement, and, eventually, to federal public accommodations legislation. Following sit-ins in Chapel Hill, the editors of the *Chapel Hill Weekly* complained that "trampling on another's rights, even when hungering for your own, isn't the way to do it." Restaurant owners in Atlanta ran a statement defending "the basic right of an individual, any individual of whatever race, creed, or color, to engage in business, to purvey any commodity or service which is lawful, to cater to a clientele of its own choosing." In defending a new, tougher anti-trespass law, passed in direct response to the sit-in movement, a Virginia state senator insisted that the law's goal was not to enforce segregation but to protect private property rights.[45]

This kind of loose rights talk was not limited to those who might not be versed in the latest constitutional doctrine. Judges also argued that there were rights at stake when the courts considered the constitutional equality claim that the sit-in protests raised. For example, in 1958 the North Carolina Supreme Court discussed the "right of an operator of a private enterprise to select the clientele he will serve and to make such selection based on color, if he so desires." Three years later, in a similar case, the same court even specified the right as based in the Constitution: "White people also have constitutional rights as well as Negroes, which must be protected, if our constitutional form of government is not to vanish from the face of the earth." U.S. Supreme Court Justice John Marshall Harlan, criticizing what he saw as the Court's undermining of the state action limitation, identified the right to discriminate as a necessary counterweight to a government interest in promoting racial equality: "Freedom of the individual to choose his associates or his neighbors, to use and dispose of his property as he sees fit, to be irrational, arbitrary, capricious, even unjust in his personal relations are things all entitled to a large measure of protection from governmental interference." Although rarely willing to go as far as segregationist ideologues wanted and to strike down policies that required business operators to serve customers regardless of race, judges recognized the value of conceptualizing this constellation of privacy, property, and associational interests as fundamental freedoms and rights.[46]

––––––––

There was nothing approaching a unified southern white position on the sit-ins. The white South was divided not only over how high a price they were willing to pay to preserve segregation, but also over whether legal prosecution of the sit-in protesters was worth the costs involved.

When it came to views on the role of the courts, the sit-ins led to some strange bedfellows. Ironically, racist southern officials and NAACP lawyers were in agreement that their interests would be best served if they could steer the confrontation into a formal legal arena. What they hoped to get out of the courts was another matter, of course. White southern leaders saw legal prosecution and punishment as the best way to demonstrate the authority of the existing power structure and suppress the uprising in their midst. NAACP lawyers saw courtroom fights over the meaning of the Constitution as a battleground where they had won before and where they could win again. In contrast, student protesters, many lunch counter operators, and racial moderates agreed that their own interests were best served by keeping the issue away from the courts. The students were concerned with losing control of their protest movement and skeptical of the potential for translating courtroom victories into on-the-ground social change. The business operators were primarily concerned about the public relations costs of sending students off to jail. Local white officials and newspaper editors wanted the issue resolved without divisive litigation and court orders. These convergences and divisions over the courts helped shape the course of the sit-in movement. The students and the civil rights lawyers had their tensions, to be sure, but they were able to settle into their uneasy but functional alliance. The divisions among their opponents proved more consequential.

The students were the ultimate beneficiaries of these divisions. "The South countered with traditional weapons—violence, mass arrests and expulsions," noted a May 1960 report on the sit-ins published in *Ebony* magazine. "But the effectiveness of these weapons [was] limited by a split in the white South and the vagueness of the law. Merchants, leery of offending Negro shoppers, were reluctant to press charges. Emboldened by the confusion in the white ranks and the enthusiastic support of most Negro leaders, the students pressed their advantage and won victories in some cities." An editorial in a Shaw University publication found some wry humor in the situation:

This new show of spirit on the Negroes' part is not being met with total resistance but with dissention among their enemies and with loyalty and aid from here-to-fore unknown supporters. If the white man needs proof that he is disunified he needs only to look at the list of people backing the student protesters. For this disunity we thank him.[47]

FIVE

The Justices

The clash between Negro customers and white restaurant owners is clear; each group claims protection by the Constitution and tenders the Fourteenth Amendment as justification for its action. Yet we leave resolution of the conflict to others, when, if our voice were heard, the issues for the Congress and for the public would become clear and precise. The Court was created to sit in troubled times as well as in peaceful days.

—JUSTICE WILLIAM O. DOUGLAS, JUNE 1964[1]

"The Court is our greatest educational institution," explained Alexander Bickel, Yale law professor and one of the nation's leading legal commentators, in the spring of 1963. "It may bring a question up to the forefront of public consciousness, reduce it, and play with it—a sort of cat and mouse game, perhaps—until there comes a moment of inarticulable judgment, of political feel, not at all different from the sense of timing that other political officers have, when the time seems ripe for a final adjudication. And the Court will then act."[2]

Bickel's description nicely captures the way in which the Supreme Court generally operated under the leadership of Earl Warren, Chief Justice of the United States from 1953 to 1969, in cases involving contentious national issues such as school desegregation, the rights for the criminally accused, and voting rights. Once the justices sensed the moment was right to act, they offered bold new interpretations of the Constitution in all these areas. Yet the sit-in cases broke pattern. Even when the time was surely "ripe" by the Warren Court's typical standards, when the civil rights movement had transformed the cultural and political land-scape of the nation, the Court refused to take the next expected step in the cases involving appeals of criminal convictions for involvement in lunch counter sit-in demonstrations. Between 1960 and 1964, the Court ducked, again and again, a major civil rights issue that was win-ning widespread public support. The justices believed that minimal-ist holdings were best in these cases, at least for a time. Chief Justice Warren explained the strategy as "taking these cases step by step, not reaching the final question until much experience had been had." The Court overturned convictions of the sit-in protesters, but always on narrow grounds, reserving the difficult constitutional question that was at the core of the sit-ins: Did the equal protection clause of the Fourteenth Amendment require racially nondiscriminatory service in private businesses that cater to the general public?[3]

The puzzle is, then, why the Court never decided the constitu-tional question, even after public opinion had clearly swung behind the equality principle put forth by the sit-ins. By the middle of 1963, an overwhelming majority of Americans supported equal access to eat-ing facilities. Although not all of these people believed it the respon-sibility of the federal government to ensure equality in this realm of life, approval of proposed federal civil rights legislation was at about 50 percent—roughly the same level that approval of school desegre-gation had reached in 1954, when the Supreme Court issued *Brown v. Board of Education*. In the coming months, approval of the Civil Rights Act increased steadily; after it passed the House in February 1964, two in three Americans supported the bill. In 1964, when Congress was about to pass the Civil Rights Act and the Court faced the last of the sit-in cases, a majority of the nation lived under state or local laws requiring nondiscriminatory access to public accommodations. De-spite this transformation taking place outside the Court, by late 1963 a majority of the justices stood poised to squarely reject the students' constitutional claim. The sit-in cases stand as the great—and largely forgotten—aberration of the Warren Court.[4]

Why did the sit-in cases give the justices, usually such stalwart de-fenders of the civil rights movement, so much difficulty? To under-stand these cases requires attention to the dynamics of Supreme Court decision making. Supreme Court justices have always been affected by major political, cultural, and social changes. "The great tides and cur-rents which engulf the rest of men do not turn aside in their course and pass the judges by," Benjamin Cardozo famously wrote. None of the Court's most significant decisions can be understood without recognizing the role of external pressures on the Court. The Supreme Court's understanding of the Constitution responds to social movement achievements, political developments, and durable changes in public opinion. This much is clear. Yet this truism about the role of the courts must be placed alongside another one. When it comes to disputes over the meaning of the Constitution, the American people and their elected representatives struggle with the same constitutional principles as the justices do, but the justices approach questions of constitutional interpretation from a distinctive perspective. This is in part a product of the fact that justices typically represent elite opinion: they have usually been to top universities and law schools, and they tend to circulate in social circles populated by the powerful and wealthy. It is also a product of the distinctive set of analytical tools that judges work with. The Supreme Court reflects society, but it does so imprecisely. Sometimes the Court is a step ahead of public opinion. Sometimes it is one or more steps behind. Only by balancing these two dynamics can one explain the puzzle of the sit-in cases.[5]

When the justices approached the constitutional claim of the sit-ins, they saw the same basic issues that captured the attention of the American people. They appreciated the powerful egalitarian message of black students sitting at lunch counters, denied their share of American citizenship for no reason other than the color of their skin. They supported the passage of federal legislation ending this shameful situation once and for all. But they also faced concerns that were particular to their places in the institution perched at the apex of the American judicial system. The justices worked with a distinctive tool, the language of constitutional doctrine, with its particular categories of analysis and reliance on precedent. And they were moved by distinctive institutional interests, the most significant of which was an overriding concern with protecting the legitimacy and integrity of the judicial process. The justices differed among themselves as to the nature, import, and relative weight of these factors, but taken as a whole they explain why the Court remained apart from much of the rest of the nation when it came to the fundamental constitutional question raised by the sit-ins.

This chapter breaks down the Supreme Court's confrontation with the sit-in cases into four acts. Act One examines two cases, each originating in challenges to racial discrimination that predated the sit-in movement, that arrived at the Court in late 1960 and early 1961, in the aftermath of the sit-ins. The justices decided these cases in the shadow of the sit-in movement. They offer insight into the justices' understanding of the key constitutional issues around the time of the sit-in movement. Act Two looks at the first appeal of student criminal convictions from the sit-in movement to reach the Court, in late 1961. The particular facts of these cases allowed the Court to overturn student convictions, but to do so on relatively narrow grounds. These cases revealed growing division among the justices. Act Three centers on a series of cases decided in 1963, in which the Court continued to find ways to overturn protester convictions without squarely facing the looming constitutional issue. The Court used these cases to strike out at official segregationist policy while avoiding the more difficult question of the constitutional status of discrimination in the private sphere. The fourth and final act came the following year, in a group of cases in which there did not appear to be a way to side with the students without facing the constitutional question. In the most important of these cases, *Bell v. Maryland*, a majority of the justices were ready to decide the constitutional issues. At first, a majority formed to deny the students' constitutional claim. A remarkable series of last-minute vote switches created a majority to come out the other way, in favor of students on broad constitutional grounds. Ultimately, however, when the decision came down in June 1964, the Court was fractured. Although six justices finally addressed the core constitutional issue, they split evenly on whether this meant the students won or not. The three remaining justices found, yet again, a way to side with the students while avoiding the constitutional question. At the end of the chapter, I return to the question with which I began: Why did the sit-in cases take such a different course from the other major issues the Warren Court confronted?

Act One: *Boynton & Burton* (1960–61)

In the period after the sit-in movement had started but before any of the appeals of criminal convictions from the protests had made their way to the Supreme Court, the justices considered two cases involving racial discrimination in public accommodations. Although each stemmed from incidents that occurred before the 1960 sit-ins, the student movement informed the justices' and the public's response to these cases.

Boynton v. Virginia

The first case arrived at the Court in early 1960. Bruce Boynton, an African American student at Howard University Law School in Washington, DC, was heading home to Alabama for holiday break in December 1958 when he requested service in the whites-only section of a restaurant located in the Richmond, Virginia, bus terminal. Boynton explained to a waitress who directed him to the black section that as an interstate passenger he had a legal right to eat there. (The Supreme Court had issued a line of decisions, dating back to 1941, holding that federal law prohibited racial discrimination in interstate railroad travel.) The manager asked him to leave, and Boynton refused. The manager then contacted the police and Boynton was charged with trespass. A Virginia judge found him guilty and fined him ten dollars. Boynton's appeals eventually brought the case to the Supreme Court, which accepted the case for review on February 23, 1960, in the midst of the explosion of lunch counter sit-ins across the South. The justices heard arguments in *Boynton v. Virginia* the following October.[6]

The NAACP Legal Defense Fund took on the case, and Thurgood Marshall argued it before the Supreme Court. In its brief to the Court, LDF urged the Court to take the opportunity to resolve the larger constitutional issues: Could operators of privately owned public accommodations run a segregated business and ask the state to step in when customers transgressed this policy? Marshall pressed on the Court the constitutional arguments he and his fellow LDF lawyers had developed the previous spring in response to the sit-ins.[7]

LDF received surprising support from Eisenhower's Justice Department, which participated as amicus curiae in the case and urged the Court to accept LDF's constitutional claim. In the government's brief, filed in September 1960, Solicitor General J. Lee Rankin argued that the Court should strike down any state enforcement of racially discriminatory treatment in public accommodations. Although a conspicuously bold argument for the U.S. government to be making, at the time most observers saw it as simply the latest in a line of Justice Department amicus briefs, reaching back to *Shelley v. Kraemer* in 1948 and continuing through the school desegregation cases, when the federal government aligned itself with LDF. The difference here was that when it came to the state action issue of the sit-ins, this was the most ambitious argument the federal government would make before the Supreme Court.

As the Court faced more rounds of sit-in cases in the following years, the Justice Department pulled back, urging the justices to overturn protester convictions through more modest, marginal adjustments to the state action doctrine.[8]

In its December 1960 ruling in *Boynton*, the Court refused the urging of LDF and the Justice Department to declare state enforcement of private discrimination unconstitutional in this context, opting instead to dispose of the case on statutory grounds. Justice Hugo Black wrote for a seven-justice majority, holding that the Interstate Commerce Act's nondiscrimination requirement applied to a restaurant within a terminal that was specifically designed to serve interstate passengers. There were "persuasive reasons" to avoid the constitutional question, Black noted. He concluded with a pointed disclaimer: "Because of some of the arguments made here it is necessary to say a word about what we are not deciding"—namely, the legal status of racial discrimination in "a wholly independent roadside restaurant." In others words, the Court was not expressing an opinion on the constitutional question looming over the sit-in movement. The Court, predicted *New York Times* Supreme Court reporter Anthony Lewis, will avoid this issue "as long as possible, because it is an explosive one."[9]

The fact that two justices—Charles E. Whittaker and Tom C. Clark —dissented in *Boynton* was another example of how the issue of discrimination in public accommodations challenged existing patterns at the Supreme Court. Since the 1940s, the justices had made an effort to speak with one voice when the Court decided cases involving racial segregation. *Shelley*, the 1948 case striking down judicial enforcement of racially restrictive covenants, had been unanimous (although three of the justices had recused themselves from the case, presumably because they owned property with racial restrictions in the deeds). *Brown* was unanimous, as were its key predecessors striking down segregation in higher education. In desegregation rulings that followed *Brown*, the Court made a point of emphasizing its unity, by issuing unsigned per curiam rulings and, most dramatically, in *Cooper v. Aaron*, the 1958 Little Rock school desegregation case, by having all nine justices sign the Court's opinion as a show of unity against white southern defiance of *Brown*. When it came to the justices' reading of the kinds of discrimination prohibited by the equal protection clause, the Warren Court justices were basically in agreement. Where they agreed less, however, was in the question of the reach of the equal protection clause—the state action question. *Boynton*, noted Lewis, was "the first time in some years that the court had been divided in a racial segregation case." For the Warren Court, cases involving racial discrimination in public accommodations would be uniquely divisive. Minor cracks among the justices on these issues would grow into angry fissures in the coming years.[10]

Burton v. Wilmington Parking Authority

The second case in this first act of the Supreme Court's confrontation with the sit-ins involved a privately run restaurant located in a city-owned parking garage that refused to serve blacks. In August 1958, in Wilmington, Delaware, William H. Burton, an African American and a member of the city council, parked his car in a city-owned garage and walked into the Eagle Coffee Shoppe, which was located in the garage, where he was refused service. He challenged the restaurant's discriminatory policy in court. Here he ran headlong into the state action limitation of the Fourteenth Amendment. The restaurant was a private business, so Burton sued the city for operating a parking garage that leased space to a business that discriminated. The question, then, was whether the relationship between the city and the restaurant was strong enough to hold the city responsible for the restaurant's policy. The Delaware trial court found that Burton had been subject to unconstitutional racial discrimination. The state's supreme court reversed that decision, holding that the restaurant acted in a "purely private capacity" and thus was not constrained by the Fourteenth Amendment.[11]

Burton fared better at the U.S. Supreme Court. In a 6–3 decision, issued in April 1961, the justices sided with Burton (and the solicitor general, who filed an amicus brief on Burton's behalf). The Court held that the city government had "so far insinuated itself into a position of interdependence" with the restaurant that it became a "joint participant" in the discriminatory policy. The analysis in Justice Tom Clark's majority opinion relied on a context-driven balancing test—which he described as "sifting facts and weighing circumstances"—to evaluate whether there was the necessary state involvement to rise to the level of state action under the Fourteenth Amendment. He noted the location of the restaurant in a building that was not only government-owned but was an ongoing government-run business. The mutual dependency of the parking garage and the restaurant created the necessary state action.[12]

Clark ventured further than this, however, offering an additional, and quite far-reaching, line of reasoning in his state action analysis. A state refusal to act to prevent private discrimination might itself be a form of state action under the Fourteenth Amendment, he suggested. "By its inaction, the . . . State . . . has not only made itself a party to the refusal of service, but has elected to place its power, property and prestige behind the admitted discrimination." This reference to what has been called a "permission" or "inaction" theory of state action had potentially dramatic implications. If a state could prohibit a form of private discrimination but chose not to, then it could be said that it permitted that discrimination. But once one starts down this path, it is hard to know when to stop. The permission theory of state action contains the seeds of a rejection of the entire premise of state action as defining the boundary between the private and public realms. In suggesting the existence of affirmative government obligations under the equal protection clause, Clark seemed to open the door to a reconsideration of the scope of government responsibility under the Constitution to protect people from discrimination by private actors.[13]

Perhaps recognizing the potentially radical nature of his state action analysis, Clark then pulled back. A Texan with a solidly liberal reputation on civil rights issues during his time as U.S. attorney general under President Truman and then, beginning in 1949, as a Supreme Court justice, Clark was generally not recognized for the rigor or vision of his legal analysis. Do not read too much into this opinion, he basically said in closing his *Burton* opinion. "Because readily applicable formulae may not be fashioned, the conclusions drawn from the facts and circumstances of this record are by no means declared as universal truths on the basis of which every state leasing agreement is to be tested." In a highly regulated society, "a multitude of relationships might appear to some to fall within the [Fourteenth] Amendment's embrace," he noted, but then cautioned that the only test of when state involvement with private actors was "significant" enough to justify a finding of state action was to look to "the peculiar facts or circumstances present." By the end of the opinion, Clark seemed intent on limiting his holding to the facts of the Eagle Coffee Shoppe.[14]

Writing in dissent, Justice John Marshall Harlan took the majority opinion to task. Harlan was the grandson of the justice with the same name who wrote a famous solo dissent in *Plessy v. Ferguson*, the 1896 Supreme Court decision holding that state-mandated racial segregation did not violate the Fourteenth Amendment. In his sixth year on the Court, he was emerging as the Warren Court's conservative voice, frequently warning against the bold doctrinal innovations his more liberal brethren favored. Cases involving the state action issue offered an important platform for his cautionary message. "The Court's opinion," he wrote in his *Burton* dissent, "by a process of first undiscriminatingly throwing together various factual bits and pieces and then undermining the resulting structure by an equally vague disclaimer, seems to me to leave completely at sea just what it is in this record that satisfies the requirement of 'state action.'"[15]

Commentators and scholars also expressed frustration at the expansive ambiguity of Clark's opinion. Some questioned whether the Court had gone too far. Some urged the Court to go further and apply its reasoning to lunch counters and other facilities that served the public: "We regret that [the Court] felt any necessity for hedging," wrote the editors of the *Washington Post*; the *Pittsburgh Courier*, a black newspaper, called the ruling a "defeat in a victory." And some wondered what to make of this "vague and obscure" opinion.[16]

Court watchers knew that *Boynton* and *Burton* were just the tip of the iceberg. The law on questions of segregation in public accommodations "remains unsettled at critical points, with much development evidently still ahead," noted Lewis in the *New York Times* after *Boynton* came down. In January 1961, less than a month after *Boynton* and several months before *Burton*, the Supreme Court received its first appeals in cases emerging from the sit-in movement. After *Burton* was decided, Lewis described the decision as "singularly tantalizing . . . with important, if elusive, implications for the whole problem of racial discrimination." He read the opinion as a sign that the Court was heading toward a significant expansion of its reading of state action in the upcoming sit-in cases.[17]

Act Two: The Louisiana Cases (1961)

In their first confrontations with appeals resulting from the lunch counter sit-in protests, the justices overturned the convictions of sit-in protesters, but they did so on relatively narrow grounds. The justices resisted the entreaties of the NAACP lawyers to embrace any of the vague invitations offered in Clark's *Burton* opinion. Observers assumed that the justices were waiting for that "ripe" time that Bickel described, their cautious rulings in these cases laying the foundation for a subsequent ruling that would sweep aside any state support for racial discrimination. Although the facts of these early sit-in cases allowed for relatively limited holdings, at least some of the justices began to indicate that they wanted to engage what Lewis described as "the great question," namely, "when segregation can be said to result from official sanctions and when from merely private discrimination."[18]

Of the hundreds of convictions that arose out of the 1960 sit-ins, the first to reach the Supreme Court on appeal came out of Louisiana. On March 21, 1961, while the justices were writing their opinions in *Burton*, they agreed to hear three appeals of disturbing-the-peace convictions stemming from March 1960 sit-ins in Baton Rouge. Although *Garner v. Louisiana* would eventually be decided unanimously, behind the scenes, divisions among the justices were growing and hardening, breaking apart longtime allies and drawing together usual antagonists.

When they first met to discuss whether to hear the cases, Hugo Black and Felix Frankfurter formed a rare alliance, both opposing the NAACP's constitutional argument. The two men were a study in contrasts. Black grew up in rural Alabama, where he practiced law before climbing the ranks of Alabama politics—a climb that was aided by his membership in the local Ku Klux Klan. He became a U.S. senator in 1926, and his staunch support for Franklin Roosevelt's New Deal helped get him appointed to the Court in 1937. As a justice, Black sought to make up for his lack of formal education, putting himself through a rigorous course of self-education. He also sought to make up for his ignominious history on the race issue, emerging as one of the Court's most aggressive champions of equal rights for African Americans. Frankfurter was born in Austria and came to New York City with his family at age twelve. His exceptional academic abilities got him into Harvard Law School, where he graduated first in his class and where he would soon return as a professor. During his years teaching at Harvard, he was an outspoken defender of liberal causes, including racial justice (he was an adviser to the NAACP). Once appointed to the Court in 1939, however, he became the Court's leading voice of judicial restraint, regularly warning his colleagues against weighing in on controversial social issues. This had produced some ironic moments at the high court, such as during the lead-up to *Brown*, when the ex-KKK member from Alabama was urging the Court to strike down segregation while the ex-NAACP adviser from Massachusetts was urging the Court to avoid the issue. Frankfurter and Black also differed on whether the protections of the Bill of Rights apply to the states, one of the most pressing issues during their time on the Court. They engaged in epic battles over the direction of the Court's constitutional jurisprudence throughout the 1940s and 1950s. The sit-in cases were different, however. Here, the longtime antagonists were in unusual accord. As far as the Constitution was concerned, Black insisted when the justices privately met to discuss the first sit-in cases for the first time, the "merchant can make his stores segregated or desegregated."[19]

The brilliant, irascible, and uncompromising William Douglas, who typically aligned with Black in jurisprudential battle against Frankfurter, emerged as Black's most dedicated adversary in the sit-in cases. For Douglas, the case was nothing more than a simple extension of the doctrine of *Shelley v. Kraemer*—once the police got involved, the business owner's "private" choice to discriminate became a matter of government policy, and this brought with it the constraints of the Fourteenth Amendment. When he thought the Court would deny review of the Baton Rouge cases, Douglas drafted an angry dissent. Allowing these convictions to stand would mark a "retreat" from the *Shelley* principle that judicial enforcement of private discrimination was state action, he argued. If the Court wanted to take this path, it should do so explicitly, not by refusing to review the case. "Members of both races have the right to know whether the line we once drew still exists. . . ." The Court eventually agreed to hear the cases, and Douglas filed away his draft dissent, saving its arguments for future sit-in cases.[20]

The Court heard oral arguments in the Louisiana cases in October 1961. Jack Greenberg, recently promoted to director-counsel of LDF after Thurgood Marshall's appointment as a federal appeals court judge, argued the students' case. He led with the constitutional argument that Douglas was making behind closed doors, that Marshall had offered in *Boynton*, and that the NAACP would push in all the subsequent sit-in cases: *Shelley* established that the authority of the state—in the form of arrests and prosecutions—could not be used to protect racial discrimination by businesses that served the public. This position received powerful endorsement from the New York City Bar Association, which submitted an amicus brief urging the Court to "meet squarely" the constitutional issue, resolve the "present uncertainty," and extend *Shelley* to the sit-in cases.[21]

Alongside the state action claim, Greenberg also gave the Court an alternative way to overturn the convictions—one that the justices would gratefully accept. The facts of the case, he argued, failed to show that the protests met the legal threshold for a disturbing-the-peace conviction. All the Baton Rouge demonstrators did was sit down and ask to be served. There were no counter-protesters. There was no evidence of a public disturbance. Louisiana could not claim that the mere breaking of a segregation custom was itself a disturbance of the peace. To do so would mean, in effect, that the students "were convicted of being Negroes at a white lunch counter," Greenberg told the justices, and this the state could not do under the equal protection clause. For this reason, he argued, the convictions could be overturned for a lack of evidence.[22]

Louisiana's assistant district attorney offered several lines of argument in defending the breach-of-peace convictions. These arguments echoed claims that opponents of the sit-in movement had been making since February 1960, and they would be replayed in the Supreme Court litigation in the sit-in cases in the coming years. They included, first, an emphasis on the imminence of violence in the sit-in protests. "In almost every instance of the staging of a militant 'sit-in demonstration' violence had occurred with resulting fist fights between members of the two races," Louisiana claimed in its brief. This kind of insistence that the sit-ins were riots in the making was commonplace among southern state authorities. Although these characterizations required some rewriting of recent history (most sit-ins did not lead to violence) and a self-serving elision of the fact that the violence that did occur was always initiated by white segregationists, they were effective at drawing attention to the substantial public disorder that the sit-in protests often ignited. Agree or disagree with the students' cause, the state lawyers insisted, one must recognize the responsibility of the state and local government to ensure the law and order of its communities. This argument, as we will see later in the chapter, increasingly resonated with certain members of the Supreme Court in the years to follow.[23]

Louisiana's attorney offered another argument when the justices responded skeptically toward his portrayal of the facts. He accused the NAACP lawyers of scheming to explode the state action limitation on the Fourteenth Amendment—a doctrinal path with dangerous consequences. Louisiana, he insisted, was not discriminating. "We have enacted no statute which requires segregation in these places." The state was just enforcing race-neutral policies designed to protect the peace of the community. He warned against declaring that "as a matter of law . . . the property of all persons engaged in every type of business, no matter how large or how small, has become public in nature."[24]

A final argument Louisiana's attorney pressed was that the rights of the business owner needed protection too. He compared the student sit-ins to the "sit-down" factory labor strikes of the 1930s and 1940s and described them as "a seizure of the owner's property in an effort to coerce him into submitting to their demand." The core issue of the case came down to "whether or not in our country, a private property owner still has the right to admit or deny access to his property or to restrict in some fashion the use of that property for any reason that he may choose." And he warned against taking away from the people their "right to privately discriminate or, to state it correctly, . . . the right to associate, and the corresponding right not to associate, with whomsoever they please for whatever reason they please, that is guaranteed to *them* by the Constitution."[25]

When the justices met to discuss the cases following oral argument, Douglas wanted to issue a broad constitutional ruling that would overturn the disorderly conduct arrests as violating both the First and Fourteenth Amendments. The issue was simple for Douglas: "A state cannot restrict either by statute or by judicial decision the use of a public place to one race." To rule otherwise would be to make the same mistake the Court did in *Plessy v. Ferguson*. It "would fasten segregation in a constitutional way on all the private enterprises in the south and perhaps in other areas as well." Chief Justice Warren and Justice William Brennan indicated some degree of support for this position.[26]

Black and Frankfurter aligned against Douglas, and, by Douglas's estimate, they had the support of Harlan and Clark. Frankfurter told the justices that this was a time to "creep along rather than be general." The Louisiana cases, he explained in a letter to the Chief Justice, "should be disposed of on the narrowest allowable grounds." Because "we are all fully conscious of the fact that it is just the beginning of a long story," the Court should "make of this a little case." In urging this gradual path, Frankfurter had influential backing from the U.S. Justice Department. Although in the previous term Eisenhower's solicitor general had called on the Court to strike down any state enforcement of racial discrimination in public accommodations, the solicitor general under the Kennedy administration, Archibald Cox—a labor law expert who had been teaching at Harvard Law School—took a more cautious approach. His amicus brief asked the Court to resolve the issue in favor of the students "without involving broader and largely uncharted questions concerning the meaning of 'State action.'"[27]

On December 11, 1961, two months after oral arguments, the justices unanimously overturned the convictions of the Baton Rouge protesters. "We find it unnecessary to reach the broader constitutional questions presented," Warren explained in his opinion for the Court. The Court rejected Louisiana's argument that the mere act of refusing to leave the lunch counter when asked to do so amounted to a disturbance of the peace under Louisiana law. The protesting students, Warren explained, "not only made no speeches, they did not even speak to anyone except to order food; they carried no placards, and did nothing, beyond their mere presence at the lunch counter, to attract attention to themselves or to others." Thus, the Court concluded, the convictions were "so totally devoid of evidentiary support" that they violated the students' constitutional right to due process of law. Since the Supreme Court usually allows state courts the last word when it comes to measuring the evidence required to support a state-law criminal conviction, this was an exceptional holding.[28]

Three justices wrote concurring opinions in *Garner*. Frankfurter questioned Warren's reading of the Louisiana statute, but he ultimately agreed that the prosecution lacked evidence. Harlan and Douglas wrote more significant concurrences. Each disagreed with Warren's conclusion that a peaceful violation of a community custom could never be sufficient grounds for a breach-of-peace conviction. Harlan's main argument was that the prosecutions of the sit-in protesters raised First Amendment concerns. He went so far as to analogize the sit-ins to "a public oration from a soapbox," although he ultimately concluded that a prosecution for a sit-in protest did not necessarily violate the First Amendment, since the amendment does not protect "demonstrations conducted on private property over the objection of the owner." (In the Baton Rouge cases, the lunch counter managers never explicitly demanded that the protesters leave.) Nonetheless, Harlan insisted, the First Amendment prohibited state prosecutions under a "general and all-inclusive breach of the peace prohibition" that had the effect of restricting speech.[29]

Douglas brushed aside his colleagues' concerns about moving too quickly in the sit-in cases. "The constitutional questions must be reached," he declared at the opening of his concurrence. True to his reputation as a jurist with little patience for crafting carefully reasoned legal opinions, Douglas offered a grab bag of rationales for why the state should be held responsible for violating the equal protection rights of the protesting students. Without actually citing *Shelley* (none of the *Garner* opinions mentioned it), he alluded to its concern with states using their authority to effectuate racial discrimination in the private realm. For Douglas, the case boiled down to a simple fact: "The police are supposed to be on the side of the Constitution, not on the side of discrimination." Douglas also argued that the Court should recognize pervasive community customs and practices as a form of state action. "Though there may have been no state law or municipal ordinance that in terms required segregation of the races in restaurants," he wrote, "it is plain that the proprietors in the instant cases were segregating blacks from whites pursuant to Louisiana's custom. Segregation is basic to the structure of Louisiana as a community; the custom that maintains it is at least as powerful as any law. . . . [W]here the segregation policy is the policy of a State, it matters not that the agency to enforce it is a private enterprise."[30]

Finally, Douglas staked out a broad claim for rethinking the constitutional responsibilities of public accommodations. He offered two overlapping reasons why, when it came to applying the equal protection clause of the Fourteenth Amendment, restaurants should be distinguished from other private enterprises. First, restaurants require state licenses to operate, and "[a] license to establish a restaurant is a license to establish a public facility and necessarily imports, in law, equality of use for all members of the public." Second, public accommodations have a distinctive responsibility in American society. "Restaurants, though a species of private property, are in the public domain," he explained. They have a "public consequence"; they are "affected with a public interest." As such, they should be treated like state-operated public facilities, the protections of the equal protection clause fully applied. In the coming years, Douglas's *Garner* concurrence provided a guiding light for civil rights lawyers who sought to make the case that discrimination in public accommodations violated the Constitution.[31]

"For those who had hoped for a sweeping expansion of state action under the fourteenth amendment," Warren's "drab" reasoning was a "disappointment," wrote law professors Kenneth Karst and William W. Van Alstyne. Yet, they added, "there was something for everyone in the *Garner* case." CORE praised the "historic" ruling as "the dawn of a new day of equality," and in Baton Rouge, where the *Garner* case originated, members of the group launched a new round of sit-in protests on the day the Supreme Court decision came down. Others lauded Warren for his cautious judicial statesmanship. The Court left the issue "to the consciences of the people concerned," Eugene Patterson, editor of the *Atlanta Constitution*, approvingly noted. "Delaying the ultimate decision permits legal thought to be clarified and may increase the chances of wisdom when an issue is resolved," added the *New York Times'* Anthony Lewis. Southern state officials downplayed the ruling, saying it had no effect on the sit-in convictions that they continued to pursue on appeal, since they were based on trespass convictions or breach-of-peace convictions in which they insisted they had sufficient evidence.[32]

All agreed that *Garner* was but an early chapter in this unfolding constitutional controversy. "The decision settles none of the constitutional questions raised by the demonstrations," noted the Supreme Court reporter for the *Washington Post*. "Instead, it indicates that the

Court intends to approach these cases cautiously and to put off as long as possible a ruling on the difficult issues." *Garner* "marks only the beginning of the court's problems in this controversial legal area," explained another newspaper account, noting that the Supreme Court was considering seven other sit-in cases for review and "countless others are on their way up."[33]

Reading the tea leaves, some observers assumed that Douglas, whose *Garner* concurrence was filled with what Professors Karst and Van Alstyne described as "dazzling moves," charted a course that the rest of the Court would soon follow. "The feeling is that when the justices reach the question of segregation in private businesses such as lunch counters, in cases that cannot be decided on technical grounds, they will declare the practice unconstitutional," reported the *New York Times*. The editors for the *Washington Post* endorsed Justice Douglas's broad concurrence as "the most pertinent and generally satisfying rationale" for the sit-in cases.[34]

Act Three: The Sit-In Cases of 1963

Despite these optimistic predictions, the reworking of the state action doctrine that seemed in the offing in the 1961 *Burton* and *Garner* cases never took place. In some ways, the 1961 cases were the high-water mark of the Court's reconsideration of the contours of the state action doctrine in response to the sit-in movement. The Court never picked up on the tantalizing hints in *Burton* and never coalesced around any of Douglas's invitations in his *Garner* opinion. The justices continued to find ways to overturn the convictions of the protesters without deciding the larger constitutional question. These decisions, complained one law professor, "were not convincing of anything except the Court's patent desire to avoid deciding the troublesome question."[35]

Yet the way in which the justices went about avoiding the constitutional question in the next round of sit-in cases, which the Court decided in the spring of 1963, is revealing. It demonstrated their continued unwillingness to directly confront the students' challenge to traditional legalistic definitions of public and private space or their insistence that the human dignity costs of private racial discrimination be recognized as a component of the constitutional analysis. The unwillingness of the majority of the justices to do what so many people expected of them and declare the sit-in prosecutions a violation of the Fourteenth Amendment was a product of the distinctive concerns the justices faced in the early 1960s, particularly a concern with protecting the legitimacy of the Supreme Court.

The 1963 cases involved appeals of trespass convictions for protests in cities across the South: Birmingham, Durham, New Orleans, and Greenville, South Carolina. These cases showed the sharpening divisions within the Court with regard to the sit-in cases. Behind-the-scenes battles were increasingly breaking out into the open. Douglas had already publicly declared his frustration with the Court's cautious approach. Now others did the same. On the other side, the justices who were most skeptical of the argument that the students had a viable constitutional claim were becoming more adamant and more outspoken about their concerns. Justice Harlan, who in his *Garner* concurrence had discussed situations in which sit-in protests might fall under the protection of the First Amendment, now focused his energies on warning against what he viewed as the Court's willingness to manipulate facts and law to overturn protester convictions. And Justice Black expressed growing unease with the direction of the civil rights movement. His concerns that the sit-in protests threatened the property rights of white proprietors would lead him to articulate a passionate defense of the state action limitation of the Fourteenth Amendment.

In early November 1962, the Court heard three days of arguments in this new round of sit-in cases. Oral arguments were a largely predictable debate between LDF lawyers, who argued for overturning the convictions because they violated the Fourteenth Amendment and on various other, more limited grounds, and the lawyers for the states, who argued that the prosecutions were race-neutral efforts to protect private property rights and the public peace.

Solicitor General Cox once again urged minimalist resolutions. Greenberg had pleaded with Kennedy administration lawyers to stand behind LDF's position. The primary obstacle proved to be Cox, who believed not only that the justices were not ready to accept such an argument, but that they should not accept it. To ask the Court to abandon a doctrine that had been in place since the late nineteenth century, Cox recalled, "took an awful, awful gulp, according to my views of the law and the need to preserve the ideal of law." He felt that expanding the state action doctrine to cover privately operated public accommodations would have problematic consequences. How, he asked Greenberg, could the courts distinguish a private social gathering from having dinner at a restaurant? Wouldn't LDF's position lead to more violence as business owners took it upon themselves to enforce their discriminatory policies? As Cox recalled, "Here my philosophy about the role of judges and the prestige of the Court, the legitimacy of the Court's decisions, did play an important role." Greenberg was unimpressed. "If you believe in your position, write it up in the *Harvard Law Review*," he said. "But now you're the Solicitor General of the United States, and it is the policy of the Kennedy administration to oppose discrimination wherever it can." Other lawyers in the Justice Department, including Burke Marshall, head of the Civil Rights Division, were more sympathetic to LDF's constitutional argument. But Cox had the final word.[36]

Following a lively oral argument, notable in particular for Justice Black's obvious skepticism toward the students' constitutional claim, the justices met in their private conference. Warren led off the discussion by explaining that the student convictions should be overturned, although he believed the Court could do so on narrow grounds once again. Black agreed, but, he added, "if it is necessary," he was prepared "to meet these cases on their merits." His views on the constitutional issue were clear: "a store owner as a home owner has a right to say who can come on his premises and how long they can stay." And with that right came the option to call on the police to enforce it. Harlan, Clark, and Potter Stewart all signaled their support for Black's position on the constitutional question.[37]

On May 20, 1963, the Supreme Court issued its rulings. The Court's decisions in the cases from Greenville, Durham, and Birmingham turned on the fact that at the time of the protests, these cities had ordinances on their books requiring segregation in public eating places. Although no protesters were arrested for violating these patently unconstitutional ordinances, their mere existence meant that the private business's choice to discriminate should not be considered a truly "private choice," wrote the Chief Justice. By retaining their segregation laws, the city "has thus effectively determined that a person owning, managing or controlling an eating place is left with no choice of his own but must segregate his white and Negro patrons." Because the choice to discriminate was not a truly private one, the state could not use its authority to enforce it, even if it did so through a racially neutral trespass law. Warren sidestepped the tricky question of whether the store manager refused to serve black patrons because of the city ordinance or because he personally agreed with this policy, concluding such inquiries irrelevant in this situation: "When a state agency passes a law compelling persons to discriminate against other persons because of race, and the State's criminal processes are employed in a way which enforces the discrimination mandated by that law, such a palpable violation of the Fourteenth Amendment cannot be saved by attempting to separate the mental urges of the discrimi-nators."[38]

In the New Orleans case, where there was no applicable segregation ordinance, the Court located the hand of discriminatory government authority in the public statements by the chief of police and mayor asserting that the city had a responsibility to prevent the sit-ins. "As we interpret the New Orleans city officials' statements," wrote War-ren, "they here determined that the city would not permit Negroes to seek desegregated service in restaurants. Consequently, the city must be treated exactly as if it had an ordinance prohibiting such conduct." For purposes of the Court's state action analysis, official public sup-port of private segregation, even indirectly, was the same as a govern-ment segregation policy. "An official command" supporting segregat-ing businesses, Warren concluded, "has at least as much coercive effect as an ordinance." Just as in the Greenville case, "the voice of the State direct[ed] segregated service," and this the Constitution did not allow.[39]

As the Court circled closer to the state action issue that lay at the core of the sit-in cases, divisions among the justices only widened. In a concurring opinion, Douglas continued to demand a bold judicial resolution of the issue. "We should not await legislative action before declaring that state courts cannot enforce this type of segregation," he asserted, alluding to the federal civil rights bill that the Kennedy ad-ministration had recently proposed, which included a provision that would prohibit racial discrimination in public accommodations across the nation. He reiterated arguments from his *Garner* concurrence, de-scribing possible paths for overturning the students' convictions on constitutional grounds. These included the following: extending *Shel-ley* to public accommodations; recognizing that because public accom-modations serve an essential "public interest," they must assume ad-ditional responsibilities (including equal protection constraints); and locating state action in the government licensing of public accommo-dations. Douglas concluded: "There is no constitutional way, as I see it, in which a State can license and supervise a business serving the public and endow it with the authority to manage that business on the basis of apartheid, which is foreign to our Constitution."[40]

Justice Harlan also wrote a separate opinion. Unlike Douglas, who believed the Court was too beholden to established state action doc-trine, Harlan felt the 1963 decisions went too far in weakening a ven-erable and valuable doctrine. He emphasized the limits of the Court's holding, noting that it did not "question the long-established rule that the Fourteenth Amendment reaches only state action." And it did not hold that the state violates the equal protection clause when it enforced "trespass laws in relation to private business establishments from which the management, of its own free will, has chosen to exclude persons of the Negro race."[41]

Harlan also took the opportunity to defend the "vital functions in our system" that the state action doctrine served. At issue in these cases was "a clash of competing constitutional claims of a high order: liberty and equality." It was Harlan's concern that liberty was being undervalued. "Freedom of the individual to choose his associates or his neighbors, to use and dispose of his property as he sees fit, to be irrational, arbitrary, capricious, even unjust in his personal relations are things all entitled to a large measure of protection from governmental interference. This liberty would be overridden, in the name of equality, if the strictures of the Amendment were applied to governmental and private action without distinction." He also worried that another constitutional principle was being lost in his liberal colleagues' eagerness to remake the state action doctrine: federalism. He urged the Court to recognize "that there are areas of private rights upon which federal power should not lay a heavy hand and which should properly be left to the more precise instruments of local authority."[42]

Harlan basically accused the majority of undermining the state action doctrine without quite admitting it. To declare that a state law can have the effect of removing the possibility of private choice in restricting the use of private property, "however unregenerate a particular exercise of that right may be thought," was to effectively destroy the right to that choice. "The dilution or virtual elimination of that right cannot well be justified either on the premise that it will hasten formal repeal of outworn segregation laws or on the ground that it will facilitate proof of state action in cases of this kind." He attacked the "inexorable rule" the Court created—one that did not depend on a factual assessment of whether the law indeed compelled the private discrimination or not—as "reflect[ing] insufficient reckoning with the demands of history."[43]

Having rejected the majority's assumption that the mere existence of the segregation policy was enough to remove the possibility of treating the discrimination as the product of private choice, Harlan then turned to the facts of the particular cases before the Court. In the Greenville case, he found sufficient evidence that the business manager acted because of the ordinance. In the Birmingham and Durham cases, he found no such evidence and therefore argued that the convictions should be upheld. In the New Orleans case, Harlan interpreted the public statements of local officials as efforts to preserve the peace rather than segregation; he called for a new trial to assess the connection between the mayor and police chief's statements and the store manager's actions.[44]

The 1963 sit-in decisions show the justices avoiding the difficult constitutional question of the sit-ins by focusing on misbehavior by southern state actors. They used the sit-in cases to create incentives for the southern states to get rid of any hint of official segregation. The Court would overturn any conviction, even if based on an ostensibly private discriminatory choice, if the local government had on the books a law requiring segregated public accommodations. The fact that the prosecutions of sit-in protests were not made under these laws was irrelevant to the Court's analysis. If there were no segregation laws on the books, any expressed support of segregation by local officials would do the job. Official action in support of segregation, rather than the student demand for service, was the illegality the Court needed to counter.[45]

In order to "present as united a front as possible," Warren explained in a letter to Douglas, he was willing to "leav[e] some facets of the problem to be dealt with next Term." The next term, the Court would face a new group of sit-in cases, none of which could be disposed of based on the reasoning the Court had deployed thus far. *Bell v. Maryland* presented the constitutional issue in its starkest terms. The protest occurred not in the Deep South, where the pervasive nature of explicit official support for racial segregation and the intertwined nature of segregation custom and law made for many opportunities to locate discriminatory state action, but in Maryland, where segregation was less firmly embedded in custom and policy. In *Bell*, it appeared that the justices finally had a sit-in case in which there was no way to avoid the constitutional issue.[46]

Act Four: *Bell v. Maryland* (1964)

Battle Lines Drawn

"The great battle of the 1963 Term was fought . . . over the Sit-In Cases," wrote Justice Brennan's clerks in a memo they prepared at the term's end. These cases "were argued on the first day of the Term and decided on the last, and were the subject of fierce debate for much of the time in-between." When the justices at the close of the previous term agreed to hear a new series of sit-in cases, they assumed these cases would be the ones in which they finally confronted the state action issue they had been carefully avoiding since the sit-in movement began. As Brennan's clerks described the situation, "In view of the prevalence of sit-in demonstrations throughout the country and the heated emotions aroused by the issue of racial discrimination in places of public accommodation, the Court, led by Justice Black, thought it imperative that a definitive constitutional ruling be announced as to whether such demonstrators could constitutionally be convicted of trespass."[47]

Bell had its origins in the arrest of twelve African Americans for a sit-in protest at a Baltimore restaurant in 1960. After being told they would not be served and asked to leave, the group took seats in the restaurant and again requested service. The owner called the police. The police refused to arrest the protesters until the restaurant owner obtained a warrant for their arrest. The owner went to the police station, where a police magistrate issued the warrant. The magistrate then called the restaurant and talked to the leader of the protest, who agreed to come to the police court and submit to a trial. At trial in March 1961, the protesters were convicted under Maryland's criminal trespass statute. The following January, the Maryland Court of Appeals, the state's high court, upheld the conviction.[48]

"Community custom did not dictate the result in the Bell case," argued Maryland in its brief at the Supreme Court. "No evidence was produced before the trial court to show the existence of an overriding custom or 'climate' of segregation in the community causing unequal enforcement of otherwise innocuous State laws solely to exclude Negroes on the basis of their race." The existence of segregation laws on the books (as in the Greenville case) or public proclamations of support for segregation practices (as in the New Orleans case) was not available here. Indeed, Maryland argued in its brief, at a number of the restaurants the protesters targeted prior to their arrest, they were served without incident. The restaurant owner who chose to press trespass charges against the protests professed to be "in sympathy" with the objectives of the protesters, if not their methods.[49]

When faced with the *Bell* case in the fall of 1963, the justices were prepared to face the constitutional issue—and to rule against the protesters. They did so despite the fact that Solicitor General Cox had submitted an amicus brief urging the Court to once again avoid "the unsettled and far-reaching" constitutional questions and decide the cases on narrower grounds. The convictions should be overturned, the government argued, because the students were not properly notified that their presence in the public accommodations was unlawful.

The brief justified such a narrow, formalistic reading of the state trespass laws because First Amendment rights were at stake and because the laws "are here applied against peaceful conduct which is, if illegal, plainly not immoral. They proscribe acts which the State has a doubtful interest in condemning." Justice Department lawyers walked right up to a conclusion that the use of trespass prosecutions to protect racial discrimination in this context was unconstitutional, but then stepped back, if only slightly—legality is not morality; while state enforcement of private discrimination is of "doubtful" interest, it is not necessarily unconstitutional.[50]

Cox, who had been urging caution in the sit-in cases from the beginning, now had an additional reason for urging the Court to avoid the constitutional issue: Congress was considering a Kennedy administration–backed civil rights bill that included a provision banning racial discrimination in public accommodations, and he thought it best if the Court allowed Congress to take the lead. Douglas privately mused that the solicitor general probably believed that if the Court issued a ruling that treated private property as "sacrosanct," then "the opposition to the public accommodation bill will use that opinion to kill the bill."[51]

Oral arguments in the cases, which the Court heard on October 14 and 15, 1963, fell into what was now a familiar pattern. LDF attorney Greenberg parried questions about the limits of his arguments against state enforcement of private discrimination. Does it apply to the home? asked Justice Stewart. No. A private club? No (assuming it was a "genuinely private club" and not a "sham"). A buying cooperative? Not sure about that one. A church? No. Greenberg found himself making strong claims on behalf of the right to discriminate in areas of society that are truly private, but then using this partial concession to strengthen his central argument: that a public accommodation—"a place fully open to the public, fully subject to regulation"—is in a distinct category.[52]

Arguing on behalf of the U.S. government, Ralph Spritzer, assistant to the solicitor general, explained that he would not discuss "whether there should be a redefinition of the concept of state action" because this "broad constitutional issue" was not necessary to resolve the case. The convictions could be overturned on "more limited principles"—in this case, the argument that the trespassing law was unconstitutionally vague. In sidestepping the state action issue, the government was being "mindful of the fact" that the president was advocating and Congress was considering legislation "directed at the very problems which underlie this kind of litigation."[53]

At their conference following oral argument, Warren expressed some regret about the position in which the Court found itself. He had hoped the justices would be able to "take these cases step by step, not reaching the final question until much experience had been had." But now, in these cases, "that course seems to me to be impracticable."[54]

In three of the cases, a majority of the justices voted to overturn convictions on narrow grounds, as they had done before. But in the remaining two—*Bell* and *Robinson* (the Florida case)—the justices voted 5–4 to affirm the trespass convictions based on the principle that the Fourteenth Amendment does not apply to private discrimination and that a restaurant owner's policy of whom to serve was a private choice. Voting to affirm were Justices Black, Clark, Harlan, Stewart, and Byron White. Black was the most outspoken in his opposition to the NAACP's constitutional position. He once again spoke about his father's right to serve whom he wanted in his Alabama general store. As the senior justice in the majority, Black assigned himself the opinion of the Court affirming the convictions. A frustrated Douglas once again accused the Court of resurrecting *Plessy v. Ferguson* with its decision.[55]

According to an account Brennan's law clerks prepared based on Brennan's descriptions of the justices' private conference, the "discussion was very heated, not only because of the importance of the issue and the fervor with which views were held on both sides, but also because the minority Justices feared that the affirmance might have a crippling effect on prospects for Congressional passage of the Civil Rights Bill." These justices, led by Brennan, sought to delay the opinion in the hope that either Congress would pass the bill or, if the bill failed, one of the majority might be convinced to switch sides. (Brennan thought White was most likely.) Black, in contrast, was particularly concerned with what he saw as a growing threat to law and order from the strengthening civil rights protest movement. He believed that the Court had a responsibility to decide the issue as quickly as possible.[56]

The debate continued at a later conference. Arthur Goldberg—who had replaced Justice Frankfurter on the Court in late 1962 and quickly aligned himself with Warren and Brennan in the ongoing battle over the sit-in cases—made another plea for the Court to resolve the cases on narrow grounds, following the path laid out in the solicitor general's brief. "I fear the results of this opinion," he warned. To permit discrimination in public places would "set back legislation indefinitely." Considering the pending civil rights bill, "it would be a great disservice to the nation to decide this issue 5–4." It would be a "tragedy." Black refuted his arguments point by point and held his majority.[57]

The discussion then turned to whether they should invite the solicitor general to present the government's position on the state action question, since the government's brief had carefully avoided this issue. This, too, divided the Court. The Black-led group saw it as nothing more than a delay tactic (which it clearly was). Stewart defected from the majority on this issue and gave Brennan the fifth vote he needed. Black, Clark, Harlan, and White signed a dissent to the Court's request for the solicitor general's position on "the broader constitutional issues."[58]

Four days after the Court requested further briefing from the solicitor general, President Kennedy was assassinated, and Lyndon Johnson became the nation's new president. Jack Greenberg and Joseph Rauh, the liberal activist and lawyer who was arguing one of the sit-in cases before the Supreme Court, met with Johnson's assistant for civil rights to urge the new administration to embrace the NAACP's legal arguments in the sit-in cases. "We argued," Greenberg recalled, "that Cox was obliged to advocate the position of the United States, not his personal philosophy." Although Johnson's assistant was concerned that pressing Cox too hard on this issue might result in "his exploding and resigning," the solicitor general, urged by Attorney General Kennedy and Burke Marshall, eventually submitted a brief to the Court that placed the federal government in basic alignment with the NAACP's position.[59]

Filed on January 17, 1964, the new Justice Department brief argued that segregationist customs, which were largely the product of generations of discriminatory policy, were different from the run-of-the-mill choices private actors made in running their daily lives. "The State must scrupulously avoid continuing to support, even indirectly, a stigma serving no function but to preserve public distinctions of caste which the [Reconstruction] Amendments promised to eliminate." (The government brief also located a Florida statute requiring segregated toilet facilities, which would allow the Court to unanimously overturn the convictions in *Robinson* on narrow grounds.)[60]

Undeterred by this new, bolder intervention by the federal government, Justice Black moved ahead with his original plan. He circulated a draft of his majority opinion in early March 1964. Harlan praised Black's opinion as "a splendid job, and eminently right," and Clark described it as "just right" and expressed his hope that it would soon be released. Black's majority was "absolutely solid and indestructible," Clark assured Goldberg. Brennan abandoned the idea of further delaying the decision. In his "grave fears" that the ruling would hinder the pending congressional legislation, Brennan was joined by the Chief Justice, but not Douglas or Goldberg.[61]

Black's draft opinion squarely rejected the argument that the Constitution prohibited a store operator from calling on the police to enforce his choice of whom to serve, even if his choice was driven by racial prejudice. As long as the state did not enforce its trespass laws "with an evil eye and a prejudiced heart and hand," the equal protection requirement was met. "We do not believe that the Amendment was written or designed to interfere with a property owner's right to choose his social or business associates, so long as he does not run counter to a valid state or federal regulation." Here Black was making clear that he saw private property rights as a limit on the courts in their reading of the Fourteenth Amendment, but not on state legislatures or Congress when they passed public accommodations laws. The nuances of this legal position risked being subsumed, however, by his sweeping proclamations in defense of property rights, such as when he declared that to recognize the students' constitutional claim "would overturn the whole history of this country" because it would "take away a man's property" without compensation.[62]

Douglas countered with a scathing dissent. He opened: "Never in our cases, unless it be the ill-starred *Dred Scott* decision, has property been more exalted in suppression of individual rights." Douglas also accused the majority of making "corporate management the arbiter of one of the deepest conflicts in our society."[63]

The normally measured Chief Justice drafted a dissent that contained all the anger of Douglas's. He attacked the majority for "interpos[ing] principles of privacy and protection of property rights between Negro petitioners and the right to equal treatment in public places" and predicted the ruling would undermine "the future development of basic American principles of equality." With regard to the department store policy of serving African American customers everywhere but when seated at the lunch counter, Warren wrote:

The store might as well have offered to feed only Negroes who would crawl in on their hands and knees, or, as in other caste systems, who would purchase food under conditions that would not cause their shadow to fall on the food of whites. It saddens me deeply to think that this Court, which has so far advanced the notion of equal dignity of all men before the law, would sanction the right so publicly first to shame and then to punish one who merely seeks that which any white man takes for granted. Irrespective of the activity of other branches of our Government, the courts, and particularly this Court, cannot escape the responsibility imposed by the Constitution to assure all Americans the basic right of equal protection under the laws.

Warren challenged Black's excessive reverence for the property rights of business owners, writing that "the important civil right of equal access to public places is a right which the Constitution forbids a State to deny in the name of private property." The Fourteenth Amendment protects against the loss of "that little bit of humanity" that is lost "each time a state-sanctioned inferior status is publicly thrust upon" a person—a line that echoed the famous reference in his *Brown* opinion about the damages segregated schooling inflicted on the psyches of black children. "I cannot in conscience be a part of a return to a tradition which so belongs to the past," Warren concluded.[64]

Around this time, with the angry debate over the sit-in cases echoing in the halls of the high court, Brennan's clerks hatched an escape plan. Maryland, they learned, had recently passed a public accommodations law. Further research found that Baltimore, where the protest in *Bell* had taken place, had had a similar regulation in place for two years. What if this new law were read to apply retroactively, thereby vacating pending sit-in convictions? According to the clerks' account, "The new idea evoked a favorable, or at least interested, reaction from Justice Brennan and others to whom it was presented."[65]

For the time being, the Court continued to move ahead on the assumption that Black would be writing a majority opinion in *Bell* upholding the trespassing convictions. Justice Harlan wrote to Black that he was anxious to announce their decision "without further unnecessary delay." In mid-April, Brennan began writing a dissenting opinion, arguing that the convictions should be overturned because of the passage of the state and local public accommodations laws. Goldberg circulated a dissent arguing that the Fourteenth Amendment prohibited the trespass convictions. Tensions steadily rose. Black told Goldberg that "the whole tone of your opinion would have to be changed in order to make it the temperate kind of reasoned argument any opinion of this Court should have in this highly emotional field." Black was hoping to have the opinions ready to be handed down on May 4. Brennan and Warren were still working on their dissents and asked for more time. Black reluctantly agreed to push back *Bell*'s release yet again.[66]

Brennan's draft dissent included strong language condemning the Court's intervention in the national debate over the civil rights bill. "We cannot be blind to the fact that today's opposing opinions on the constitutional question decided will inevitably enter into and perhaps confuse that debate." He declared it an "error" to "reach[] out to decide the question." The justices "unnecessarily create the risk of dealing the Court a 'self-inflicted wound'—because the issue should not have been decided at all." This language would be deleted in subsequent drafts, likely the price paid to get the Chief Justice and Justice Goldberg to join his opinion. (Douglas remained committed to a strong opinion supporting the constitutional claim of the sit-in protesters.) Brennan concluded his draft dissent noting that although he believed the constitutional question should not be decided, he "felt obliged, since the Court has done so, to express my position on that issue." He joined the opinions of his fellow dissenters—Douglas, Goldberg, and Warren—that decided the constitutional question in favor of the protesters.[67]

In response to Brennan, Black added new language to the opening of his majority opinion: "The case does not involve the constitutionality of any existing or proposed state or federal legislation requiring restaurant owners to serve people without regard to color."[68]

The drafting done, the decision was scheduled to come down on Monday, May 18.

Realignment

On Friday, May 15, as the final drafts of the *Bell* opinions circulated between the justices' chambers, the alignments that had been set the previous fall shifted. At the private conference of the justices, Clark indicated that he wanted more time to consider Brennan's approach based on the retroactive application of Maryland's public accommodations law. Angry at this last-minute defection from a majority opinion he felt so strongly about, Black said little in the short, tense meeting. Douglas, who believed just as strongly as Black that the constitutional issue needed a clear judicial response, declared he would not join Brennan's opinion. At the end of the conference, there appeared to be a majority of votes to overturn the convictions but no majority on the legal reasoning by which this was to be done.[69]

Persuaded by Brennan's concern that upholding the convictions would undermine the pending federal civil rights legislation, on May 27, Clark informed the justices that he was joining Brennan's opinion. Brennan followed this with a memorandum explaining that since there were enough votes to overturn the convictions without facing the constitutional issue, he would no longer be joining the opinions of Douglas, Goldberg, and Warren. Justice Brennan's clerks began reworking his dissent into a judgment (if not an opinion) of the Court.[70]

"Oh shit!" Douglas exclaimed when he arrived at the Court and learned what had happened. He immediately challenged Brennan's claim to have a majority, explaining that he would only sign on to an opinion that ruled on constitutional grounds. By Douglas's count, this meant that a majority of the Court opposed Brennan's sidestepping resolution. "I suffered a real shock," Douglas wrote Brennan, "when I realized you were in dead earnest in vacating *Bell* and remanding it to the State court and thus avoiding the basic constitutional question. I guess I underwent a real trauma when I realized that the spirit of Felix [Frankfurter]"—a devotee of the idea that the Court should avoid constitutional rulings whenever possible—"still was the dominant force here."[71]

Black wrote a scathing dissent to Brennan's opinion, arguing that since the majority of the six justices who reached the constitutional merits of the case believed the convictions should be upheld, the decision of the Court was to affirm, not vacate or reverse. Harlan judged the tone of the draft dissent "unnecessarily harsh" and urged him to adopt more moderate language. With Douglas's support, Black also countered Brennan by proposing that the Court accept for review a new set of sit-in cases with the goal of finding a case in which there was no way to avoid the constitutional issue. Black argued that the Court should fast-track the cases, holding a special summer session of oral arguments if necessary.[72]

Before Black's desperate plan to find a way to decide the constitutional question could be put into effect, there was yet another turn in this amazing drama. Clark, who Brennan had been able to lure away from the Black majority with his late discovery of a legal off-ramp, now declared himself willing to decide the constitutional question in favor of the students. Exactly why Clark performed this about-face was not fully clear. It might have been a negative reaction to Black's extraordinary efforts to force the issue upon the Court; it might have been a late reassessment of the merits of the constitutional issue; it may have been what Brennan's clerks described as "the consummately executed bluff of a skilled Texas poker player" whose real goal was to force the Court into another sidestep of the central constitutional question.[73]

Bluff or not, Clark circulated his draft opinion. It was a stunning reversal of positions, as aggressively supportive of the NAACP's constitutional argument as anything Douglas had written. (Douglas, always the hero in his own mind and memoirs, claimed that the opinion "was conceived in my office in a talk I had with Clark.") Clark's finding that a trespassing prosecution for a sit-in protest violated the equal protection clause relied on the same catch-all reasoning he had deployed several years earlier in *Burton v. Wilmington Parking Authority*: When a state is involved in private choice "to a significant extent," that is state action; in *Bell*, the "totality of circumstances" met the necessary quantum of state action. Clark described the Fourteenth Amendment as creating "a constitutional right in all Americans, regardless of color, to be treated equally by all branches of Government." He quoted approvingly a legal scholar who described access to public accommodations as having become "a piece of the fabric of society." Racially discriminatory treatment, when hardened into a community "standard," is "foreign to the equal Protection Clause."[74]

Clark insisted that nothing in his bold opinion should be read to undermine the need for the federal civil rights bill, which at this point had passed in the House of Representatives and was moving toward passage in the Senate. Indeed, he insisted that the Court's decision should only reinforce the need for federal legislation. Clark concluded his opinion with a call to Congress to "implement the Fourteenth Amendment as well as our decision, drawing the guidelines necessary to practical administration." Although the Court must deal with issues "on a case-to-case basis," Congress "is better advised as to the necessary steps to be taken and in the give and take of the legislative process can fashion an Act that will meet the necessities of the situation."[75]

On June 11, Warren informed the other justices that Clark was now writing the opinion of the Court.[76]

Endgame

Sitting on the bench on June 15, Justice Stewart was irritated. In his six years on the high court, the Ohio Republican had established himself as a generally centrist vote, valuing careful legal reasoning and respect for judicial precedent over the ideological wars some of his colleagues seemed intent on waging. He was listening to the Chief Justice announce the Court's decision in *Reynolds v. Sims*, one of a series of landmark cases uprooting malapportioned legislative districts across the nation and establishing the new constitutional requirement of a one person–one vote standard in drawing legislative district lines. Stewart felt the Court had gone too far in the reapportionment cases. Its ruling was a "fabrication" of a new constitutional requirement. It was, he wrote in his dissenting opinion, "a long step backward into that unhappy era when a majority of the members of this Court were thought by many to have convinced themselves and each other that the demands of the Constitution were to be measured not by what it says, but by their own notions of wise political theory"—a reference to the "*Lochner* Era" of the late nineteenth and early twentieth centuries. While unhappily listening to Warren in *Reynolds*, he was also thinking about the sit-in cases. In Stewart's eyes, they were yet another liberal effort to fabricate a new constitutional rule that aligned with their sympathies. And because of Clark's last-minute defection, he was about to lose here as well. So he decided to reshuffle the cards once again. When he got back to his chambers, he announced he would sign on to Brennan's opinion in the sit-in cases. He just could not stand to see the Clark opinion prevail, he explained to his clerks. With Stewart on board, Brennan would now write the opinion of the Court, overturning the sit-in convictions based on the subsequent passage of local and state public accommodations laws. Stewart, Clark, Goldberg, and Warren would join Brennan's opinion, the latter two also expressing their position that the prosecutions violated the Fourteenth Amendment. (Warren would withdraw his opinion and join Goldberg's.)[77]

The final decision was handed down on June 22, 1964. Brennan's opinion of the Court noted that the passage of Baltimore and Maryland antidiscrimination laws meant that these sit-ins "would not be a crime today." State and local law "now vindicates their conduct and recognizes it as the exercise of a right, directing the law's prohibition not at them but at the restaurant owner or manager who seeks to deny them service because of their race." Although the public accommodations laws included no provision explicitly applying them retroactively, those who passed these laws "probably did not desire that persons should still be prosecuted and punished for the 'crime' of seeking service from a place of public accommodations which denies it on account of race." Considering these changed legal circumstances, it would be unjust to allow the convictions to stand, Brennan concluded. Applying the common law doctrine of "abatement," which prohibits prosecution for something that is no longer a crime, Brennan vacated the convictions and sent the case back to Maryland's high court. ("Until that time," Jack Greenberg noted, "I had never heard of abatement and neither had any of our cocounsel.")[78]

The six justices who were willing to answer the core constitutional question in *Bell*—Douglas, Goldberg, and Warren on one side; Black, Harlan, and White on the other—all believed that the Court had a responsibility to offer a clear, principled resolution to the sit-in controversy. This would help restore law and order to a national situation that they feared risked spiraling out of control. They differed sharply, however, on whether those who were demanding change or those who were committed to preserving the status quo were the culprits of the disorder. In the context of the sit-in cases, the question came down to which party was the primary lawbreaker, the discriminating proprietor or the sit-in demonstrator. This question had a circularity to it, of course, because locating the source of the breakdown of the rule of law required a prior judgment about what the law actually required in this situation. The crucial question, then, was which party was acting outside the law. And the answer to this question turned more on the justices' attitudes toward direct-action protest as a tactic for claiming a new legal right than it did on the abstract question of whether the discriminatory choice was truly private.[79]

The concurrences by Douglas and Goldberg, in which they argued that the right to nondiscriminatory service in public accommodations was constitutionally protected, laid out the terms of the problem. "We have in this case a question that is basic to our way of life and fundamental in our constitutional scheme," Douglas wrote. "No question preoccupies the country more than this one; it is plainly justiciable; it presses for a decision one way or another; we should resolve it. The people should know that when filibusters occupy other forums, when oppressions are great, when the clash of authority between the individual and the State is severe, they can still get justice in the courts." Douglas expressed as much concern with preserving order and law as his more conservative colleagues. "When we default, as we do today, the prestige of law in the life of the Nation is weakened."[80]

Douglas was disgusted. As he explained in a letter to Goldberg, "I have more or less consistently resisted efforts to avoid pressing demanding constitutional adjudications for reasons technical, picayune, or otherwise." He was particularly angry at Brennan for doing exactly this. Brennan had apparently said that he had only written his opinion urging an overturning of the convictions without facing the constitutional issue as a tactic to try to derail Black's majority. According to Douglas, who spilled his feelings, as he often did, into a "memorandum for the files," Brennan had said he would not file his opinion if a majority of the Court "held that the sit-ins were constitutional." But he changed his mind after Stewart accused Brennan of having written his opinion for reasons of expediency rather than principle. For that reason, Brennan felt compelled to stand by his opinion, even when Clark's defection from the Black camp created a majority to decide the case in the students' favor on the constitutional merits. Thus, Douglas complained, Brennan "had been somewhat shamed into sticking to the position he had taken."[81]

In the end, Black's dissent held only White and Harlan. Although Black told his clerks that he, unlike Douglas, had no desire to attack his colleagues, the final opinion proved otherwise. It was long, impassioned, bristling with anger. "It would betray our whole plan for a tranquil and orderly society," Black asserted, "to say that a citizen, because of his personal prejudices, habits, attitudes, or beliefs, is cast outside the law's protection and cannot call for the aid of officers sworn to uphold the law and preserve the peace." To prohibit trespassing prosecutions in these cases would "penalize citizens who are law-abiding enough to call upon the law and its officers for protection instead of using their own physical strength or dangerous weapons to preserve their rights." Reading the Fourteenth Amendment to require business owners to serve blacks would "severely handicap a State's efforts to maintain a peaceful and orderly society," which was the primary responsibility of government. His opinion then took an apocalyptic turn, reflecting Black's pessimism toward the rising tide of protests taking place across the nation. "The Constitution does not confer upon any group the right to substitute rule by force for rule by law," he wrote. "Force leads to violence, violence to mob conflicts, and these to rule by the strongest groups with control of the most deadly weapons." Black concluded with a point that critics of the sit-ins frequently made: that in the risk to protect against discrimination, other rights were being undervalued. "At times the rule of law seems too slow to some for the settlement of their grievances," he explained. "But it is the plan our Nation has chosen to preserve both 'Liberty' and equality for all. On that plan we have put our trust and staked our future."[82]

Black, the ex-politician, knew how to play to an audience, and during the opinion announcements, he "was in rare form," reported the *New York Times*. "He mixed drama, wit and savage ridicule of the Goldberg opinion as he extemporized on his written views." Black also noted, in a sarcastic aside, that if Goldberg were right, and the Fourteenth Amendment had prohibited racial discrimination in public accommodations all along, then the heroic battle to pass civil rights legislation in Congress had been "a work of supererogation."[83]

Response to *Bell* was predictably mixed. The *Washington Post* editors described Brennan's opinion as written "ingeniously if not altogether convincingly," while the Goldberg and Douglas opinions were "illuminating and persuasive." The conservative *Chicago Tribune* editorial page, still fuming over the reapportionment decision from a week earlier, took the opportunity to attack the Court, seeing the willingness of three "hotspurs of the high bench" to rule in favor of the students' Fourteenth Amendment claim as further evidence of the Court's trend toward "judicial absolutism." Conservative commentator William F. Buckley attacked the "practical effect" of the sit-in cases as "encourag[ing] anyone at all to believe that he may with impunity enter somebody's premises and, for as long as he desires, lie down on the hall carpet." In Alabama, editors of the *Montgomery Advertiser*, having spent the last decade condemning Justice Black for his role in *Brown*, now celebrated the homecoming of their wayward son. "The essence of the Black opinion was that the proprietor had an all-American right to throw the bums out and that his right to bigotry was sacred," wrote the *Montgomery Advertiser*. After quoting at length from Black's dissent, the editors noted, "Many will not believe it came from Black. They will insist that it was from the state papers of George Wallace," Alabama's archsegregationist governor.[84]

Why Did the Supreme Court Pull Back?

What explains the uncharacteristic hesitancy of the Warren Court in the sit-in cases to support a reading of the Fourteenth Amendment that the sit-in movement had forced onto the nation's consciousness and the civil rights movement now made both viable and urgent? The American people were ready. The time was ripe. But the Court would not follow—not this time. In fact, for much of the 1963–64 Court term, five of the justices were ready to squarely face the state action issue and *reject* the students' constitutional claim. What happened?

Congress's struggle with the Civil Rights Act influenced the Court's assessment of the sit-in cases. But it is not quite the case, as often assumed, that the Court would have stepped forward if Congress had not. The reality was more complicated. In the early fall of 1963, with passage of the Civil Rights Act still uncertain, a solid majority of the justices were willing to reject the students' constitutional claim and uphold their convictions. A majority of the Court was willing to deny the constitutional challenge to racial discrimination in public accommodations even when Congress was not moving ahead with the issue. The pending civil rights bill played a clearer role, however, in moving the Court in the spring of 1964. When passage of the bill looked more certain, some in Black's majority worried that rejecting the students' constitutional claim would undermine the passage of the law. When they abandoned Black's majority, the *Bell* decision was left fractured. And the state action dilemma that the sit-ins had pressed upon the nation's legal agenda was left unresolved.

The justices' perception of the constraints imposed by constitutional doctrine offers another factor in the Court's hesitancy to embrace the students' Fourteenth Amendment claim. The justices were concerned with the limits of existing constitutional doctrine and the consequences of a broad constitutional ruling on areas of law beyond racial discrimination in public accommodations. Apart from Douglas, all the justices expressed some apprehension regarding these issues. The words of caution from influential voices—Solicitor General Cox first and foremost, but also various law professors and commentators—made a major reworking of the state action doctrine appear more risky and minimalist resolutions more attractive. Apart from Douglas—who was never one for coalition building in the first place and whose sway over his colleagues in the sit-ins cases was limited by his unwillingness to entertain the doctrinal and institutional concerns with which even his most liberal colleagues struggled—the Warren Court's leading liberals never matched the commitment of Black and his allies in the sit-in cases. Black never wavered, and his confidence in his constitutional position pulled other justices along. The same did not occur on the other side. Brennan, so often the pied piper of the liberal wing of the Warren Court, did not play this role in the sit-in cases. The same could be said for the Chief Justice. Their commitment to the students' constitutional claim was always negotiable.

As Black's paean to "peaceful and orderly society" in his *Bell* dissent indicates, another factor in the ultimate failure of the constitutional claim put forth by the students in the sit-in cases was the justices' discomfort with disruptive forms of social protest. A number of the justices had serious concerns with extrajudicial methods of resistance, and this colored their assessment of the constitutional issues in the sit-in cases. Much of the Warren Court's hesitancy in the sit-in cases was a product of skepticism, even antagonism, toward the civil rights movement's efforts to bypass litigation and lobbying as the primary mode of social change in favor of direct-action protest—a pivot the sit-in movement of 1960 had initiated.

No one on the Court felt this antagonism toward social protest more deeply than Justice Black. For Black, the issue was first and foremost a question of protecting the rule of law. In conference discussions, he referenced the need to protect the associational rights of private citizens as a basic tenet of an orderly society. In his files relating to the October term 1963 sit-in cases, he kept a collection of newspaper clippings filled with stories of the escalating tensions resulting from efforts to integrate public accommodations. One story told of the owner of a Maryland restaurant who, with the aid of several friends, "hurled" a dozen civil rights demonstrators from his restaurant. Another told of a Florida hotel manager who poured acid into the hotel pool in order to force "integrationists" out of the water. When the protesters were driven from the water, "club-swinging policemen rained blows on the heads, backs, and shoulders of the Negroes." Yet another story described the growth of "anti-white gangs" in Harlem, including ominous references to the training of black youths in martial arts. In *Bell* and subsequent civil rights protest opinions, Justice Black returned again and again to his belief that liberties ultimately suffer when protesters take to the streets. "Minority groups, I venture to suggest, are the ones who always have suffered and always will suffer most when street multitudes are allowed to substitute their pressures for the less glamorous but more dependable and temperate processes of the law," he wrote in a 1965 dissent. As his wife recorded in her diary, Black believed the Court needed to issue a strong, clear ruling defining the limits of the Fourteenth Amendment because "the Negroes . . . continue to break the law in the belief the Supreme Court will sustain the legality of their claims."[85]

Black's defense in the sit-in cases of the existing boundaries of state action as necessary to protect social order marked something of a new direction for the justice. In his earlier decisions, he had been quite ambitious in expanding the Court's conception of state action in order to extend constitutional constraints further into the private sphere. When he confronted the state action question in the context of civil rights protests, Black's doctrinal views changed.[86]

Black rarely talked about pending cases outside the Supreme Court, but he made an exception in the sit-in cases. As convictions from sit-in protests worked their way through the appeals process, "Black recognized what was coming, and he didn't like it," one clerk noted. These cases bother him, another clerk recalled. "He was adamant, arguing that we have a system of private property in this country." People around him heard over and over that story of his father's general store and how he had a right to serve whom he wanted. "Black liked a certain orderliness to his life," explains one biographer. "He was very conscious of the security of his person, and he viewed anyone coming uninvited to his house almost as a bodily assault against which one was entitled to protection."[87]

Among the justices, Black felt this skepticism toward direct-action protest and civil disobedience most deeply, but he was certainly not alone. Prior to signing on to Black's *Bell* dissent, Justice White drafted a brief dissent in which he warned that treating a state trespass conviction derived from a private discriminatory choice as impermissible state action "would be nothing short of an invitation to private warfare and a complete negation of the central peace-keeping function of the State." For at least some of the justices, a sharp discomfort with direct-action protest contributed to their opposition to using the sit-in cases as a platform for a reconsideration of the state action doctrine.[88]

One of the most striking elements of the Supreme Court's confrontation with the sit-in cases was the fact that the issue seemed to become more divisive for the justices over the period from 1960 to 1964. Even as the sit-ins and subsequent civil rights demonstrations were having their intended effect on the nation by moving public opinion behind the cause of federal intervention on behalf of civil rights, the constitutional challenge raised by the sit-ins was pulling the Court apart. Most notably, Justices Douglas and Black, longtime allies in battles against McCarthyism and school segregation, could not have been further apart when it came to the sit-in cases. Douglas came out early in support of the students' constitutional claim. Black feared the property rights of the businesses were being overlooked, a concern that only strengthened as the protests of the civil rights movement gained momentum. Whereas the school desegregation cases had brought the Court together, the sit-in cases now pulled it apart. The battles over the sit-ins previewed the divides in the Court that would become commonplace in the coming years as the civil rights battlefront moved beyond dismantling of de jure segregation to confronting racial discrimination in the private marketplace, where property, privacy, and associational rights pressed back against equality claims.

An irony lies at the heart of the sit-in cases. Among the achievements of the sit-ins was to inspire a massive social protest movement, which, in turn, pressured Congress to pass landmark civil rights legislation. But these very achievements made the Court more divided and ultimately less likely to give the movement a sweeping constitutional victory. Civil rights activists and many Supreme Court observers kept predicting that the Court was about to issue the breakthrough ruling in which it found the students' demands justified in the equal protection clause of the Fourteenth Amendment. It was not to be. There was to be no *Brown*-like judicial breakthrough in the sit-in cases. The problem of racial discrimination in public accommodations was left to Congress to resolve.

SIX

The Lawmakers

Men and women who conscientiously challenged a form of discrimination which they believed was unconstitutional and which the Congress of the United States, in large part as a result of their challenge, made unlawful, ought not be punished for what history will surely record as a courageous public service. *WASHINGTON POST, DECEMBER 1964*[1]

In this final chapter, I turn to the people who crafted, debated, and made into law the Civil Rights Act of 1964. Of the provisions in this landmark legislation—which included voting rights protections, increased federal involvement in school desegregation, and nondiscrimination requirements for recipients of federal funding and for private employers—none was recognized as more important or more controversial at the time of passage than Title II, the section that prohibited racial discrimination in restaurants, hotels, and other public accommodations. With the passage of the Civil Rights Act, Congress would do what the Supreme Court had not: provide a national remedy for the claim to nondiscriminatory treatment that the sit-in protesters had demanded four years earlier at lunch counters across the South.

Unlike other episodes in the legal history of the sit-ins, the Civil Rights Act has received voluminous attention in historical and legal scholarship. In this chapter, I turn from the more familiar elements of this history: the mobilization of civil rights forces behind the bill, the months-long Senate filibuster, President Johnson's application of his famously persuasive "treatment" on recalcitrant members of Congress, the curious story behind the addition of "sex" to the employment nondiscrimination provision. I focus instead on the constitutional questions that the sit-in movement pressed so powerfully on the nation and the role they played in the struggle for a federal public accommodations law.[2]

I consider two constitutional issues in particular. The first is the core constitutional claim of the sit-ins: whether the Fourteenth Amendment prohibits racial discrimination in privately owned public accommodations. Although some of the Supreme Court justices and the lawyers who argued before them viewed congressional action as a way to avoid this troublesome constitutional question, that is not quite right. A federal public accommodations law would help the *courts* avoid the issue, but members of Congress would still need to determine whether the law should be based on its authority to enforce the Fourteenth Amendment, the most obvious constitutional basis for civil rights legislation. (Section 5 of the Fourteenth Amendment gives Congress "power to enforce, by appropriate legislation, the provisions of" the Fourteenth Amendment.) In the end, Congress, like the Supreme Court in the sit-in cases, found a way to avoid the difficult constitutional question. The version of Title II that Congress passed relied on the commerce clause as its primary authority, with the enforcement provision of the Fourteenth Amendment relegated to a limited, secondary basis of authority. When the U.S. solicitor general stood before the Supreme Court to defend Title II, he convinced the justices to focus exclusively on the commerce power basis for the law. In yet another unexpected turn in the legal history of the sit-ins, the national ban on racial discrimination in public accommodations—Congress's greatest contribution to racial equality in nearly a century—was upheld by the Supreme Court not as an effort to enforce the constitutional guarantee of equality but as a regulation of interstate commerce. This chapter explains this strange constitutional turn of events. It explains why Congress passed on this historic opportunity to assert a reading of the Fourteenth Amendment that aligned with the emergent constitutional norm that the 1960 lunch counter sit-ins had produced: that racial discrimination in public accommodations violated the most basic requirements of the Constitution.

The second constitutional issue I examine in this chapter is the question of whether a law prohibiting racial discrimination in public accommodations violates the constitutional rights of business owners. In an earlier chapter, I labeled this a claim of a "right to discriminate." Usually dismissed as a last-gasp constitutional stand by the losing side (which it was, in large part), I argue that this claim played an important role in the debate over the public accommodations bill. Although the claim of a right to discriminate lost as an argument against the Civil Rights Act, and although it would basically be laughed out of the Supreme Court in subsequent litigation challenging Title II, in the lawmaking process it resonated (and continues to resonate) in surprising ways across the ideological spectrum.

I conclude the chapter by returning to the Supreme Court. Here I consider how the justices assessed the work of Congress and its effect on the thousands of sit-in cases that remained on appeal.

The Kennedy Administration and Public Accommodations Legislation

When the sit-ins first spread across the South in 1960, the possibility of a federal public accommodations law was, in the words of one observer, "so remote that a discussion of it is largely academic." Not only was the constitutional foundation for such a law unclear, but the very idea of a federal nondiscrimination requirement in public accommodations was highly controversial and, considering the power held by long-serving southern senators and their ability to use the filibuster, unlikely to pass. Previous efforts to pass anti-lynching and anti-poll tax legislation had died in the Senate, as did the effort to create a permanent fair-employment commission in the 1940s. The civil rights bills that did get through, in 1957 and 1960, were more symbol than substance, offering mostly ineffectual protections for voting rights, and even these only got through because of the efforts of Senate Majority Leader Lyndon Johnson of Texas, who believed these legislative achievements would help legitimate him as a viable presidential candidate outside the South.[3]

As late as February 1963, when President Kennedy first called on Congress to pass comprehensive civil rights legislation, he urged expanded federal intervention for voting rights and school desegregation, but not public accommodations. Kennedy acknowledged discrimination in public accommodations as a problem of constitutional dimension, noting that "no act is more contrary to the spirit of our democracy and Constitution than the barring of that citizen from restaurants, hotels, theaters, recreational areas and other public accommodations and facilities." But at this point he did not see a significant federal role in resolving this constitutional wrong. He touted federal efforts against discrimination in eating facilities connected to interstate transportation and on federal property, but then concluded that when it came to other private businesses, the federal government's role would be to "continue to encourage and support action by state and local communities, and by private entrepreneurs." Three years after the first sit-ins in Greensboro, Kennedy believed that neither Congress nor the country was ready for a public accommodations law.[4]

Later that spring, when the Kennedy administration began drafting a new civil rights bill, administration officials remained divided over whether to include a public accommodations provision. Justice Department lawyers—including Attorney General Robert Kennedy, Deputy Attorney General Nicholas Katzenbach, and Assistant Attorney General for the Civil Rights Division Burke Marshall—believed it necessary. Several senior presidential aides opposed it as too politically risky.[5]

Three developments changed the calculus of federal civil rights policy making on the issue of public accommodations. First was the failure of the approach Kennedy initially favored, federal encouragement of local solutions. In the years since the sit-in movement began, there was steady progress on the local level in moving business owners away from practices of racial discrimination. By 1963 this trend appeared to be stalling. There were also growing concerns over the uneven results produced by local negotiations, with some businesses desegregating while others did not. (Department stores and drugstores with lunch counters generally desegregated first. Restaurants were often slower.) The resulting patchwork frustrated business owners who felt the burdens of desegregation were not being fairly distributed. These frustrations help explain why, when civil rights legislation became a real possibility, business interests never organized in concerted opposition. Indeed, chain store operators complained that early versions of the federal public accommodations law did not go far enough in their coverage.[6]

Another critical development was the civil rights campaign in Birmingham in the spring of 1963. "Project C" (for confrontation), as Martin Luther King Jr. and the leaders of the Southern Christian Leadership Conference referred to it, was a meticulously planned protest campaign in what King deemed "the most segregated city in America." Birmingham was known for its brutal segregationist police commissioner Eugene "Bull" Connor and its history of legal and extralegal retribution against anyone who challenged its white supremacist practices. The frequent bombings of black churches and the homes of civil rights activists earned the city the nickname "Bombingham." Project C leaders decided to focus their protest on Birmingham's white business community, particularly the department and drugstore operators who ran still segregated lunch counters. Connor lashed out, as the civil rights leaders predicted he would, ordering his police force to put an end to the demonstrations. Birmingham police allowed police dogs to attack the protesters, used high-pressure fire hoses to toss them around like rag dolls, and carted them off to jail by the thousands.[7]

With the dramatic protests and harsh police crackdown in Birmingham attracting national headlines and dominating nightly newscasts, the Kennedy administration was desperate to do something that could reduce the increasingly volatile situation in the South. Fears of domestic unrest were amplified by concerns about the costs these episodes had on the international reputation of the United States, as its Cold War rivals eagerly publicized the hypocrisies of the supposed global defender of freedom. Kennedy administration officials came to believe that the only way the public accommodations dilemma was going to be resolved was through federal regulation. As the president explained in his May 1963 press conference—where, for the first time, he added public accommodations legislation to his list of needed federal civil rights reforms—the nation had to "develop a legal remedy" for "those who feel themselves, or who are, as a matter of fact, denied equal rights." It is because they lack a legal remedy that "they take to the streets and we have the kinds of incidents that we have in Birmingham." Alexander Bickel observed, "A new climate of national opinion was created on the streets of Birmingham." These pressures forged the national support that would result in the passage of the Civil Rights Act in the following year.[8]

A third development was the Supreme Court's ongoing struggles with the sit-in cases. An internal memorandum drafted by Kennedy administration officials in May 1963 noted that a Court ruling upholding the convictions of sit-in protesters could ignite new protests. A bold federal effort to end public accommodations discrimination would respond to "the wide frustrations and anger which such a decision would create." Several days later, the Court announced another round of sit-in decisions, which once again reversed the convictions for sit-in protests while again avoiding a broad constitutional ruling. President Kennedy then referenced these decisions in explaining his support for a public accommodations bill.[9]

Once the administration committed itself to public accommodations legislation, two key issues remained. One was how to get the bill through Congress. In the late spring of 1963, there was much urgency but not much optimism that the bill would make it through the Senate.

The other issue was where in the Constitution to locate congressional power for this kind of regulation.[10]

The Constitutional Debate over Title II: Regulating Commerce or Enforcing Equal Protection

This then brings us to a central question of this chapter: Why, in this landmark assault on racial inequality, did Congress bypass the Four-teenth Amendment, the one provision of the Constitution specifically designed and always understood to serve that end? Explaining this cu-rious turn of events requires a careful examination of Kennedy admin-istration officials who drafted and justified Title II and the members of Congress who then debated the constitutional basis for this provision. Based on their reading of judicial precedent and the difficulties the Su-preme Court was having with the sit-in cases, these key actors in fram-ing Title II felt that justifying the law on the basis of Congress's power to enforce the equal protection clause was a risky proposition. Concern about the boundaries of the equal protection principle—and particu-larly of how a sweeping legislative assertion of the principle might af-fect the Court's own efforts to protect equal protection rights—steered proponents of the legislation toward the commerce power and away from the Fourteenth Amendment. Defenders of the commerce clause approach argued that congressional power to regulate interstate com-merce included authority to prohibit racial discrimination in public accommodations. In the end, relying on the commerce power—the ba-sis for a broad array of federal legislation, from regulating railroads to protecting the rights of industrial workers to attacking prostitution and protecting consumer safety—seemed a surer way of protecting the law against constitutional challenge in court.

Initially, however, two factors favored the Fourteenth Amendment approach. First was what might be called constitutional common sense. Those who framed and ratified the Fourteenth Amendment under-stood it as primarily intended to deal with the legacy of slavery and the problem of racial inequality. The same could hardly be said of the commerce clause. Advocates of the Fourteenth Amendment approach attacked the commerce clause rationale as disingenuous. As Republican Senator John Sherman Cooper from Kentucky explained, "If there is a right to the equal use of accommodations held out to the public, it is a right of citizenship and a constitutional right under the 14th Amend-ment. It has nothing to do with whether a business is in interstate commerce." The Fourteenth Amendment is "the obviously most relevant source of national power," asserted Professor Gerald Gunther of Stanford Law School in a letter to the Justice Department. "The proposed end-run" of relying on the commerce clause "suggests an inclination toward disingenuousness, cynicism and trickery as to constitutional principles. . . ." To many, it simply made sense that such a foundational civil right came under the constitutional equal protection provision. This was the provision on which *Brown* was based, and civil rights supporters saw desegregation in public accommodations as a natural extension of the attack on segregated schools and other public facilities.[11]

A second factor bolstering the case for the Fourteenth Amendment rationale was the partisan heritage of the respective constitutional clauses. Democrats tended to be more enthusiastic about the commerce power, which harkened back to their party's achievements in the New Deal. Most of the landmark legislation of the 1930s had been passed under Congress's commerce clause authority. Republicans, by contrast, retained some skepticism toward these New Deal policies and the expansive vision of the commerce power on which they rested. They feared that basing this landmark civil rights legislation on the commerce clause risked expanding that clause's reach in other areas of economic regulation. Furthermore, they tended to view the Fourteenth Amendment as a centerpiece of the constitutional legacy of the party of Abraham Lincoln. It was this Republican identification with the Fourteenth Amendment that, in part, motivated the Kennedy administration, early in the debate over the framing of Title II, to emphasize both constitutional bases for the law: it was a way to attract bipartisan support, which was essential because the southern wing of the Democratic Party would be leading the opposition to the bill.[12]

In the spring of 1963, during the early stages of the framing of Title II, it appeared that these factors would ensure the prominence of the Fourteenth Amendment justification. President Kennedy, in his June 19 message to Congress calling for passage of the sweeping civil rights bill, highlighted both the Fourteenth Amendment and the commerce power as the bases for Title II. The attorney general made the same point when he defended the bill before various congressional committees.[13]

After a brief period of additional political assessment and legal research, however, administration support shifted toward the commerce power. By the fall of 1963, administration officials clearly regarded the Fourteenth Amendment as a secondary constitutional basis for congressional action.

Why this move away from the Fourteenth Amendment and toward the commerce clause? Legislative strategy played a role. In the Senate, the Commerce Committee was far friendlier terrain for civil rights than the Judiciary Committee. Senator Warren Magnuson of Washington, a supporter of the civil rights bill, chaired the predominantly liberal Commerce Committee. Archsegregationist James Eastland of Mississippi chaired the Judiciary Committee, which was known as the "graveyard of civil rights legislation." Drafting the legislation as a regulation of interstate commerce justified sending it directly to the Commerce Committee, thereby avoiding Eastland's graveyard. (In the House, the dynamic was reversed. Emanuel Celler, a New York Democrat and a strong civil rights proponent, chaired the liberal-dominated House Judiciary Committee, while Oren Harris, an Arkansas segregationist, chaired the House Commerce Committee. Kennedy officials who drafted the bill made sure to include what one called "judicial words," particularly in its preamble, to justify sending it to the House Judiciary Committee.)[14]

More important in advancing the commerce power justification for Title II, however, was the legal assessment of the leading lawyers in the Kennedy administration and the academic advice they received. In a May 1963 memorandum outlining the upcoming legislative battle over federal civil rights legislation, Burke Marshall emphasized the obstacle posed by the state action doctrine and predicted that the Supreme Court was going to reject the NAACP's Fourteenth Amendment claim in the pending sit-in cases. Solicitor General Cox had been struggling with the state action doctrine in his arguments before the Supreme Court in the sit-in cases, attempting to balance the administration's official posture of opposition to racially discriminatory practices with his instinctively cautious approach to the development of constitutional doctrine. As the administration's public accommodations law took shape, Cox echoed Marshall's advice and urged deference to existing Court doctrine. Cox, a labor law specialist who was intimately familiar with the National Labor Relations Act—a particularly far-reaching exercise of the commerce power—was confident that the justices would have no trouble upholding Title II on commerce clause grounds.[15]

The Kennedy administration's position was also influenced by the recommendations of Harvard Law School professor Paul A. Freund, a highly valued legal adviser to the administration. Freund's crucial contribution was to frame the commerce clause approach as more limited than the Fourteenth Amendment approach. "Any decision overruling the *Civil Rights Cases* [the seminal Supreme Court decision establishing the state action limitation on the Fourteenth Amendment] has implications for judicial power and duty that transcend the immediate controversy," he warned in a brief submitted to the Senate Commerce Committee. The commerce clause "is primarily a grant of legislative power to Congress, which can be exercised in large or small measure, flexibly, pragmatically, tentatively, progressively, while guaranteed rights, if they are declared to be conferred by the Constitution, are not to be granted or withheld in fragments."[16]

These influential arguments pushed Attorney General Kennedy to advocate the commerce clause as the primary basis for Title II. As the Title II debate evolved, he would continue to assert his view that the Fourteenth Amendment basis was sufficient and would be upheld in the Supreme Court, yet he would increasingly emphasize that the Fourteenth Amendment was best treated as a secondary justification. Picking up Freund's point, Kennedy argued that the commerce power gave Congress more discretion to limit the scope of the law, an argument specifically aimed toward attracting congressional moderates. In the end, the Kennedy administration's constitutional arguments, motivated primarily by strategic concerns but bolstered by constitutional analysis, proved persuasive in Congress.

The Fourteenth Amendment in Congress

The most committed proponents of resting Title II squarely on the Fourteenth Amendment's enforcement power came from an eclectic group of pro–civil rights liberals in Congress. In early May 1963, prior to the administration drafting its own bill, House Judiciary chairman Celler held hearings on public accommodations legislation, with discussion focused primarily on congressional power under the Fourteenth Amendment. On May 23, the day after President Kennedy announced that he was considering broader civil rights legislation, Senator Cooper joined Thomas J. Dodd, Democrat from Connecticut, in sponsoring public accommodations legislation based on the Fourteenth Amendment. Their bill had broad application, covering all businesses that operated under state or local licensing. Then, in early June, John Lindsay, leader of civil rights supporters among Republican House members (and future mayor of New York City), introduced his own civil rights bill, which included a public accommodations provision based on the Fourteenth Amendment. One of the points these lawmakers offered in defense of the Fourteenth Amendment approach was a direct reversal of Professor Freund's argument: that the Fourteenth Amendment, not the commerce clause, was less susceptible to regulatory overreach. The Fourteenth Amendment, they insisted, offered a more conservative approach that would better protect choice and privacy in the private sphere.[17]

The Senate bill sparked a heated debate on the constitutional basis for the public accommodations law in the pages of the *New York Times* between columnist Arthur Krock and Columbia Law professor Herbert Wechsler. Krock praised the Cooper-Dodd bill for directly facing the "'moral' principle" of the issue—as opposed to the commerce clause approach, which treated this principle as "divisible." Krock offered a generous reading of Supreme Court Fourteenth Amendment doctrine, suggesting that a bill based on the Fourteenth Amendment had a better chance of being upheld in the Court than a bill based on the commerce clause. Wechsler was not persuaded. "One need not be a lawyer," he lectured in a letter to the *Times*, "to perceive that the fact that a state requires a lunchroom to obtain a license as a means of protecting the public health does not make the lunchroom a state agency," referencing the state action issue that a Fourteenth Amendment justification raised. "It puts the matter with excessive charity to say that this is a submission which is most unlikely to persuade the Supreme Court and, what is more important, should not do so." In contrast, "ever since the thirties a unanimous Supreme Court has sustained the broad reach of the power over commerce. . . ." Wechsler also rejected Krock's "moral" argument, noting that there was no endorsement of discrimination when Congress limits itself to powers defined in the Constitution. In response, Krock stood his ground: "Let a layman but venture an opinion on a legal issue which the Supreme Court has often dealt with but not finally resolved, and law professors are certain to pounce on him for ignorant temerity." He then quoted from Professor Gunther's letter defending the Fourteenth Amendment justification for Title II.[18]

Debate between the dueling rationales for Title II came to a head in the fall of 1963, when liberal House members sought to expand Title II's coverage under a Fourteenth Amendment rationale. In September 1963, with the optimistic afterglow of the March on Washington shattered by the national outcry over the bombing of a Birmingham church that took the lives of four African American children, Robert W. Kastenmeier, a Democratic congressman from Wisconsin, proposed a bold extension of Title II. His version drew on the Fourteenth Amendment as the constitutional basis for a bill that not only included a wider array of public accommodations but also went beyond public accommodations, prohibiting racial discrimination in private schools, law firms, and medical associations. The requisite state action for Fourteenth Amendment regulation was based on the government licenses these businesses required to operate. In defending his proposal, Kastenmeier denounced the strategic nature of the Kennedy administration's commerce clause–based bill, which prohibited discrimination in restaurants and hotels while allowing it in "barber shops, beauty parlors, many other places of recreation and participation sports, unless such places serve food." Although Kennedy administration officials believed Kastenmeier's bill threatened their careful orchestration of the civil rights bill, Celler supported it, believing a stronger initial bill would strengthen their bargaining position when it came time to make the compromises that would be needed to pass the bill.[19]

Fearing such an expansion would sink the bill, the Kennedy administration launched a counter-campaign. Its centerpiece: the commerce clause. In his October 1963 testimony before the House Judiciary Committee and then in a press conference that followed, Robert Kennedy, having fully abandoned his earlier inclination to base the law on the Fourteenth Amendment, now insisted that the commerce power was the only appropriate basis for Title II. Not only did this provide stronger constitutional authority for a subsequent legal challenge, but—and here was his key point—the commerce power was the more limited, conservative approach. Drawing on Freund's constitutional analysis, Kennedy argued that Kastenmeier's proposed expansion would capture "all kinds of businesses . . . private hospitals, and private schools, and every kind of business conceivable, lawyers, doctors, and everything. I think that is dangerous." He then made the connection between this coverage issue and the constitutional basis for the law—a connection that would become the centerpiece of the administration's position going forward. He wondered if such a bill would, in effect, convert private businesses into "an instrument of the State," which would raise all sorts of new complications for the courts. Would every fired employee be entitled to the due process protections? "What if religious schools want to read the Bible?" he asked, noting that Supreme Court had recently held required Bible recitation in public schools a violation of the Fourteenth Amendment. In language aimed directly at moderate Republicans, Kennedy declared that the revised bill created "more power than I want, and more power than anybody should have, in my judgment, under our system of government."[20]

The attorney general wrote a memorandum to the president in which he suggested that the sweeping coverage pressed by the Fourteenth Amendment advocates "is probably unconstitutional and in any event brings under federal control for some purposes such business establishments as lawyers' offices, doctors' offices, and other licensed establishments. It should be deleted." Title II, he emphasized, should focus on hotels, theaters, places of amusement, places that serve food, and gas stations. Reliance on the Fourteenth Amendment was appropriate only where there was unquestionable state action, such as in application to places in which state law required segregation. Kennedy thus revised his constitutional interpretation to align with his legislative strategy.[21]

The administration won this battle. Robert Kennedy and the Justice Department worked with Celler and William McCulloch, the senior Republican on the House Judiciary Committee, to find an acceptable middle ground that would address the reservations of congressional moderates while maintaining the protections necessary for effective civil rights reform. The commerce clause rationale for Title II, framed by the administration as the less far-reaching approach, became a central tool for attracting these moderates. The alternative Fourteenth Amendment–based bill was soon abandoned. By the end of 1963, supporters of the bill lined up behind the commerce clause rationale. The Fourteenth Amendment remained in the legislation, but only as a secondary rationale.[22]

By the time the Senate debated the Civil Rights Act for eighty-one days in the spring of 1964, there was little dispute over the constitutional foundation for Title II. The triumph of the commerce clause rationale was the product of a concerted campaign, led by constitutional lawyers in the Justice Department and in academia and, eventually, by the attorney general. Constitutional assessment, legislative strategy, and partisan politics all contributed to the demotion of the Fourteenth Amendment basis for Title II into a secondary role.[23]

Title II and the Right to Discriminate

Opponents attacked Title II not only for going beyond congressional power, but also for infringing upon individual liberty. While courts treated these as quite different claims, in the constitutional debate over the Civil Rights Act that took place on the floor of Congress and around the nation, the two were often impossible to separate. (One suspects that when Senator Richard Russell attacked Title II as "the most unconstitutional 66 words conceived by man," he was not just questioning commerce clause doctrine.) In a dissenting report accompanying an early House version of the bill, opponents derided it for ignoring basic protections of the Bill of Rights: "One freedom is destroyed by governmental action to enforce another freedom." "The free and uncontrolled use of private property is essential to freedom," announced one southern senator. Title II "would deny American citizens the freedom of choice—the freedom to select their own personal associates and business customers," declared another. This new language of segregationism—a language of freedom, liberty, choice, associational rights—had rippled across the South in response to the sit-ins and now became the centerpiece of Jim Crow's last stand.[24]

But the challenge to public accommodations based on a claimed right to discriminate was not limited to southern segregationists. Senator Barry Goldwater of Arizona justified his vote against the bill largely on his constitutional reservations toward Title II. A year earlier, Goldwater had consulted a lawyer based in Phoenix named William Rehnquist (who would later become a justice on the Supreme Court), who advised Goldwater that he believed the law to be unconstitutional. Goldwater then turned to Yale Law professor Robert Bork, who had recently published an article in the *New Republic* attacking public accommodations legislation as violating personal liberties. Bork wrote a seventy-five-page brief for Goldwater outlining the constitutional infirmities of the civil rights bill.[25]

In his *New Republic* article, Bork sought to separate himself from segregationist opponents of civil rights policy. He described the proposed legislation as based in "justifiable abhorrence of racial discrimination," and he lamented that most critics of the law were "southern politicians who only a short while ago were defending laws that enforced racial segregation" and hence only opportunistic libertarians. Yet, Bork insisted, one may stand opposed to racial discrimination and still see something amiss in public accommodations law. "It is not whether racial prejudice or preference is a good thing but whether individual men ought to be free to deal and associate with whom they please for whatever reasons appeal to them," he wrote. "The trouble with freedom is that it will be used in ways we abhor." State-enforced segregation was wrong, but so was state-enforced integration in certain spheres of private relations. The principle behind the proposed civil rights law, Bork explained, "is that if I find your behavior ugly by my standards, moral or aesthetic, and if you prove stubborn about adopting my view of the situation, I am justified in having the state coerce you into more righteous paths. This is itself a principle of unsurpassed ugliness."[26]

Goldwater was likely drawing on Bork's analysis when he justified his own opposition to the proposed federal public accommodations law. "There is a limit on how far we can go without upsetting the constitutional rights to freedom of association," the senator explained. "I believe deeply in integration. But I believe that it must be brought about in accordance with our Constitution and the fundamental concepts of freedom." In a dramatic speech delivered on the floor of the Senate as the Civil Rights Act was about to pass, Goldwater, then the front-runner for the 1964 Republican presidential nomination, explained his continued opposition to a bill that, by the spring of 1964, had widespread support nationally. Although "unalterably opposed to discrimination or segregation on the basis of race," the Constitution, he claimed, compelled him to oppose the public accommodations and fair employment provisions. His primary constitutional argument was that the civil rights law went beyond Congress's constitutional authority and violated the rights of the states. But he also emphasized that the law threatened to "destroy the freedom of all American citizens." Its enforcement would necessitate measures that threatened the creation of a "police state" and the "destruction of a free society." He opposed "any threats to our great system of government and the loss of our God-given liberties."[27]

Bork's libertarian critique found a receptive audience in another U.S. senator, North Carolina's Sam J. Ervin Jr. Like Goldwater, Ervin argued that members of Congress should take seriously their oaths to obey the Constitution by refusing to vote for legislation that they believe to be unconstitutional, regardless of what the Supreme Court said on the issue. As to Title II, Ervin wrote that "few more blatantly unconstitutional and unwise pieces of legislation have ever been proposed." Like Goldwater, his constitutional concerns centered predominantly on congressional power and the need to preserve state control over matters of local concern. But, also like Goldwater, he insisted that individual liberties were at stake. "Truly, in the midst of the cynical debate on how best can sections of the Constitution be stretched beyond their traditional understanding to encompass the aims of certain social theorists, there is all too little discussion of the immense price in personal liberty and freedom that will be the cost of such so-called reform."[28]

Despite the fervor with which it was put forth, the idea of a right to discriminate, at least in the context of public accommodations, was roundly rejected. A majority of members of Congress put aside the constitutional reservations aired by Goldwater, Ervin, and others, and voted overwhelmingly for the Civil Rights Act. For the law's backers, strong public support for the law and generations of judicial precedent and societal practice conclusively refuted the idea that discrimination in public accommodations merited constitutional protection. How, asked Representative William McCulloch, could one say that Congress was "invading privacy, overturning the sanctity of private property, destroying personal liberties, or in other ways acting in an illegal manner," when in banning racial discrimination in public accommodations it was just doing what many states had been doing for generations? As a question of constitutional contestation in the political arena, the case for the right to discriminate in public accommodations relied upon an assumption that these services function in society in a way that was so personal and private that they require affirmative protection against government antidiscrimination regulations. By the early 1960s, in large part because of the efforts of those who took part in the sit-in movement, this argument simply failed on its merits.[29]

Yet we should not be too quick to dismiss the right to discriminate as nothing more than a disingenuous effort to protect Jim Crow in more palatable language. For one, segregationists and libertarians were not the only ones to pronounce the importance of this right. Title II supporters were anxious to show that they too recognized that there were limits to how far into private social relations civil rights policy should reach. Robert Kennedy and his legal advisers expressed this concern through their argument in favor of the commerce power as a more limited basis for Title II than the Fourteenth Amendment. Often civil rights advocates declared their commitment to protecting private autonomy more directly: by embracing their own version of a right to discriminate. This general principle was given concrete legal form in the coverage of Title II. The need to attract moderate Republicans to the bill effectively put a limit on the scope of coverage for Title II. Exempted from coverage was any "private club or other establishment not in fact open to the public." Also excluded from coverage in Title II was any establishment that provided lodging in which there are no more than five rooms for rent and in which the owner also lives. This became known as the "Mrs. Murphy" exemption.[30]

Mrs. Murphy's exemption appeared at the start of the debate over Title II. George Aiken, Republican senator from Vermont, urged the administration to revise the bill so that Title II would apply to "the Waldorf and other large hotels but permit the 'Mrs. Murphys' all over the country to rent their rooms to those they choose." Attorney General Kennedy indicated the administration's willingness to consider the exemption during his first round of testimony before the House Judiciary Committee in June 1963. When asked for its "legal" and "moral" basis, he explained that the federal government was not "attempting to become involved in social relationships." For the hypothetical "Mrs. Murphy," the business establishment "becomes virtually a social operation" and therefore should not be covered by a law intended to regulate economic relations in the public sphere. Liberal activist Joseph Rauh gave a passionate plea for privacy rights before the same committee. "What is there in this country that we prize as much as any other right?" he asked. "It is the right in our own home to do as we see fit. Those of us who have been in the civil rights movement have also been fighting for civil liberties, for the right of privacy, for the right to be let alone."[31]

When questioned at a news conference later that summer about whether he was committed to the exemption, President Kennedy deflected the question with a touch of constitutional humor: "The question would be, it seems to me, whether Mrs. Murphy had a substantial impact on interstate commerce." Beneath this deft laugh line was a more serious point, which was the same one his brother would make in the coming months: that the limits of the commerce power protected against overly intrusive civil rights regulation.[32]

"There is no desire to regulate truly personal or private relationships," explained Senator Hubert Humphrey when debate on the civil rights bill began in the Senate in the spring of 1964. "The so-called Mrs. Murphy provision" involves relationships "of a closer and more personal nature than in the case of major commercial establishments." It involves "balancing the right of privacy of one who hires out rooms in his own residence and the obligations of a proprietor who maintains a public lodging house."[33]

Humphrey and other supporters of the Civil Rights Act accepted that there were indeed privacy concerns at stake and insisted that these interests be protected when the lawmakers decided how broad to make Title II's reach. Thus, all sides accepted that a civil rights law that interfered with personal associational choices would be constitutionally suspect. The critical issue was what kinds of activities were personal enough to merit protection from antidiscrimination requirements. Supporters of Title II saw the limitations on the law's reach as responding to legitimate concerns about the personal liberty interests at stake.

Back to the Supreme Court

The Supreme Court had two more major decisions to make before the constitutional debate sparked by the sit-ins finally reached its endpoint. First, the justices had to give an answer to those who challenged Title II as beyond Congress's constitutional authority and as an infringement on the personal liberty of business operators. Second, they had to figure out what to do with the thousands of appeals still pending from prosecutions of sit-in protesters.

Congressional Authority

Legal challenges to the Civil Rights Act came immediately. On the day the bill was signed into law, the executive director of the Mississippi Innkeepers Association told a *Wall Street Journal* reporter to expect "a great many test cases starting in Mississippi that will go all the way to the U.S. Supreme Court." Louis W. Hollis, executive director of the national office of the Citizens' Council of America—a white supremacist organization based in Jackson, Mississippi—claimed that "most businessmen feel the law will be declared unconstitutional and are going to treat it like they did [*Brown*]": they were going to defy it.[34]

Moreton Rolleston, a Georgia lawyer and owner of the Heart of Atlanta Motel, filed his lawsuit challenging the Title II just hours after President Lyndon Johnson signed the Civil Rights Act. He was so intent on being the first person to challenge the law that when he found the courthouse closed, he tracked down the federal district court clerk at home. Rolleston lost his first round of litigation, but was able to get the Supreme Court to hear his appeal.[35]

In Alabama, a local lawyer advised the Birmingham Restaurant Association that the best chance to challenge the law would be to identify a restaurant that operated with as limited a relation to interstate commerce as possible. This would give challengers the strongest case to argue that the public accommodations provision was beyond congressional authority to regulate commerce. The group settled on Ollie's Barbecue, a restaurant with an almost exclusively local clientele that reserved its seating area to whites and required African American customers to use the take-out window. Its owner, Ollie McClung, was committed to maintaining his service policy. "I didn't feel the Lord felt we should change our method of doing business," he explained.[36]

A special three-judge federal district court consisting of three Alabama judges with little sympathy for civil rights ruled in McClung's favor, striking down Title II as beyond the authority of Congress. "Of course, we express no opinion as to the wisdom of the legislation and confine our consideration to the constitutionality of the provisions with which we are concerned," the court explained. It then went on to declare that to read the commerce clause so broadly as to cover a restaurant such as Ollie's Barbeque would put the "rights of the individual to liberty and property . . . in dire peril."[37]

The Supreme Court allowed expedited review of both the *Heart of Atlanta* and *McClung* cases. The justices heard oral arguments in early October 1964, and just two months later the Court unanimously upheld Title II as a legitimate exercise of the commerce power.[38]

The Court reserved the question, however, of whether the Fourteenth Amendment provided the necessary authority for the law. While recognizing that the legislative history drew on both rationales, Justice Clark wrote in his opinion for the Court that it was unnecessary to evaluate the Fourteenth Amendment claim. "Since the commerce power is sufficient for our decision we have considered it alone."[39]

Although the majority chose not to address whether the Fourteenth Amendment provided constitutional authority for Title II, a majority of the justices, it appears, would have been willing to uphold Title II on that basis if they felt it necessary to do so. For those justices who concluded in the sit-in cases that the Fourteenth Amendment prohibited racial discrimination in public accommodations—Chief Justice Warren and Justices Douglas and Goldberg—congressional enforcement in this area was straightforward: Congress obviously had the power to enforce a judicially recognized equal protection right. But for those justices who refused to stretch the state action doctrine this far—particularly Justice Black—the constitutional issue was different, raising some thorny questions about the relationship between the Court and Congress on questions of constitutional interpretation. How can a justice recognize congressional authority to enforce a Fourteenth Amendment right that the same justice has refused to recognize as contained in that amendment? The answer: Allow Congress some measure of interpretive latitude in defining state action when it exercises its Fourteenth Amendment enforcement powers. In other words, even some of those who affirmed the principle of the state action doctrine as defined in the *Civil Rights Cases* challenged that decision's holding with regard to congressional power and public accommodations. They recognized that a congressional definition of state action might go beyond a judicial definition.

In conference discussion on the sit-in cases, Justice Black noted, "I would have no difficulty in sustaining a state law or a federal law under the Fourteenth Amendment (despite the *Civil Rights Cases*) that would prevent racial discrimination and require a retailer to serve all people." In his dissent in *Bell v. Maryland*, where he denounced the legal defiance of the sit-in protesters and rejected their Fourteenth Amendment claim, he repeatedly referenced congressional power under the Fourteenth Amendment to prohibit discrimination in public accommodations. Black's approach appeared to have the support of most of the other justices who sided with him in rejecting the Fourteenth Amendment claim of the lunch counter protesters.[40]

Justice Douglas tended to adjust his views of congressional authority to enforce the Fourteenth Amendment according to the leverage it could bring for his own interpretation of that amendment. When he sought to sway his brethren to his position on the constitutional claim of the sit-in protesters, he insisted that the opposing position would limit congressional authority to act. "If we hold that restaurants and other businesses serving the public cannot discriminate against people on account of race, Congress can 'enforce' that construction of the Fourteenth Amendment," he wrote his colleagues in October 1963. "But if we hold that this kind of discrimination is beyond the purview of the Fourteenth Amendment, there is nothing for Congress to 'enforce' and the Civil Rights Cases are vindicated." At this point, Brennan agreed with Douglas—a decision upholding protester trespass convictions would mean that Congress lacked authority to ban discrimination in these settings. Later that term, however, when Douglas recognized that he did not have the votes for his reading of the equal protection clause, he took a sharply different line. "Congress by reason of [its Fourteenth Amendment enforcement power] has some leeway to define what due process requires in protection of federally protected rights. Moreover, Congress has authority to define what is 'state' action within the meaning of the Fourteenth Amendment in order to protect federal rights against dilution."[41]

With such apparent willingness to recognize congressional authority under the Fourteenth Amendment—a willingness that garnered much more agreement among the justices than the state action issue in the sit-in cases—why did the Court not take this path? One factor was the forceful arguments of Solicitor General Cox. In defending Title II before the Court, he urged the justices to ignore the Fourteenth Amendment and focus on the commerce power. The problem of public accommodations discrimination is "a commercial problem of grave national significance," Cox told the justices. Even when Justice Goldberg suggested that it was also a moral problem, Cox continued to present the law as concerned primarily with the effects on interstate commerce caused by public accommodations discrimination. "The constitutionality of Title II under [the commerce clause] is sustained by principles that are so familiar because they have been enacted over and over again, applied indeed throughout our entire history. . . . We do not seek the extension of any existing principles here. . . . [W]e invoke no new doctrine."[42]

Cox's position proved persuasive with the justices. "We should not concern ourselves with the Fourteenth Amendment," Warren stated at the start of the justices' conference discussion on *Heart of Atlanta* and *McClung.* Black told his colleagues, "I would prefer to go on the Fourteenth Amendment, but I think that Congress limited the act to the commerce clause. Otherwise, I would be for overruling the *Civil Rights Cases.*" Harlan rejected the Fourteenth Amendment basis for Title II, but did so in a way that suggested he distinguished between the congressional adoption of the Court's state action standard and a congressional effort to define the standard for itself. Brennan agreed, noting in conference discussion that in Congress "the 'state action' definition followed the *Civil Rights Cases,* and that these cases must go on the commerce clause."[43]

Only Douglas and Goldberg insisted that the question of congressional authority under the Fourteenth Amendment needed to be faced. Each wrote a concurring opinion locating authority for Title II in both the commerce clause and the Fourteenth Amendment. As Clark read the opinion of the Court in the *Heart of Atlanta* case, Goldberg passed a note to Douglas: "It sounds like hamburgers are more important than human rights."[44]

The Right to Discriminate

Both Title II challenges that made it to the Supreme Court emphasized claims of a right to discriminate. McClung's lawyers argued that Title II infringed upon business owners' "rights to their property and in their liberty to use it as they choose—rights which are expressly included within the due process clause of the Fifth Amendment." The due process clause protects "the freedom of a business enterprise to select its patrons and customers," regardless of the grounds for that decision.

"It is a part of a man's civil rights that he be at liberty to refuse business relations with any person whomsoever, whether the refusal rests upon reason, or is the result of whim, caprice, prejudice, or malice."[45]

In *Heart of Atlanta*, Rolleston advanced a more eclectic constitutional basis for his claimed right to discriminate. Not only did Title II's antidiscrimination requirement run afoul of the due process clause; it also constituted an uncompensated taking of property in violation of the Fifth Amendment. Rolleston claimed to have located yet another constitutional footing for the right to discriminate in the Thirteenth Amendment's prohibition on involuntary servitude: "When an individual is either coerced into working for another or punished for failure to do so, the inescapable conclusion is that such employment amounts to involuntary servitude."[46]

Relying on the Thirteenth Amendment as a shield against antidiscrimination law is a strange, indeed perverse idea. This is the amendment that liberated America's slaves. During Reconstruction, Congress used it to pass pioneering civil rights legislation. As the Justice Department put it in its brief in *Heart of Atlanta*, to argue that this same amendment "placed discrimination in public accommodations wholly beyond the reach of both federal and State law is nothing short of absurd."[47]

Yet in the early 1960s, this unusual Thirteenth Amendment argument featured prominently in the debate over the appropriate line between antidiscrimination policy and personal liberties. Rolleston relied extensively on the scholarship of a man named Alfred Avins, a native New Yorker whose libertarian scholarship quickly gained the attention of southerners who were searching for legal footholds from which to make their stand against the civil rights movement. Avins argued that the drafters of the Thirteenth Amendment intended to promote liberty, not equality. As applied to the issue at hand, he wrote: "A waitress can no more be required to wait on all persons who come into her shop without discrimination than can a cotton picker be required to pick cotton for all who want his services without discrimination."[48]

Avins's unlikely argument received considerable attention. Senator Strom Thurmond from South Carolina embraced it. Arthur Krock, the conservative *New York Times* columnist and Kentucky native, also championed it. As the Civil Rights Act was moving toward passage in the spring of 1964, Krock published editorials urging consideration of the potential costs to "individual freedom of choice" posed by the pending legislation. "The intolerance with which the bill is urged in the name of tolerance" was cause for concern, Krock wrote. He praised

Avins for having drawn attention to the liberty costs of the civil rights bill, "a great constitutional issue . . . which has been carefully avoided or strangely neglected."[49]

For all the efforts that Avins, Thurmond, Krock, and the lawyers in *Heart of Atlanta* and *McClung* put into the Thirteenth Amendment and other liberty-based constitutional arguments against public accommodations laws, courts easily set them aside. The Supreme Court in *Heart of Atlanta Motel* dispatched the argument in all of four sentences. In his concurrence, Justice Black gave it a footnote: "The motel's argument that Title II violates the Thirteenth Amendment is so insubstantial that it requires no further discussion."[50]

The Court was only marginally less dismissive in its treatment of the other possible constitutional bases for the claim of a right to discriminate. It referenced and summarily rejected all claims that Title II infringed constitutional protections of property or liberty. Justice Black did little to hide his irritation with these arguments, which he characterized as claiming "that the broad power of Congress to enact laws deemed necessary and proper to regulate and protect interstate commerce is practically nullified by the negative constitutional commands that no person shall be deprived of 'life, liberty, or property, without due process of law' and that private property shall not be 'taken' for public use without just compensation." There was simply no basis to challenge Title II on either due process or takings grounds. His assessment of the takings argument could have been used for practically every judicial evaluation of the right to discriminate during the civil rights era: it "does not even come close."[51]

Title II, like all public accommodations legislation, gave rise to valid concerns about personal liberty and property rights—this was a point on which practically everyone, even many of the law's most fervent defenders, agreed. Both friends and foes of the civil rights cause generally accepted that, in some form, people had a right to discriminate. But, despite the efforts of segregationists and libertarians, this was simply not the sort of legal claim the courts recognized, at least not when used to challenge a law that did nothing more than tell a business that served the general public to stop using race as a criteria for service.

"Sit-In Cases Die"

The same day the Court upheld Title II, the justices issued a ruling in what would be the last of the sit-in cases. *Hamm v. City of Rock Hill*, an appeal of trespass convictions from a South Carolina sit-in, gave the

Court an opportunity to consider the effect of the passage of the Civil Rights Act on thousands of pending appeals of convictions related to sit-ins that had taken place over the preceding years. The Civil Rights Act said nothing on this question. It prohibited racial discrimination in public accommodations going forward, but made no reference to its effect on pending criminal prosecutions deriving from past acts of racial discrimination.[52]

None of the justices were interested in dragging these difficult cases out any further, but they were sharply divided over whether the Civil Rights Act affected them. In *Hamm*, a five-justice majority came together to create a tenuous legal rationale for what they understood to be a just and necessary legal conclusion. Despite the general presumption against applying statutes retroactively absent explicit guidance on the issue, the majority found grounds for doing just this.

In holding that the passage of the Civil Rights Act abated the pending sit-in convictions, the Court expanded (or, according to the dissenters, transformed) the tactic that Justice Brennan had deployed in *Bell v. Maryland*. In that case, Brennan argued that Maryland's subsequent passage of a public accommodations law had the effect of nullifying the state's prior convictions related to demands for nondiscriminatory service. The difference in *Hamm* was that the relevant public accommodations law came from a different government than the one responsible for the initial criminal conviction. In *Bell*, the state had prosecuted the sit-in protesters under state trespass laws, and the state had passed the public accommodations law. In *Hamm*, the state had prosecuted the sit-in protesters under state trespass laws, but the abatement was read into a federal law.

In his opinion of the Court, Justice Clark wrote: "The great purpose of the civil rights legislation was to obliterate the effect of a distressing chapter of our history. . . . The peaceful conduct for which petitioners were prosecuted was on behalf of a principle since embodied in the law of the land." He wrote with evident relief at the possibility of clearing the books of the appeals: Since the constitutional question of whether the equal protection clause "bar[s] criminal trespass convictions where . . . they are used to enforce a pattern of racial discrimination . . . is not free from doubt, and since we have found Congress has ample power to extend the statute to pending convictions we avoid that question by favoring an interpretation of the statute which renders a constitutional decision unnecessary." The Supreme Court used the Civil Rights Act to make all these pending convictions simply go away. "The law the sit-inners had helped to create had protected them," Jack Greenberg noted with satisfaction.[53]

Justice Black would have none of this. "I do not find one paragraph, one sentence, one clause, or one word in the 1964 Act on which the most strained efforts of the most fertile imagination could support" the majority's abatement argument, he wrote in his dissent. For Black, the Court's ruling, in effect, condoned what he saw as the sit-in protesters' lawless behavior. "One of the chief purposes of the 1964 Civil Rights Act was to take such disputes out of the streets and restaurants and into the courts." Justice White expressed similar outrage at the Court's acceptance of civil disobedience: "Whether persons or groups should engage in nonviolent disobedience to laws with which they disagree perhaps defies any categorical answer for the guidance of every individual in every circumstance. But whether a court should give it wholesale sanction is a wholly different question which calls for only one answer."[54]

"Sit-In Cases Die," read the headline of a front-page *New York Times* article. The editors of the *Chicago Tribune* attacked the decision as "a new excursion in legislation by judicial fiat." "The court's ex post facto application of the [Civil Rights Act] will turn all defendants loose" in the thousands of cases still on appeal, lamented the editors. The *Washington Post* editors professed to be "astonishe[d] by the hostility and scorn" that characterized the dissents. "Men and women who conscientiously challenged a form of discrimination which they believed was unconstitutional and which the Congress of the United States, in large part as a result of their challenge, made unlawful, ought not be punished for what history will surely record as a courageous public service." John Lewis, a leader of the Nashville sit-ins who had become chair of SNCC, declared *Hamm* "the most heartening thing since SNCC was founded." Greenberg estimated that the ruling would have the effect of nullifying some three thousand cases currently on appeal. LDF's next task, he said, was to coordinate "a massive mop-up operation to secure the release of all these defendants."[55]

Implementation

The public accommodations provision of the Civil Rights Act of 1964 was remarkably effective. To the surprise of many at the time, it was implemented quickly and with relatively little controversy. In sharp contrast to *Brown*, few white southerners called for outright defiance. "It is the law," said Allen J. Ellender, U.S. senator from Louisiana and staunch defender of segregation. Any southern resistance to the Civil Rights Act "must be within the framework of the orderly processes established by law." Defiance outside the legal process, he insisted, would be "foolhardy and indefensible."[56]

It was "a sad day for individual freedom," Rolleston lamented when the Supreme Court ruled against him. McClung declared himself "shocked." But both accepted the Court's ruling. "With my grandchildren there won't be any problems at all," Rolleston told reporters. "They won't even know there were any." McClung explained, "As law-abiding Americans, we feel we must bow to this edict." On the day the opinion came down, he served five African Americans without incident. In major cities across the South, operators of segregated public accommodations responded to the passage of the law with some relief. They wanted segregation and they wanted profits. By 1964, with federal law as cover, they were willing to give up on the former to preserve the latter.[57]

There was still defiance, of course. The implementation of Title II required the consent of thousands of individual private businesses, many run by people who strongly opposed racial integration. In St. Augustine, Florida, restaurants and hotels initially complied with the law, thankful to move beyond the protests and shutdowns, but pressure from a local white supremacist group led a number to resegregate. They only came back into compliance after a district court issued an injunction ordering the white supremacists to stay away from the businesses. Across the South, there were scattered reports of whites leaving their jobs rather than abiding by the new Title II requirements. There were some incidents of violence against people seeking nondiscriminatory service. And there were efforts to turn public accommodations into private clubs that would be exempted from Title II. About a hundred restaurants in the Shreveport, Louisiana, area, for example, formed the "Northwest Louisiana Restaurant Club," requiring membership cards (which were only given to whites) for admittance.[58]

Yet these were exceptions. Most Americans, including those who fought so hard against the Civil Rights Act, fell into line with the new national requirement that private eating establishments and hotels no longer practice racial discrimination, and they did so with little drama and minimal resistance.

Why did a white South that for the past decade had fought so hard against school desegregation now come, by and large, to accept the new law of the land? A key reason was the collective action dynamic of integration in public accommodations. From the perspective of the southern business operator, being the first mover was risky. This was why Curly Harris, the manager of the Greensboro Woolworth, had insisted that he would only integrate his lunch counter when his competitors did the same. He assumed that if he integrated first, he would lose his predominantly white clientele to businesses that remained segregated. The way to change discriminatory business practices was to break through this collective action problem. Initially, this was done by citywide lunch counter integration agreements and by local or state public accommodations laws. Now, with the passage of the Civil Rights Act, it was accomplished on a national scale.[59]

Compliance with the new federal nondiscrimination requirement was also bolstered by the dollars and cents of the integration of public accommodations. Despite all the fears of white southern businessmen of the costs of integration, this was a legal regulation that actually proved quite profitable. The business owners' belief that segregation was necessary to retain the loyalty of their white customers was overwhelmingly wrong. Following the passage of the Civil Rights Act, retail profits across the South increased, and they did so at rates above the rest of the nation. Contrary to the fears of white business owners, white customers rarely abandoned desegregated businesses. Desegregation brought not only a larger, interracial clientele, but also the end of the protests and boycotts that suppressed business operations. Civil rights reform turned out to be good for whites, not just in terms of their moral health, but also in terms of their bottom line. "This was a revolution," writes the economic historian Gavin Wright, "in which almost all parties gained."[60]

Within a few years of the passage of Title II, the issue of racial discrimination in public accommodations—the issue that had been at the heart of so many protests between 1960 and 1964, the issue that had been the most contentious part of the debate over the Civil Rights Act—all but disappeared from the national civil rights agenda. This is not to say that race discrimination in public accommodations ended, of course. Acts of racial discrimination more subtle than outright exclusion continued—and they still continue. But as a matter of law, at least, this was a revolution that worked. It worked so well, in fact, that we no longer remember it for the revolution it was. Rarely, if ever, in American history has such a deeply contentious debate over a basic constitutional principle been wiped so thoroughly from the nation's consciousness.

Any celebration of this achievement should also recognize its limits. In the midst of the battle over discrimination in public accommodations, few questioned the importance of the issue they were fighting over. The mere fact that white southerners fought so hard to protect their "right" to discriminate confirmed the importance of the issue. Yet once the battle was won, and Title II was the law of the land, people on both sides began questioning the significance of the victory. "Desegregation of public accommodations does not basically alter the pattern of social life anywhere," observed a Mississippi restaurant operator. "That is why it has been accomplished as easily as it has." From a very different perspective, civil rights organizer Bayard Rustin arrived at much the same conclusion. "We must recognize that in desegregating public accommodations, we affected institutions that are relatively peripheral both to the American socio-economic order and to the fundamental conditions of life of the Negro people," he wrote in a widely discussed 1965 essay. The sit-ins had targeted "Jim Crow precisely where it was most anachronistic." They had toppled an "imposing but hollow structure." Or, as the African American comedian Dick Gregory once explained: "I sat in six months once at a Southern lunch counter. When they finally served me, they didn't have what I wanted." It is a funny line, with enough truth to cast a shadow over any victory celebration.[61]

The history of Title II offers yet another example of a theme that runs throughout the legal history of the sit-ins: the challenges of translating a rights claim from one arena of constitutional contestation to another. The civil rights lawyers struggled to come to terms with the defiant rights claim of the students; the justices struggled with the rights claim urged by the civil rights lawyers; and now a new translation challenge took shape, this one between the Supreme Court and Congress. The legislative arena was more receptive than the judiciary to the blend of morality, politics, and constitutional principle that characterized public debate over the sit-ins. Law-and-order concerns weakened the students' constitutional claim at the Supreme Court, where at least some of the justices feared that to accept the students' constitutional claim was to approve of their disruptive protests and to undermine the rights of property owners. In Congress, however, these concerns were less of an obstacle. Whereas judges look backward, evaluating the rights and wrongs of past actions, the job of lawmaking is more concerned with resolving issues going forward. Although some saw Title II as a judgment on the rightness of the sit-in movement, others saw it more as a policy response to a problem that had reached the stage of a national crisis.

Prior to the Civil Rights Act, the Court had led the way in advancing the cause of racial justice. The issue of public accommodations changed this. Now, for the first time since Reconstruction, Congress took the lead.

Conclusion

We will sit-in, demonstrate, sit-in some more, have prayer vigils and sit-in, sit-in, sit-in—and then we will win. DIANE NASH[1]

None of the four African American students who sat down at the whites-only lunch counter at the Greensboro Woolworth on February 1, 1960, could have imagined the events that would follow. Their lonely, defiant act of protest was a spark landing in a rain-starved forest. Others had been preparing their own fires; some had set off their own sparks. But this time, in Greensboro, the spark caught. It ignited a movement, first in Greensboro, then across North Carolina, then across the South.

The sit-ins transformed the black freedom struggle. New leaders—younger, less patient, bolder—came to the fore. Established racial justice organizations rushed to catch up with events. Lawyers who had been the vanguard of reform efforts now struggled to carve out a role in a civil rights "movement" (a label that only became commonplace after the sit-ins) in which direct-action protests rather than courtroom battles had become the primary moving force. Racial discrimination in privately owned public accommodations now stood alongside school desegregation and voting rights as the most urgent civil rights issues of the day. The battle for racial justice was revitalized and reshaped in the wake of the sit-ins.

As typically told, this is the story of the sit-ins—a heroic, innovative assertion of human dignity that set in motion a social movement whose cascading effects transformed a nation. In this book I have tried to capture this important and inspiring story. I have also sought to add another side to the story, one that loomed large at the time of the sit-ins but has largely been forgotten in the years since: how the distinctive legal issues involved in the lunch counter sit-ins shaped the protest movement; and how the protest movement, in turn, generated a national debate over these legal issues.

At the heart of this debate was a simple question: Was racial discrimination in public accommodations constitutionally permissible? To this simple question, there was no simple answer. Supporters of the student protest movement generally assumed that of course such an offensive Jim Crow practice violated the Constitution, just as surely as did segregation in schools and other state-operated facilities following the Supreme Court's decision in *Brown v. Board of Education*. Lawyers and judges, even those in sympathy with the students, were less sure. They knew the complications that the Fourteenth Amendment's state action requirement—basically an exemption of private activity from the amendment's constraints—brought to the issue. The question was not over whether the equal protection clause permitted state-enforced segregation. After *Brown* it clearly did not. The question was over the reach of the Fourteenth Amendment into the choices of those, like the operator of a department store lunch counter, who did not receive a government paycheck.

From the perspective of the students who took part in the sit-in protests and their many sympathizers across the nation, the fact that this particular act of racial humiliation was the policy of a local businessman rather than the local school board did not seem all that significant a distinction. In either case, blacks were the victims of a concerted decision to relegate them to second-class citizenship in public life. From the perspective of the lawyers and judges who viewed the issue through the lens of long-standing legal precedents and constitutional doctrine, that this particular form of racial discrimination was the product of the decision of a businessman—a private individual— was of critical importance. It placed this issue in a distinct category from the discriminatory action of a local school board. The businessman's discriminatory policy was, as a matter of constitutional law, a "private" act, and therefore not necessarily constrained by the Fourteenth Amendment.

The fact that this private act of discrimination took place in such a public place—indeed, even the legal term of art, "public accommodation," highlighted this point—indicates the reason the sit-ins placed such pressure on existing constitutional doctrine. By putting on display the value of public accommodations and the high dignitary costs of exclusion, and by demonstrating the relative normalcy of blacks sitting down at segregated eating establishments—Henry David Thoreau called this "the performance of right"—the sit-ins directly challenged the cultural norms that undergirded Jim Crow. The sit-ins exerted pressure on the cultural assumptions regarding the line between private and public action, expectations of government responsibility, and basic conceptions of social justice. Simply by sitting down at the lunch counter, the students were enacting a different social norm. When social norms diverge from legal principles, those legal principles become vulnerable. When people mobilize around a new social norm, and when they then deploy this mobilized social norm to challenge existing legal principles, legal principles usually fall.[2]

In the case of the sit-ins, the legal principle the students challenged —that race was a permissible criteria for service in public accommodations—did eventually fall, although unlike most stories of constitutional transformation in modern America, this one culminated in an act of Congress rather than a Supreme Court victory. The sit-in protesters relied on a method to express their disapproval of Jim Crow public accommodations that, while effective as a tactic of social protest, created difficulties for civil rights lawyers and ultimately alienated certain justices on the Court. The fate of the constitutional claim that emerged from the sit-ins—not a clear victory, but in no way a defeat either— demonstrates the challenges of creating an alternative interpretation of the Constitution outside the courts that not only responds to the political and ideological needs of extrajudicial actors but also offers a compelling case that can persuade judges.

Each stage of development of the legal claim of the sit-ins reshaped the claim itself, until the end result—as reflected in new business practices, a landmark civil rights law, and modified (if not transformed) legal doctrine—should be recognized as both a culmination and a transformation of the vision of social change that the students described in the midst of those heady days of protest in the spring of 1960. The students who took part in the sit-ins always insisted that while their immediate demand was simply to be served, they were ultimately interested, as Ella Baker put it, in "something much bigger than a hamburger or even a giant-sized Coke." The goal of the sit-in movement was "nothing less than the liberation of the entire country from its most crippling attitudes and habits," pronounced the great African American writer James Baldwin after spending time with student activists.

That this audacious vision was not one that could be delivered by the Supreme Court or Congress should not diminish our appreciation for what the sit-in movement did accomplish, which was nothing less than toppling a pillar of the Jim Crow regime.[3]

The resolution of the issue first given prominence by the students sitting at lunch counters in the winter of 1960 was one of the greatest achievements of the civil rights era. This book is, in part, an effort to celebrate the sit-in movement and the legal battles over discrimination in public accommodations that the movement sparked. It is an effort to draw attention to this triumphant moment in our ongoing struggle for racial justice, to better understand why this campaign for social and legal change worked, when so many others did not.

Other battlefronts in the African American freedom struggle proved far more difficult to uproot than racial exclusion in public accommodations. The powerful synergy between social protest and legal change that made the campaign against racial discrimination in public accommodations so powerful and consequential was hard to replicate in other areas. The struggle to implement *Brown* dragged out for decades, and we still face pervasive segregation in our schools. Disparities of wealth and income across racial lines persist, a particularly stubborn reminder of the continuing effects of slavery and Jim Crow. Racial disparities in our criminal justice system—from the stunning overrepresentation of racial minorities in our bloated prison populations to racially discriminatory police practices—remain one of the most significant challenges we face as a nation.

Our challenge is to find new ways combine social protest and legal claims to disrupt those practices and policies that perpetuate old inequalities and create new ones. The lunch counter sit-in movement shows that it can be done.

Acknowledgments

In the course of researching and writing this book, I have accumulated an impressive list of debts.

I have had the good fortune to be affiliated with two wonderful institutions, Chicago-Kent College of Law and the American Bar Foundation. I thank Dean Harold Krent and ABF directors Robert Nelson and Ajay Mehrotra for their encouragement and support. I also thank the people on the Chicago-Kent and ABF administrative staffs who make these institutions run and who, in ways small and large, make them such enjoyable and productive places to work. I offer a special thanks to the Chicago-Kent research librarians—particularly, Tom Gaylord, Scott Vanderlin, and Clare Willis—for their expert assistance in tracking down research materials.

I first began thinking about the legal issues involved in the sit-ins when, as a third-year law student, I had the privilege of taking a seminar with Robert Post and Reva Siegel. They inspired me to think differently about how constitutional change happens, about the ways people outside the courts make claims on the Constitution, and about the intersection of social movements and legal doctrine. From the seminar paper I wrote then, through this book, their inspiration and influence have been a constant.

I always envisioned my work on the sit-ins coming together into a book, but along the way I published a number of shorter pieces on the topic. I have drawn from these essays and articles—published in *Law and History Review, Signposts: New Directions in Southern Legal History, UC Irvine Law Review*, and *William and Mary Bill of Rights Jour-*

nal—in writing this book. I take this opportunity to thank once again the colleagues, editors, conference paper commentators, and friends who helped me with these articles: Felice Batlan, Mary Dudziak, Richard Fallon, Jon Gould, Joanna Grisinger, Sally Hadden, Sarah Harding, Martha Jones, Michael Klarman, Sophia Lee, Sanford Levinson, Kate Masur, Serena Mayeri, Patricia Minter, Laura Beth Nielsen, William Novak, Dylan Penningroth, Mark Rosen, Lucy Salyer, James Sparrow, Norman Spaulding, Kristen Stilt, Allison Brownell Tirres, Mark Tushnet, and any others I fear I have missed.

I presented material from this book at a number of conferences and workshops, including the American Bar Foundation Seminar; annual meetings of the American Society of Legal History and the Association of American Law Schools; faculty workshops at Chicago-Kent, Cornell, Duke, Marquette, University of California, Irvine, UCLA, and University of Chicago; the Northeast Regional Law and Society Meeting; the Harvard Law School Legal History Workshop; the Chicago Legal History Seminar; the Policy History Conference; the Law and Humanities Junior Scholars Workshop; the conference on "Theory and Method in Legal History" at UC Irvine School of Law; the Midwest Law and Society Retreat at the University of Wisconsin, Madison; the Harvard-Stanford-Yale Junior Faculty Forum; the University of Michigan Legal History Workshop; the *Northwestern Journal of Law and Social Policy* Symposium on Social Movements and the Law; and the conference on "Turning Points in Social Movements" at Indiana University School of Law. I thank all those who took part in these sessions for their critiques and advice on the project.

I am fortunate to have an unusually generous collection of friends who, as I neared completion of the book, were willing to read the manuscript and give me detailed, thoughtful feedback. They include Andy Baer, Kathy Baker, Felice Batlan, Jane Dailey, Joanna Grisinger, Sarah Harding, Steve Heyman, Mandy Hughett, Mike Klarman, Hal Krent, Gary Lee, Kate Masur, Ajay Mehrotra, Mark Rosen, Willa Sachs, Carolyn Shapiro, Dan Sharfstein, Allison Tirres, Jill Weinberg, Laura Weinrib, and Mary Ziegler. Research assistant extraordinaire Sarah Williams gave me her smart, thoughtful reactions to the manuscript. Faculty assistant extraordinaire Laura Caringella expertly proofread the entire manuscript and made everything look right. A group of these readers participated in a manuscript workshop at the American Bar Foundation, and I owe them a particular debt of gratitude for spending a summer afternoon helping me work through some challenges I was having pulling the manuscript together.

Michael Klarman deserves special mention. Over the years, Mike has taken the time to help me out with so much of my work, and here again he read the entire manuscript and offer page upon page of his characteristic careful and challenging comments. He has long been my most valued—and valuable—reader. In his own extraordinary scholarship and in his generosity to others, he sets the standard.

I thank Lynn Mather for inviting me to contribute to the Chicago Series in Law and Society and for her careful editorial guidance and boundless enthusiasm along the way. At the University of Chicago Press, I have had the pleasure of working with two excellent acquisition editors, John Tryneski and Chuck Myers, and Erin DeWitt expertly guided the manuscript through the copyediting process.

My parents, Meg and Jim Schmidt, to whom I dedicate this book, carefully read every word of the book manuscript, letting me know what made sense and what did not. Early in my life, my dad gave me his love of history, and my mom her love of stories and words. They have given their unwavering support to all that I have done. When it comes to being parents, they set the standard.

And, finally, I thank my wife, Erin, and our three remarkable children. Henry, Caroline, and James arrived into this world when this book was taking shape, and they have done their best ever since to delay its arrival. For this, and for everything else, thank you.

Abbreviations

AC	*Atlanta Constitution*
ADW	*Atlanta Daily World*
AN	*Amsterdam News*
ASR	*American Sociological Review*
BG	*Boston Globe*
BS	*Baltimore Sun*
CD	*Chicago Defender*
CORE	Congress of Racial Equality
CT	*Chicago Tribune*
GDN	*Greensboro Daily News*
GR	*Greensboro Record*
JNE	*Journal of Negro Education*
LDF	Legal Defense and Educational Fund
LHR	*Law and History Review*
LOC	Library of Congress
LSI	*Law & Social Inquiry*
NAACP	National Association for the Advancement of Colored People
NCCHR	North Carolina Council on Human Relations
NR	*New Republic*
NYHT	*New York Herald Tribune*
NYT	*New York Times*
PC	*Pittsburgh Courier*
SNCC	Student Nonviolent Coordinating Committee
SRC	Southern Regional Council
WP	*Washington Post*
WSJ	*Wall Street Journal*

Notes

EPIGRAPH

1. Quoted in James H. Laue, *Direct Action and Desegregation, 1960–1962: Toward a Theory of Rationalization of Protest* (Brooklyn: Carlson, 1989) (reprint of PhD diss., Harvard University, 1965), 195–96.

INTRODUCTION

1. Martin Luther King Jr., "The Time for Freedom Has Come," *NYT Magazine*, September 10, 1961, 25, 118–19, at 119.
2. Franklin McCain Oral History, Bluford Library, North Carolina Agricultural and Technical College, available at http://www.library.ncat.edu/resources/archives/four.html ("exhausted"); L. F. Palmer Jr., "Uprising for Freedom," *CD*, March 22, 1960, 9, 11, at 11 (quoting Joseph McNeil) ("do something").
3. Albert L. Rozier Jr., "Students Hit Woolworth's for Lunch Service," *Register* (North Carolina A&T), February 5, 1960, reprinted in *Reporting Civil Rights: American Journalism, 1941–1963*, vol. 1 (New York: Library of America, 2003), 431 ("I'm sorry"; "membership cards"); Palmer, "Uprising for Freedom," 11 ("just sat"); "Sitdown Leader Persists in Goal," *NYT*, March 26, 1960, 10; Paul Ernest Wehr, "The Sit-Down Protests: A Study of a Passive Resistance Movement in North Carolina" (MA thesis, University of North Carolina, Chapel Hill, 1960), 18; Miles Wolff, *Lunch at the 5 & 10* (1970; rev. ed., Chicago: Ivan Dee, 1990), 11–12.
4. Rozier, "Students Hit Woolworth's"; Marvin Sykes, "A&T Students Launch 'Sit-Down' Demand for Service at Downtown Lunch Counter," *GR*, February 2, 1960, B1; "Student Strength

Rises in Protest at Lunch Counter," *GR*, February 4, 1960, B1; "Movement by Negroes Growing," *GDN*, February 4, 1960, B1; James H. Laue, *Direct Action and Desegregation, 1960–1962: Toward a Theory of Rationalization of Protest* (Brooklyn: Carlson, 1989) (reprint of PhD diss., Harvard University, 1965), 76; Clarence Lee Harris Scrapbook #1, 22 (1980), Clarence Lee Harris Papers, Martha Blakeney Hodges Special Collections and University Archives, UNCG University Libraries, Greensboro, North Carolina.

5.   "Sitdown Leader Persists" ("scared"); Elsie Carper, "Gandhi 'Inspired' Negro Sitdowns at 5-and-10s," *WP*, April 10, 1960, E1 ("expect").

6.   SRC, "The Student Protest Movement, Winter 1960," February 25, 1960, available at http://www.thekingcenter.org/archive/document/student -protest-movement-special-report; "The South: Youth Will Be Served," *Time*, March 21, 1960, 23; SRC, "A Follow-Up Report on the Student Protest Movement After Two Months," NCCHR Records, Folder 757, Southern Historical Collection, Wilson Library, University of North Carolina at Chapel Hill; SRC, "A Chronological Listing of the Cities in Which Demonstrations Have Occurred, February 1–March 31, 1960" (appendix to "Follow-Up Report"), ibid.

7.   L. D. Reddick, "The State vs. the Student," *Dissent* 7 (Summer 1960): 219–28, at 220.

8.   "A Universal Effort," *Time*, May 2, 1960, 18; Charles H. Thompson, "Desegregation Pushed Off Dead Center," *JNE* 29 (1960): 107–11, at 107 ("brush fire"); Laue, *Direct Action*, 76–77.

9.   The best historical accounts tend to downplay, mischaracterize, or simply ignore the relevant legal issues. See, for example, David Halberstam, *The Children* (New York: Random House, 1998); William H. Chafe, *Civilities and Civil Rights: Greensboro, North Carolina, and the Black Struggle for Freedom* (New York: Oxford University Press, 1980), 79–101; Clayborne Carson, *In Struggle: SNCC and the Black Awakening of the 1960s*, 2nd ed. (Cambridge, MA: Harvard University Press, 1995), 9–18; Aldon D. Morris, *The Origins of the Civil Rights Movement: Black Communities Organizing for Change* (New York: Free Press, 1984), 188–215.

    The outstanding exception to this general neglect of the legal history of the sit-ins is Tomiko Brown-Nagin, *Courage to Dissent: Atlanta and the Long History of the Civil Rights Movement* (New York: Oxford University Press, 2011), chaps. 6–7.

    In the 1960s, by contrast, scholars and activists exhaustively examined the legal issues that the sit-ins raised. See, for example, Daniel H. Pollitt, "Dime Store Demonstrations: Events and Legal Problems of First Sixty Days," *Duke Law Journal* (1960): 315–65; "Legal Aspects of the Sit-In Movement," *Race Relations Law Reporter* 5 (1960): 935–47; William J. Kenealy, "The Legality of the Sit-Ins," in *The New Negro*, ed. Mathew H. Ahmann (Notre Dame, IN: Fides, 1961), 63–86; Earl Lawrence Carl, "Reflections on the 'Sit-Ins,' " *Cornell Law Quarterly* 46 (1961): 444–57;

Kenneth L. Karst and William W. Van Alstyne, "Comment: Sit-Ins and State Action—Mr. Justice Douglas Concurring," *Stanford Law Review* 14 (1962): 762–76; Thomas P. Lewis, "The Sit-In Cases: Great Expectations," *Supreme Court Review* (1963): 101–51; Marion A. Wright, "The Sit-In Movement: Progress Report and Prognosis," *Wayne Law Review* 9 (1963): 445–57; Monrad G. Paulsen, "The Sit-In Cases of 1964: 'But Answer Came There None,'" *Supreme Court Review* (1964): 137–70; Burke Marshall, "The Protest Movement and the Law," *Virginia Law Review* 51 (1965): 785–803; Charles L. Black, "The Problems of the Compatibility of Civil Disobedience with American Institutions of Government," *Texas Law Review* 34 (1965): 492–506; Jack Greenberg, "The Supreme Court, Civil Rights, and Civil Dissonance," *Yale Law Journal* 77 (1968): 1520–44.

10. Brown v. Board of Education, 347 U.S. 483 (1954); Boynton v. Virginia, 364 U.S. 454 (1960); Henry Hampton and Steve Fraser, *Voices of Freedom: An Oral History of the Civil Rights Movement from the 1950s through the 1980s* (New York: Bantam, 1990), 75 (quoting James Farmer).

11. On the history of common-law protections in the area of public accommodations, see Joseph William Singer, "No Right to Exclude: Public Accommodations and Private Property," *Northwestern University Law Review* 90 (1996): 1283–497; A. K. Sandoval-Strausz, "Travelers, Strangers, and Jim Crow: Law, Public Accommodations, and Civil Rights in America," *LHR* 23 (2005): 53–94.

12. 109 U.S. 3, 17 (1883). The Supreme Court referenced the essence of the state action doctrine in cases before 1883—see, for example, Virginia v. Rives, 100 U.S. 313, 318 (1879); United States v. Cruikshank, 92 U.S. 542, 554–55 (1875)—but the *Civil Rights Cases* was the Supreme Court's first direct analysis of the issue.

Section One of the Fourteenth Amendment reads in relevant part: "*No State shall* make or enforce any law which shall abridge the privileges or immunities of citizens of the United States; *nor shall any State* deprive any person of life, liberty, or property, without due process of law; nor deny to any person within its jurisdiction the equal protection of the laws" (emphasis added).

Cases expanding the limits of "state action" include Smith v. Allwright, 321 U.S. 649 (1944); Marsh v. Alabama, 326 U.S. 501 (1946); Shelley v. Kraemer, 334 U.S. 1 (1948); Terry v. Adams, 345 U.S. 461 (1953); Barrows v. Jackson, 346 U.S. 249 (1953). For a more detailed overview of developments in the state action doctrine during this period, see Christopher W. Schmidt, "The Sit-Ins and the State Action Doctrine," *William & Mary Bill of Rights Journal* 18 (2010): 767–829. For recent historical scholarship that considers the postwar development of the state action doctrine in different contexts, see Risa L. Goluboff, *The Lost Promise of Civil Rights* (Cambridge, MA: Harvard University Press, 2007); Sophia Z. Lee, *The Workplace Constitution: From the New Deal to the New Right* (New York: Cambridge University Press, 2014).

13. Plessy v. Ferguson, 163 U.S. 537 (1896); New Orleans City Park Improvement Association v. Detiege, 358 U.S. 54 (1958) (per curiam); Gayle v. Browder, 352 U.S. 903 (1956); Holmes v. City of Atlanta, 350 U.S. 879 (1955) (per curiam); Mayor and City Council of Baltimore v. Dawson, 350 U.S. 877 (1955) (per curiam).

14. The most relevant precedent for this kind of constitutional claim was *Marsh v. Alabama,* in which the Court held that for purposes of the First Amendment, a private "company town" could be treated as a state actor. Justice Black's sweeping assertion that a private actor who "opens up his property for use by the public in general" will be constrained by "constitutional rights" was frequently cited by lawyers who argued that the equal protection clause should apply to owners of public accommodations. 326 U.S. 501, 506 (1946).

15. Shelley v. Kraemer, 334 U.S. 1 (1948). While reaffirming the basic state action requirement, some civil rights lawyers and legal scholars read Chief Justice Fred Vinson's rather opaque opinion for the unanimous Court as a harbinger of a fundamental judicial reconsideration of the state action doctrine. See, for example, "The Disintegration of a Concept—State Action under the 14th and 15th Amendments," *University of Pennsylvania Law Review* 96 (1948): 402–14; William R. Ming Jr., "Racial Restrictions and the Fourteenth Amendment: The Restrictive Covenant Cases," *University of Chicago Law Review* 16 (1949): 203–38; Richard G. Huber, "Revolution in Private Law?" *South Carolina Law Quarterly* 6 (1953): 8–31.

16. See Charles L. Black Jr., "The Supreme Court, 1966 Term—Foreword: 'State Action,' Equal Protection, and California's Proposition 14," *Harvard Law Review* 81 (1967): 69–109, at 84–91; Michael Seidman and Mark V. Tushnet, *Remnants of Belief: Contemporary Constitutional Issues* (New York: Oxford University Press, 1996), chap. 3; Schmidt, "The Sit-Ins and the State Action Doctrine," 779–81; Christopher W. Schmidt, "On Doctrinal Confusion: The Case of the State Action Doctrine," *BYU Law Review* (2016): 575–628.

17. Lewis, "Sit-In Cases," 101.

18. Bell v. Maryland, 378 U.S. 226, 243 (1964) (Douglas, J., concurring).

19. On "legal consciousness," see, for example, Patricia Ewick and Susan Silbey, *The Common Place of Law: Stories from Everyday Life* (Chicago: University of Chicago Press, 1998); Susan S. Silbey, "After Legal Consciousness," *Annual Review of Law and Social Science* 1 (2005): 323–68.

20. See Hendrik Hartog, "The Constitution of Aspiration and 'The Rights That Belong to Us All,'" *Journal of American History* 74 (1987): 1013–34; Michael W. McCann, "Reform Litigation on Trial," *LSI* 17 (1992): 715–43; Reva B. Siegel, "Text in Context: Gender and the Constitution from a Social Movement Perspective," *University of Pennsylvania Law Review* 150 (2001): 297–351; Christopher W. Schmidt, "Social Movements, Legal Change, and the Challenges of Writing Legal History," *Vanderbilt Law Review En Banc* 65 (2012): 155–83; Risa Goluboff, "Lawyers, Law, and the New Civil Rights History," *Harvard Law Review* 126 (2013): 2312–35.

21. Goluboff, "New Civil Rights History," 2323. For a seminal analysis of the "transformation" of disputes across various institutional settings, see Lynn Mather and Barbara Yngvesson, "Language, Audience, and the Transformation of Disputes," *Law & Society Review* 15 (1980–81): 775–822. I discuss the literature on popular constitutionalism in chapter 3.

CHAPTER ONE

1. Quoted in Ella Baker, "Bigger than a Hamburger," *Southern Patriot* 18 (June 1960): 4.
2. Clarence H. Patrick, *Lunch Counter Desegregation in Winston-Salem, North Carolina* (SRC Pamphlet, 1960), 5 (quoting Carl Matthews).
3. "An Appeal for Human Rights," *AC*, March 9, 1960, 13.
4. Scholarly debate over why the sit-in movement spread so far and so fast has taken on an unfortunate dichotomous quality. Scholars have generally divided into two camps: those who emphasize the spontaneous qualities of the protest and those who emphasize the planning and organizing that went into the movement. In this book I try to sidestep this reductionist either-or debate by emphasizing the diversity of experiences contained within the sit-in movement.

   Scholars who highlight the spontaneous, unplanned qualities of the sit-ins echo a theme that pervaded contemporaneous accounts. "The movement has been spontaneous and contagious," asserted an influential Southern Regional Council report. SRC, "The Student Protest Movement, Winter 1960," February 25, 1960, 2, available at http://www.thekingcenter.org/archive/document/student-protest-movement-special-report. "This is not a fully organized mechanism but a loosely worked out plan mixed with a spontaneous movement," read a typical newspaper account of the early stages of the movement. Robert S. Bird, "South's Sit-Ins: A Field Report," *NYHT*, March 13, 1960, 1, 18. Subsequent scholarship that embraces this spontaneity theme includes Lewis M. Killian, "Organization, Rationality and Spontaneity in the Civil Rights Movement," *ASR* 49 (1984): 770–83; Anthony Oberschall, *Social Movements: Ideologies, Interests, and Identities* (New Brunswick, NJ: Transaction, 1993), chap. 8; Clayborne Carson, *In Struggle: SNCC and the Black Awakening of the 1960s*, 2nd ed. (Cambridge, MA: Harvard University Press, 1995), chap. 1; Francesca Polletta, *It Was Like a Fever: Storytelling in Protest and Politics* (Chicago: University of Chicago Press, 2006), chap. 2.

   On the other side of the debate are those scholars who reject this spontaneous portrait of the sit-ins by emphasizing the mobilizing efforts that predated the 1960 movement. The leading scholar here is sociologist Aldon Morris, who argued in his pathbreaking *Origins of the Civil Rights Movement: Black Communities Organizing for Change* (New York: Free Press,

1984) that the sit-in movement was the outgrowth of organizational activity, including various earlier sit-in campaigns. See also Aldon Morris, "Black Southern Student Sit-In Movement: An Analysis of Internal Organization," *ASR* 46 (1981): 744–67; Doug McAdam, *Political Process and the Development of Black Insurgency, 1930–1970*, 2nd ed. (Chicago: University of Chicago Press, 1999), 117–45.

Morris is surely right to argue that behind the pronouncements of spontaneity and independence favored by early sit-in leaders lies a more complex reality in which networks of communication and support, created and maintained by black churches and civil rights organizations, played a key role in the sit-in movement. But I believe to then assert that the movement was the product of these networks goes too far. Morris's key sources of support for his argument are interviews with leaders of movement organizations, who, unsurprisingly, emphasize their central role in the sit-in movement. Morris also treats the highly organized—and in many ways quite exceptional—Nashville student movement as representative of the larger movement. See also Kenneth T. Andrews and Michael Biggs, "The Dynamics of Protest Diffusion: Movement Organizations, Social Networks, and News Media in the 1960 Sit-Ins," *ASR* 71 (2006): 752–77, at 767 n. 27 (challenging Morris's reading of various sit-in sites).

A better approach to explaining the sit-in movement resists the impulse to reduce something as complex and varied as the sit-in movement to singular sociological categories. My account recognizes the mixture of spontaneity and planning that went into the sit-ins. It recognizes the diversity of experiences contained in the sit-in movement, and it recognizes the changes that took place in the movement as it unfolded—most obviously, the increased level of organization and planning that was required to sustain the movement after its explosive (and in important ways spontaneous) opening weeks. This approach accords with the assessment that James Robinson, Executive Director of CORE, offered in June 1960. "There is no question but that the movement began more or less spontaneously and spread rapidly across North Carolina," he noted. But after this point, when the movement spread further into the South, "spontaneity is not so clear." James R. Robinson, "The Meaning of the Sit-Ins," memorandum prepared for June 8, 1960, meeting of civil rights organizations, 1, NAACP Papers, Part III, Series A, Container 308, Folder: "Staff, Farmer, James, General, 1960, June–Sept.," LOC, Manuscript Division. My approach also aligns with the findings of a recent quantitative analysis of the diffusion of sit-in protests. Andrews and Biggs, "Dynamics of Protest Diffusion."

5.   "1958 Sit-Ins Were Successful," *AN*, February 27, 1960, 2; L. F. Palmer Jr., "'Movement' Guided by Non-Violence," *CD*, March 24, 1960, 11; Les Mathews, "Sympathy and Support in New York," *CD*, April 5, 1960, 9; Roy Wilkins, *The Meaning of the Sit-Ins*, NAACP pamphlet, September 1960, 2; August Meier, "The Successful Sit-Ins in a Border City: A Study in Social

Causation," *Journal of Intergroup Relations* 2 (1961): 230–37, reprinted in August Meier, *A White Scholar and the Black Community, 1945–1965: Essays and Reflections* (Amherst: University of Massachusetts Press, 1992), 117–26, at 119–20; Robert E. Baker, "Sit-Ins Gave Equality; Where's Opportunity?" *WP*, December 20, 1964, E3; James Farmer, *Freedom—When?* (New York: Random House, 1965), 60–62; August Meier and Elliot Rudwick, *CORE: A Study of the Civil Rights Movement, 1942–1968* (New York: Oxford University Press, 1973), 3–14, 91, 102; Morris, *Origins*, 188–94; Martin Oppenheimer, "Genesis of the Southern Negro Student Movement" (PhD diss., University of Pennsylvania, 1963), 50; Lizabeth Cohen, *A Consumers' Republic: The Politics of Mass Consumption in Postwar America* (New York: Knopf, 2003), 98–99; Thomas J. Sugrue, *Sweet Land of Liberty: The Forgotten Struggle for Civil Rights in the North* (New York: Random House, 2008), 159–60.

6. SRC, "Student Protest Movement, Winter 1960," 3; Barbara Ann Posey, *Why I Sit*, NAACP pamphlet, September 1960, NCCHR Records, Folder 758, Southern Historical Collection, Wilson Library, University of North Carolina at Chapel Hill; Clara Luper, *Behold the Walls* (Oklahoma City: Jim Wire, 1979); Morris, *Origins*, 124–25, 188–89; Martin Oppenheimer, "The Southern Student Movement: Year 1," *JNE* 33 (1964): 396–403, at 397; Ronald Walters, "The Great Plains Sit-In Movement, 1958–1960," *Great Plains Quarterly* 16 (Spring 1996): 85–94; Gretchen Cassel Eick, *Dissent in Wichita: The Civil Rights Movement in the Midwest, 1954–72* (Urbana: University of Illinois Press, 2001), 1–11; Thomas Bynum, *NAACP Youth and the Fight for Black Freedom, 1936–1965* (Knoxville: University of Tennessee Press, 2013), 95–99.

7. Oppenheimer, "Southern Student Movement," 397; SRC, "Student Protest Movement, Winter 1960," 3; Morris, *Origins*, 124–25; Taylor Branch, *Parting the Waters: America in the King Years, 1954–1963* (New York: Simon & Schuster, 1988), 272.

8. Morris, *Origins*, 198 (quoting Floyd McKissick); James Farmer Oral History Interview 1, October 1969, LBJ Library, available at http://www.lbjlib .utexas.edu/johnson/archives.hom/oralhistory.hom/Farmer/farmer1.pdf; *CORE-lator*, April 1960; Meier and Rudwick, *CORE*, 102.

    On the NAACP's post-1960 embrace of the Midwest sit-ins, see Meier and Rudwick, *CORE*, 31–33, 61–71; Morris, *Origins*, 125; "The Role of the NAACP in the 'Sit-ins,'" May 1960, NAACP Papers, Part III, Series A, Container 290, Folder: "Sit-Ins, North Carolina," LOC, Manuscript Division; Roy Wilkins, *Standing Fast: The Autobiography of Roy Wilkins* (New York: Viking, 1982), 259–60; *The Day They Changed Their Minds*, NAACP pamphlet, March 1960, 4, available at www.loc.gov/exhibits/naacp/the-civil-rights -era.html#obj19. I discuss further the NAACP's efforts amplify the role of its pre-1960 activities on the sit-in movement in chapter 2.

9. Paul Ernest Wehr, "The Sit-Down Protests: A Study of a Passive Resistance Movement in North Carolina" (MA thesis, University of North Carolina,

Chapel Hill, 1960), 19–20 ("hazy"); James H. Laue, *Direct Action and Deseg-regation, 1960–1962: Toward a Theory of Rationalization of Protest* (Brooklyn, NY: Carlson, 1989) (reprint of PhD diss., Harvard University, 1965), 147; Frank Adams with Myles Horton, *Unearthing Seeds of Fire: The Idea of Highlander* (Winston-Salem, NC: John F. Blair, 1975), 147.

10. Sykes, "A&T Students Launch 'Sit-Down' Demand"; Carson, *In Struggle*, 9.

11. Miles Wolff, *Lunch at the 5 & 10* (1970; rev. ed., Chicago: Ivan Dee, 1990), 35–36; Meier and Rudwick, *CORE*, 102; Morris, *Origins*, 199–200; William H. Chafe, *Civilities and Civil Rights: Greensboro, North Carolina, and the Black Struggle for Freedom* (New York: Oxford University Press, 1980), 84.

12. "White Students Act," *NYT*, February 5, 1960, 12; Elsie Carper, "Gandhi 'Inspired' Negro Sitdowns at 5-and-10s," *WP*, April 10, 1960, E1 ("toughs"); "Bomb Scares Halt Negro Sitdown," *AC*, February 7, 1960, 18A ("rebel yells"); "White Men Arrested at Sitdown," *GDN*, February 6, 1960, B1 ("Christian movement"); "Klan Tries to Halt Negroes' Protest," *NYT*, February 6, 1960, 20; "A&T Students Call Two-Week Recess in Protest Here," *GDN*, February 7, 1960, A1, A4; "Collegians Win Initial Victory in Bias Fight," *CD*, February 8, 1960, 3; Wolff, *Lunch at the 5 & 10*, 47–48.

13. "A&T Students Call Two-Week Recess"; "Visit Set to Probe Sitdown," *GDN*, February 9, 1960, B1; Gordon W. Blackwell, "Timeline of events related to the Greensboro sit-ins," February 16, 1960, Gordon Williams Blackwell Records, Martha Blakeney Hodges Special Collections and University Archives, UNCG University Libraries, Greensboro, North Carolina ("without conviction"); Wehr, "Sit-Down Protests," 28; Oppenheimer, "Southern Student Movement," 398; Chafe, *Civilities and Civil Rights*, 84.

14. Clarence Lee Harris Scrapbook #1, 38–40 (1980), Clarence Lee Harris Papers, Martha Blakeney Hodges Special Collections and University Archives, UNCG University Libraries, Greensboro, North Carolina; "A&T Students Call Two-Week Recess" ("cheering"); "Renew Cooperation," *GR*, February 8, 1960, A14 ("orderly and courteous"); "Counters to Remain Closed," *GDN*, February 8, 1960, B1 ("negotiation and study"); "Collegians Win Initial Victory in Bias Fight"; "Integration Armistice," *NYT*, February 8, 1960, 14; Wolff, *Lunch at the 5 & 10*, 49–53.

15. "Demonstration Grows," *GDN*, February 9, 1960, A3; "Resistance Move to Continue," *GDN*, February 12, 1960, A10; Patrick, *Lunch Counter Desegregation*, 4; Helen Fuller, " 'We Are All So Happy,' " *NR*, April 25, 1960, 13–16, at 14.

16. "Mass Negro Protests Hit Durham, Winston," *GDN*, February 9, 1960, A1, A3; "Negroes' Sitdown Hits 2 More Cities," *NYT*, February 9, 1960, 16; "N.C. Stores Close Down Counter," *GDN*, February 10, 1960, A1, A3; "N.C. Lunch Counter Bias Protest Spreads," *ADW*, February 10, 1960, 1; "Negroes Extend Sitdown Protests," *NYT*, February 10, 1960, 21; "Eggs Spray Negro in Cafe Flareup," *AC*, February 11, 1960, 12 ("no reaction"); Claude Sitton, "Negroes Extend Store Picketing," *NYT*, February 11, 1960, 22; SRC,

"A Chronological Listing of the Cities in Which Demonstrations Have Occurred, February 1–March 31, 1960" (appendix to "Follow-Up Report").

17. Morris, *Origins*, 201 ("shake up the world"); "Lunch Counter Strikes Spread to High Point," *GDN*, February 12, 1960, A1, A6; Almetta C. Brooks, "White Patrons Balk Negro Sitdowners," *GDN*, February 13, 1960, A3; "Negro Pupils Crowd Store; It Closes," *GDN*, February 14, 1960, A1.

18. "NAACP Upholds Store Picketing," *NYT*, February 12, 1960, 15; SRC, "Chronological Listing"; Edward Rodman, "Portsmouth: A Lesson in Nonviolence," in *Sit-Ins: The Students Report*, ed. James Peck (New York: CORE, 1960), 4–6, at 4.

    Although the first Hampton sit-in took place on February 10, when three Hampton Institute students sat down at the local Woolworth lunch counter, without service, for three hours, the press did not report on the protests until the following day, when more than two hundred Hampton Institute students participated in sit-ins. Donnie L. Everette and Kennell A. Jackson, "The Hampton Sit-Ins and the Southern Society," n.d., available at http://www.crmvet.org/lets/60_hamptons_sitins.pdf.

19. "41 Negroes Charged with Trespass in Raleigh Area," *GDN*, February 13, 1960, A1; "41 Negroes Seized at Lunch Counter," *AC*, February 13, 1960, 2; "Halt Is Called to Protest at Center," *GDN*, February 15, 1960, A1; "Negroes Halt Sit-Downs at Lunch Counters," *AC*, February 15, 1960, 9; "43 Negroes Fined in Raleigh Court," *NYT*, March 29, 1960, 28.

20. Claude Sitton, "Negroes' Protest Spreads in South," *NYT*, February 13, 1960, 1, 6 ("duck-tail haircuts"); Claude Sitton, "Negroes Press for Faster Desegregation," *NYT*, February 21, 1960, E3 ("delinquents"); SRC, "The Student Protest Movement: A Recapitulation," September 29, 1961, 5, available at http://www.crmvet.org/info/6109_src_sitins.pdf.

21. Wesley C. Hogan, *Many Minds, One Heart: SNCC's Dream for a New America* (Chapel Hill: University of North Carolina Press, 2007), 26 ("logical world"); Morris, *Origins*, 190; Branch, *Parting the Waters*, 260, 268–69; David Halberstam, *The Children* (New York: Random House, 1998), 25–92; Interview with James M. Lawson, Southern Oral History Program Collection #4007, Southern Historical Collection, Wilson Library, University of North Carolina at Chapel Hill.

22. "Phone Call Sparked Sit-Ins, Says Lawson," *Nashville Tennessean*, March 21, 1960, 2; Morris, *Origins*, 205–6; Branch, *Parting the Waters*, 273; Paul Laprad, "Nashville: A Community Struggle," in *Sit-Ins: The Students Report*, 6–7; Milton Viorst, *Fire in the Streets: American in the 1960's* (New York: Simon and Schuster, 1979), 107.

23. David Halberstam, "A Good City Gone Ugly," *Reporter*, March 31, 1960, 19; Rodman, "Portsmouth," 6; "N.Y. Coeds Describe Sit-Down," *AN*, March 12, 1960, 26; Halberstam, *Children*, 93–102; "Rebuffed in Nashville," *NYT*, February 14, 1960, 30; "Demonstrations in Nashville," *NYT*, February 21, 1960, 57; "Nashville Seizes 75 in Race Clash," *NYT*, February

28, 1960, 51; Robert C. Albright, "Rights Protests Spreading," *WP*, February 28, 1960, A1; "Negroes Throng Sitdown Trials," *NYT*, March 1, 1960, 20; "3 Fined in Race Demonstrations," *CT*, March 1, 1960, 2; Harrison Salisbury, "Nashville Issue Is Full Equality," *NYT*, April 18, 1960, 1, 20; Laprad, "Nashville," 7; Branch, *Parting the Waters*, 278–79.

24. "The South: Youth Will Be Served," *Time*, March 21, 1960; SRC, "Postscript to Special Report of February 25: The Student Protest Movement, Winter 1960," March 14, 1960, NAACP Papers, Part III, Series A, Container 289, Folder: "Sit-Ins, General, 1959, 1960, Jan.–May"; SRC, "A Follow-Up Report on the Student Protest Movement after Two Months," NCCHR Records, Folder 757; L. F. Palmer, "New Face of Young Negro America," *CD*, March 21, 1960, 1, 9, 11.

25. Smith v. Allwright, 321 U.S. 649 (1944); Michael J. Klarman, "The White Primary Rulings: A Case Study in the Consequences of Supreme Court Decisionmaking," *Florida State University Law Review* 29 (2001): 55–107.

26. Sweatt v. Painter, 339 U.S. 629 (1950); McLaurin v. Oklahoma State Regents, 339 U.S. 637 (1950); Brown v. Board of Education, 347 U.S. 483 (1954).
     On the growing national support for civil rights in the 1940s and 1950s, see, for example, Michael J. Klarman, *From Jim Crow to Civil Rights: The Supreme Court and the Struggle for Racial Equality* (New York: Oxford University Press, 2004); Mary L. Dudziak, *Cold War Civil Rights: Race and the Image of American Democracy* (Princeton, NJ: Princeton University Press, 2000).

27. Chafe, *Civilities and Civil Rights*, 84, 110; Patrick, *Lunch Counter Desegregation*, 3; Salisbury, "Nashville Issue Is Full Equality"; Wallace Westfeldt, "A Report on Nashville," Nashville Community Relations Conference (1960); Steven F. Lawson, "From Sit-In to Race Riot," in *Southern Businessmen and Desegregation*, ed. Elizabeth Jacoway and David R. Colburn (Baton Rouge: Louisiana State University Press, 1982), 257–81, at 262–63.

28. Ben H. Bagdikian, "Negro Youth's New March on Dixie," *Saturday Evening Post*, September 8, 1962, 15–19, at 15.

29. Howell Raines, *My Soul Is Rested: The Story of the Civil Rights Movement in the Deep South* (New York: Putnam, 1977), 73 (Lewis); Chafe, *Civilities and Civil Rights*, 113 ("tears"); Wehr, "Sit-Down Protests," 21–22 ("genuine hero"). See also Julian Bond, "Introduction," in Juan Williams, *Eyes on the Prize* (1987; reprint, New York: Penguin, 2013), xi; Howard Zinn, *SNCC: The New Abolitionists* (Boston: Beacon Press, 1964), 18; Fuller, " 'We Are All So Happy.' "

30. Fuller, " 'We Are All So Happy,' " 13; Fredric Solomon and Jacob R. Fishman, "Action and Identity Formation in the First Student Demonstration," *Journal of Social Issues* 20 (April 1964): 36–45, at 39; Zinn, *SNCC*, 18; Henry Hampton and Steve Fraser, *Voices of Freedom: An Oral History of the Civil Rights Movement from the 1950s through the 1980s* (New York: Bantam, 1990), 56 (interview with Joseph McNeil).

31. Fuller, "'We Are All So Happy,'" 13 ("unintellectual"); Bagdikian, "Negro Youth's New March," 18 ("heroes"); Claude Sitton, "Racial Problems Put to President," *NYT*, April 18, 1960, 21 (Eisenhower letter); Martin Luther King Jr., Statement to the Press, Youth Leadership Conference, Raleigh, North Carolina, April 15, 1960, available at http://www.thekingcenter.org/archive/document/mlk-student-sit-ins.
32. Robert Coles, "Social Struggle and Weariness," *Psychiatry*, November 1, 1964, 305–15, at 313 ("optimistic").

    See generally Michael Biggs, "Who Joined the Sit-Ins and Why: Southern Black Students in the Early 1960s," *Mobilization: An International Journal* 11 (2006): 321–36 (finding that movement activists were significantly more optimistic about the potential for racial progress than those who did not join the movement). Studies of racial attitudes in the early 1960s found that African Americans generally underestimated the extent of white opposition to desegregation. Donald R. Matthews and James W. Prothro, "Southern Racial Attitudes: Conflict, Awareness, and Political Change," *Annals of the American Academy of Political and Social Science* 344 (1962): 108–21, at 112–13; Ruth Searles and J. Allen Williams, "Negro College Students Participation in Sit-Ins," *Social Forces* 40 (1962): 215–20, at 218–19.
33. Henry Lee Moon, "New Emancipation: The Atlanta Conference," *Nation*, June 5, 1954, 484 ("entire South"); Christopher W. Schmidt, "'Freedom Comes Only from the Law': The Debate over Law's Capacity and the Making of *Brown v. Board of Education*," *Utah Law Review* (2008): 1493–559, at 1544–57; Chafe, *Civilities and Civil Rights*, 5, 16, 57–59.
34. Klarman, *From Jim Crow*, 349; Gerald N. Rosenberg, *The Hollow Hope: Can Courts Bring about Social Change?* (Chicago: University of Chicago Press, 1991), 49–52; Sitton, "Negroes Press for Faster Desegregation." On the reaction to *Brown* in North Carolina, see Chafe, *Civilities and Civil Rights*, 5, 56–108.
35. "'We'll Pay Your Fines!'" *AN*, March 5, 1960, 1 ("too slow"); Bagdikian, "Negro Youth's New March," 16 ("failure"); Leslie Dunbar, "Reflection on the Latest Reform of the South," *Phylon* 22 (1961): 249–57, at 252 ("disillusion and disgust"). On the Greensboro Four, see Solomon and Fishman, "Action and Identity Formation," 37; Jacob R. Fishman and Fredric Solomon, "Perspectives on the Sit-In Movement," *American Journal of Orthopsychiatry* 33 (1963): 874–75. See also Max Freedman, "The South Smoulders: Colour Bar at Drug Stores," *Guardian* (London), February 29, 1960, 17; Chafe, *Civilities and Civil Rights*, 72–81, 100–113; Claude Sitton, "Negro Sitdowns Stir Fear of Wider Unrest in South," *NYT*, February 15, 1960, 1, 18; Interview on *Meet the Press*, April 17, 1960, in *The Papers of Martin Luther King, Jr.*, vol. 5, ed. Clayborne Carson et al. (Berkeley: University of California Press, 1992), 434 [hereinafter *King Papers*]; Daniel H. Pollitt, "Dime Store Demonstrations: Events and Legal Problems of First Sixty

Days," *Duke Law Journal* (1960): 315–65, at 319; James McBride Dabbs, "Dime Stores and Dignity," *Nation*, April 2, 1960, 289; Zinn, *SNCC*, 27.

36. Halberstam, "Good City Gone Ugly," 18. According to James Robinson, executive secretary of CORE, the "snail's pace" of school desegregation "is the reason that persons who believe in brotherhood in the South—Negro and white—are now ready to proceed in a more direct fashion and not to wait upon decisions which go court to court, year by year, and achieve, in most cases, merely token integration. The present popularity of direct action, therefore, is traceable to the Supreme Court [school desegregation] decision." Robinson, "Meaning of the Sit-Ins," 4.

37. Robert L. Carter, "The Warren Court and Desegregation," *Michigan Law Review* 67 (1968): 237–48, at 246–47 ("fathered"); J. Harvie Wilkinson III, *From* Brown *to* Bakke: *The Supreme Court and School Integration: 1954–1978* (New York: Oxford University Press, 1979), 3 ("sired"); Morton J. Horwitz, *The Warren Court and the Pursuit of Justice* (New York: Hill and Wang, 1998), 15 ("initiated"). For a study of the modern legal academy's attitude toward *Brown* and the Warren Court generally, see Laura Kalman, *The Strange Career of Legal Liberalism* (New Haven, CT: Yale University Press, 1996).

It is worth noting that academic historians have tended not to buy the grandiose portrayals of *Brown*'s impact that characterize the work of lawyers and legal scholars. Historians generally have not refuted these accounts so much as simply ignored them. With bottom-up social history the methodology of choice within the profession in the late 1970s and 1980s, particularly among scholars of African American history and the civil rights movement, historians tended to be skeptical toward the very idea that elite-level politics and formal legal change were central factors in the lives of everyday people. *Brown* might have offered some vague inspiration or consolation for local movement actors, but their lives had little connection to the NAACP and its courtroom battles. The law, at least in its formal manifestations of courts and lawyers, was, for the most part, irrelevant to the everyday struggles of grassroots activists. See Kenneth W. Mack, "Bringing the Law Back into the History of the Civil Rights Movement," *LHR* 27 (2009): 657–69, at 657–58.

38. Rosenberg, *Hollow Hope*, 39–169; Klarman, *From Jim Crow*, 344–442; Michael J. Klarman, "*Brown*, Racial Change, and the Civil Rights Movement," *Virginia Law Review* 80 (1994): 7–150; Michael J. Klarman, "*Brown v. Board of Education*: Facts and Political Correctness," *Virginia Law Review* 80 (1994): 185–99; Michael J. Klarman, "How *Brown* Changed Race Relations: The Backlash Thesis," *Journal of American History* 81 (1994): 81–118.

39. Rosenberg, *Hollow Hope*, 140–41; Klarman, *From Jim Crow*, 374.

40. See, for example, Michael W. McCann, "Reform Litigation on Trial," *LSI* 17 (1992): 715–43; Tomiko Brown-Nagin, *Courage to Dissent: Atlanta and the Long History of the Civil Rights Movement* (New York: Oxford University

Press, 2011), 7–11, 135; Christopher W. Schmidt, "Divided by Law: The Sit-Ins, Legal Uncertainty, and the Role of the Courts in the Civil Rights Movement," *LHR* 33 (2015): 93–149.

41. Klarman, *From Jim Crow*, 368.
42. Bagdikian, "Negro Youth's New March," 18 ("no answer"; "stodgy"); Halberstam, "Good City Gone Ugly," 18 ("dissatisfied").
43. James Lawson, "From a Lunch-Counter Stool," April 1960, reprinted in *Black Protest Thought in the Twentieth Century*, 2nd ed., ed. August Meier, Elliott Rudwick, and Francis Broderick (Indianapolis: Bobbs-Merrill, 1971), 308–15, at 310–15 ("well-meaning"); Halberstam, "Good City Gone Ugly," 18 ("legal redress"). Lawson attacked the NAACP throughout the spring of 1960, often in quite blunt terms. "This movement is not only against segregation," he stated at one point. "It's against Uncle Tom Negroes, against the N.A.A.C.P's over-reliance on the courts; and against the futile middle class technique of sending letters to the centers of power." Nat Hentoff, "A Peaceful Army," *Commonweal*, June 10, 1960, 275–78, at 275.
44. Michael Walzer, "A Cup of Coffee and a Seat," *Dissent* 7 (1960): 111–20, at 116–17.
45. Wehr, "Sit-Down Protests," 18.
46. Sykes, "A&T Students Launch 'Sit-Down' Demand"; Solomon and Fishman, "Action and Identity Formation," 38; see also Martin Oppenheimer, *The Sit-In Movement of 1960* (New York: Carlson, 1989), 37.
47. "Leader of Sit-In Movement Hailed by Negro Newspapermen," *WP*, May 22, 1960, C12; "Showdown," *AN*, May 7, 1960, 1.
48. L. F. Palmer, "Uprising for Freedom," *CD*, March 22, 1960, 9, 11, at 9 ("too worried"); Walzer, "A Cup of Coffee," 119 ("brainwashed"); Alvin Adams, "Aim Fall Sit-Ins at 'Unfinished' Work," *CD*, June 18, 1960, 22 ("subordination"); Lerone Bennett Jr., "What Sit-Downs Mean to America," *Ebony*, June 1960, 35–40, at 40 ("Mamma"). See also Jack L. Walker, "The Functions of Disunity: Negro Leadership in a Southern City," *JNE* 32 (1963): 227–36, at 231–32. On generational divides within the African American activist community during the civil rights era, the essential work is Brown-Nagin's study of Atlanta, *Courage to Dissent*.
49. Edward B. King Jr., "Equal Rights," letter to the editor, *Raleigh News & Observer*, April 28, 1960; L. F. Palmer, "Violence Fails to Halt 'Sit-In,'" *CD*, March 23, 1960, 9; "A Passive Insister: Ezell Blair Jr.," *NYT*, March 26, 1960, 10; Chafe, *Civilities and Civil Rights*, 94.
50. Ralph McGill, "New Laws, Old Fears," *Reporter*, June 9, 1960, 31–34, at 32.
51. Chafe, *Civilities and Civil Rights*, 111–12; Adams, "Aim Fall Sit-Ins." In line with most accounts from the time of the sit-ins, Chafe emphasizes the extent of support older blacks in Greensboro had for the students. *Civilities and Civil Rights*, 131–35, 137. Morris makes the same claim on a more general level. *Origins*, chap. 9. According to a survey of student activists in May 1960, few of their parents discouraged their participation and most

encouraged it. Wehr, "Sit-Down Protests," 84, 101. Students also reported financial and moral support from black businessmen. Ibid., 84. I discuss black community support further in chapter 4.

There was occasional organized black opposition to the sit-ins: some black newspapers, including the *Charlotte Post* and *Atlanta World*, initially opposed the protests. For the most part, however, whatever resistance there was from the black community was expressed through quieter forms of disapproval. Wehr, "Sit-Down Protests," 83; "Georgia Negro Unit Opposes N.A.A.C.P.," *NYT*, April 16, 1960, 18; Walker, "Functions of Disunity," 229. I consider African American opposition to the sit-ins in more detail in chapter 5.

52. For example, the Freedom Rides in 1961, while raising hard questions of strategy and personal safety, had the benefit of having clearly defined federal law on the side of the protesters. The Supreme Court had issued a long line of decisions on the issue at the heart of the Freedom Rides: the right to non-segregated service on interstate transportation. Mitchell v. United States, 313 U.S. 80 (1941); Morgan v. Virginia, 328 U.S. 373 (1946); Henderson v. United States, 339 U.S. 816 (1950); Boynton v. Virginia, 364 U.S. 454 (1960). Unlike the sit-ins, the Freedom Rides were in direct response to a Supreme Court decision. A precursor to the Freedom Rides, the 1947 Journey of Reconciliation, was designed specifically to test the *Morgan* decision, and the Freedom Rides were a response to the failure to enforce the 1960 Supreme Court decision in *Boynton*. See Raymond Arsenault, *Freedom Rides: 1961 and the Struggle for Racial Justice* (New York: Oxford University Press, 2006), 92–93.

53. Cohen, *A Consumers' Republic*; Searles and Williams, "Negro College Students Participation"; Carson, *In Struggle*, 13.

54. Martin Luther King Jr., "The Burning Truth in the South," *Progressive* 24 (May 1960): 8, reprinted in *King Papers*, 5:449; Raines, *My Soul Is Rested*, 76 (interview with Franklin McCain); Dabbs, "Dime Stores and Dignity," 289, 291; Major Johns, "Baton Rouge: Higher Education—Southern Style," in *Sit-Ins: The Students Report*, 13 ("a small thing"). On Nashville, see Halberstam, *Children*, 90–91; Raines, *My Soul Is Rested*, 98 (interview with John Lewis).

55. Louis E. Lomax, "The Negro Revolt Against 'The Negro Leaders,'" *Harper's* (June 1960): 41–48, at 48; Lewis M. Killian and Charles M. Grigg, "Rank Orders of Discrimination of Negroes and Whites in a Southern City," *Social Forces 39* (1961): 235–39; Jack L. Walker, "Protest and Negotiation: A Case Study of Negro Leadership in Atlanta, Georgia," *Midwest Journal of Political Science* 7 (1963): 99–124, at 109–11.

56. "Cafe Push Spreads to Tennessee," *AC*, February 20, 1960, 2 ("the papers"). On the importance of the media in spreading the sit-ins, see Oppenheimer, "Genesis," 61–62; Laue, *Direct Action*, 81; Wehr, "Sit-Down Protests," 25; Gene Roberts and Hank Klibanoff, *The Race Beat: The Press,*

the Civil Rights Struggle, and the Awakening of a Nation (New York: Knopf, 2006), 222–27; Andrews and Biggs, "Dynamics of Protest Diffusion," 764, 769–70.

57. Bagdikian, "Negro Youth's New March," 16 ("strange fever"); Wehr, "Sit-Down Protests," 25; Morris, *Origins*, 196–97; McAdam, *Political Process*, 138; Walzer, "A Cup of Coffee"; Oberschall, *Social Movements*, 226–28; Searles and Williams, "Negro College Students Participation," 219; Laue, *Direct Action*, 82.

58. Morris, *Origins*, 196–203. Biggs finds that church attendance actually correlated with *less* involvement in civil rights protest—although being a member of a church that was part of a civil rights activist network increased the probability of being involved in the movement. "Who Joined the Sit-ins," 330.

59. Morris, *Origins*, 188–215; McAdam, *Political Process*, chap. 6. But see Andrews and Biggs, "Dynamics of Protest Diffusion," 763 (questioning the prominence of SCLC as a driving force in the sit-in movement based on a statistical comparison of cities that had sit-in protests and cities that did not).

60. "Youth Leadership Meeting," available at http://www.crmvet.org/docs/6004_sncc_call.pdf; Baker, "Bigger than a Hamburger." At the conference, Baker struggled with SCLC leaders who hoped to organize the students as a youth branch of their organization. She ultimately prevailed in ensuring the SNCC would remain independent from any existing civil rights groups. James Forman, *The Making of Black Revolutionaries* (New York: Macmillan, 1972), 216–17; Carson, *In Struggle*, chap. 2; Barbara Ransby, *Ella Baker and the Black Freedom Movement: A Radical Democratic Vision* (Chapel Hill: University of North Carolina Press, 2003), 239–47.

61. "Delegates to Youth Leadership Conference," April 21, 1960, available at http://www.crmvet.org/docs/6004_shaw_delegations.pdf; Sitton, "Racial Problems Put to President," 21; "142 Students Push Integration Drive," *AC*, April 18, 1960, 5; Ted Dienstfrey, "Conference on the Sit-Ins," *Commentary* 30 (January 1960): 524–28.

62. Morris, *Origins*, 218–20. See generally Carson, *In Struggle*.

63. Doug McAdam, "Tactical Innovation and the Pace of Insurgency," *ASR* 48 (1983): 735–754, at 743. See also Oberschall, *Social Movements*, 225–26.

64. Oppenheimer, "Southern Student Movement," 399. See also Alvin C. Adams, " 'And Then We'll Win,' Vows Sit-In Students," *CD*, March 29, 1960, 7.

65. Bagdikian, "Negro Youth's New March," 16 ("release"); Willard Clopton, "Campuses Get Noisy in Behalf of Lunch Sit-Ins," *WP*, April 23, 1960, D1 ("truce with honor"); "Sit-In," NBC White Paper, No. 2, aired on December 20, 1960, at 19:45 ("needed"); Zinn, *SNCC*, 14 ("Devil").

66. Bagdikian, "Negro Youth's New March," 16. Accounts of jail experiences ran the spectrum, from horrific to tedious to humorous. Patricia Stephens, who was jailed in Tallahassee, recalled writing songs, poems, and articles

with her fellow protesters during her time in jail. "Leader of Sit-In Movement Hailed by Negro Newspapermen." A white civil rights activist who had "been arrested so many times I've given up counting," recounted, "Some of those police know the handwriting on the wall, laugh about the whole thing with us. Others are real sadists. Turn on the hot air in summer to burn you up or let you freeze in winter, or mess your food up, and swear, can they swear!" Robert Coles, "Serpents and Doves: Non-Violent Youth in the South," in *Youth: Change and Challenge*, ed. Erik Erikson (New York: Basic Books 1963), 203.

67. Walzer, "A Cup of Coffee," 112 ("cup of coffee"); "Negroes Extend Sitdown Protests" ("leave a tip"); "Negroes Fight Back in the South," *AN*, February 16, 1960, 1 ("We don't care"); Hentoff, "A Peaceful Army," 277 ("visible results").

68. "Some Negroes Served," *NYT*, March 8, 1960, 23; Patrick, *Lunch Counter Desegregation*, 6, 12; "Sit-Down Action Wins Two Victories," *CD*, March 9, 1960, 2; "Sit-Ins Break Oklahoma Bias," *CD*, March 19, 1960, 3; "Both Races Accept Move by 5 Stores," *NYT*, March 20, 1960, 1; "Freeze & Thaw," *Time*, March 28, 1960, 26; "Galveston Becomes Second Texas City to Desegregate Its Lunch Counters," *WP*, April 6, 1960, A14; SRC, "Postscript"; SRC, "A Follow-Up Report"; Laue, *Direct Action*, 77.

   For a quantitative analysis of the connection between sit-in protests and lunch counter desegregation, see Michael Biggs and Kenneth T. Andrews, "Protest Campaigns and Movement Success: Desegregating the U.S. South in the Early 1960s," *ASR* 80 (2015): 1–28.

69. Laue, *Direct Action*, 77; "Nashville Protest Resumes," *NYT*, April 12, 1960, 29; Salisbury, "Nashville Issue Is Full Equality," 20; Laprad, "Nashville," 8; C. Eric Lincoln, "The Strategy of a Sit-In," *Reporter*, January 5, 1961, 20–24, at 22; "'Segregation on Death Bed,'" *CD*, April 30, 1960, 1 ("best organized"); "Bombing Rips House, Hosp. in Nashville," *ADW*, April 20, 1960, 1; "Blast Home of Sit-In Lawyer," *CD*, April 30, 1960, 12; NBC, "Sit-In"; Oppenheimer, *Sit-In Movement*, 124–30; "Sit-In Results," *NYT*, May 15, 1960, E12; Robert S. Bird, "Key to Racial Calm: 'Preparation,'" *NYHT*, May 15, 1960, 1, 26.

70. "It Happened in Nashville," *Reporter*, May 26, 1960, 2–4 ("carefully chosen"; "eating a hamburger"); "The Nashville Story," *CT*, May 13, 1960, 12 ("dignity"); "Negroes Win Dining Rights in Nashville," *CT*, May 11, 1960, A1; "Nashville Integrates Six Lunch Counters," *NYT*, May 11, 1960, 1; Robert S. Bird, "Local Eating Going Well in Nashville," *NYHT*, May 12, 1960, 24; "Sit-In Results"; "Sit-Ins Win in Tennessee," *AN*, May 14, 1960, 1; "Settlement in Nashville," *Time*, May 23, 1960.

   Other cities followed Nashville's carefully crafted approach to integrating their lunch counters. Patrick, *Lunch Counter Desegregation*, 19–22; Lawson, "From Sit-In to Race Riot," 266–67; Oppenheimer, *Sit-In Movement*, 129.

71. Susanna McBee, "2 Drug Outlets, 3 Major Stores Desegregate Arlington Counters," *WP*, June 23, 1960, A1; Susanna McBee, "More Dining Places Drop Racial Bars," *WP*, June 24, 1960, A1; Anthony Lewis, "7 Restaurants Open to Virginia Negroes," *NYT*, June 24, 2016, 1, 19; Susanna McBee, "Most Eating Places Drop Racial Bar," *WP*, June 25, 1960, A11; J. W. Anderson, "Open Lunch Counters Set Precedent," *WP*, June 26, 1960, E2; Oppenheimer, *Sit-In Movement*, 121–23; "More Counters Open in Southern Cities," *AN*, July 16, 1960, 4; "Two Stores Integrate Counters," *GDN*, July 26, 1960, B1 ("quietly"); Editorial, "A Quiet Denouement," *GDN*, July 27, 1960, A8 ("sky"); "'Sit-Iner' Says '13' to Go in Greensboro," *CD*, August 13, 1960, 20; Wolff, *Lunch at the 5 & 10*, 167–76; "Sit-Ins Victorious Where They Began," *NYT*, July 26, 1960, 1, 19.

    There were also reports of desegregated service at several lunch counters in Tallahassee in early June. "Report Florida Sit-In Victory," *CD*, June 11, 1960, 1.

72. Laue, *Direct Action*, 88; Oppenheimer, "Genesis," 271–72; Margaret Price, "Why Some Areas Solve 'Sit-Ins,'" *CD*, July 2, 1960, 8. See also Claude Sitton, "Stores in South Prosper with Integrated Counters," *NYT*, June 6, 1960, 1; Margaret Price, "Toward a Solution of the Sit-In Controversy" (SRC report), May 31, 1960, NAACP Papers (microfilm), Part 21, Reel 21, Frame 783; United States Commission on Civil Rights, *Freedom to the Free* (Washington, DC: Government Printing Office, 1963), 177.

73. *CORE-lator*, April 1960, 1; "Sit-In Staff Opens Ga. Office," *CD*, May 30, 1960, 4 (Barry quotation); Dunbar, "Reflection," 255; Clayborne Carson interview with David Richmond, April 10, 1972, William Henry Chafe Oral History Collection, David M. Rubenstein Rare Book & Manuscript Library, Duke University. See also Coles, "Serpents and Doves," 190; Maurice Pinard, Jerome Kirk, and Donald von Eschen, "Processes of Recruitment in the Sit-in Movement," *Public Opinion Quarterly* 33 (1969): 355–69, at 369.

74. "Negro Protest Lead to Store Closing," *NYT*, February 7, 1960, 35; "Sitdown Leader Persists in Goal," *NYT*, March 26, 1960, 10; "Protest Move Hits Virginia," *CD*, February 16, 1960, A1; Halberstam, "Good City Gone Ugly," 19; "Negro Sitdown Protest Spreads in South," *NYHT*, February 21, 1960, 21; "Lunch Places in South Close or Serve Negroes Standing," *BS*, February 21, 1960, 3 ("claim a victory").

    Not all agreed on whether the creation of interracial committees was an accomplishment for the movement or not. Lawson dismissed them as a waste of time. Helen Fuller, "Southern Students Take Over," *NR*, May 2, 1960, 14–16, at 16. For analyses of these committees, see Oppenheimer, *Sit-In Movement*, 52–54; Charles M. Grigg and Lewis M. Killian, "The Bi-Racial Committee as a Response to Racial Tensions in Southern Cities," *Phylon* 23 (1962): 379–82.

75. "Sit-Downs: Arrests Are Setting Stage for More Court Action," *NYT*, April 3, 1960, E7; Wehr, "Sit-Down Protests," 44; McAdam, "Tactical Innovation," 744.

76. "Children in Sit-In," *NYT*, June 18, 1960, 11; Oppenheimer, "Southern Student Movement," 401; Knoxville Area Human Relations Council, "A Chronology of Negotiations for Lunch Counter Desegregation in Knoxville, Tennessee," July 18, 1960; Merrill Proudfoot, *Diary of a Sit-In* (Chapel Hill: University of North Carolina Press, 1962); Cynthia Griggs Fleming, "White Lunch Counters and Black Consciousness: The Story of the Knoxville Sit-Ins," *Tennessee Historical Quarterly* 49 (1990): 40–52.

77. Baker, "Bigger than a Hamburger"; Oppenheimer, "Southern Student Movement," 402; Griffin v. Maryland, 378 U.S. 130 (1964); Elsie Carper, "Wade-Ins Next in Fight on Bias," *WP*, June 24, 1960, A14.

78. Posey, *Why I Sit*; Statement Submitted by the Student Nonviolent Coordinating Committee to the Platform Committee of the National Democratic Convention, July 7, 1960, available at http://www.crmvet.org/docs/6007 _sncc_demconv-platform.pdf.

CHAPTER TWO

1. "NAACP Sits Down with the 'Sit-Inners,'" *AN*, March 26, 1960, 1, 24, at 24.

2. Clarence Mitchell to Roy Wilkins, April 18, 1960, NAACP Papers, Part III, Series A, Container 289, Folder: "Washington Bureau," LOC, Manuscript Division.

3. LDF was formed in 1940 as a formally, if not functionally, independent, tax-exempt litigation arm of the NAACP. In order to preserve its tax-exempt status, in 1957 LDF became completely independent of the NAACP. Mark V. Tushnet, *Making Civil Rights Law: Thurgood Marshall and the Supreme Court, 1936–1961* (New York: Oxford University Press, 1994), 310–11. For an inside account of the relations between the NAACP and LDF, which became increasingly tense in the 1960s, see Jack Greenberg, *Crusaders in the Courts: How a Dedicated Band of Lawyers Fought for the Civil Rights Revolution* (New York: Basic Books, 1994).

4. When discussing attitudes within the NAACP toward any civil rights issue, it is important to acknowledge divisions within the organization. The NAACP was never monolithic. Considerable intra-organizational variation could be found on a number of levels: national office versus local branches; southern versus northern; rural versus urban; leaders versus rank-and-file members. See, for example, *Long Is the Way and Hard: One Hundred Years of the NAACP*, ed. Kevern Verney and Lee Sartain (Fayetteville: University of Arkansas Press, 2009).

   On support for the students by local NAACP leaders, see William H. Chafe, *Civilities and Civil Rights: Greensboro, North Carolina, and the Black Struggle for Freedom* (New York: Oxford University Press, 1980), 84; Stephen

Tuck, *Beyond Atlanta: The Struggle for Racial Equality in Georgia, 1940–1980* (Athens: University of Georgia Press, 2003), 155; Tomiko Brown-Nagin, *Courage to Dissent: Atlanta and the Long History of the Civil Rights Movement* (New York: Oxford University Press, 2011), 355; Thomas Bynum, *NAACP Youth and the Fight for Black Freedom, 1936–1965* (Knoxville: University of Tennessee Press, 2013), 100–106.

5. Brown v. Board of Education, 347 U.S. 483 (1954); "A Historic Decision for Equality," *Life*, May 31, 1954, 11, 14; Editorial, "Emancipation," *WP*, May 18, 1954, 14.

6. "The Tension of Change," *Time*, September 19, 1955, 25; Brown v. Board of Education, 349 U.S. 294 (1955); Richard Kluger, *Simple Justice: The History of* Brown v. the Board of Education *and Black America's Struggle for Equality* (New York: Knopf, 1976), 746–47 ("damned good"); Tushnet, *Making Civil Rights Law*, 268 ("licked"). See also Roy Wilkins and Thurgood Marshall, Memorandum to Emergency Regional Conference, June 4, 1955, NAACP Papers (microfilm), Part 3, Series C, Reel 14 ("In the overwhelming majority of instances, it can be expected that compliance without legal action will be the rule, perhaps grudgingly and reluctantly in some areas, but compliance, nevertheless.").

7. "Declaration of Constitutional Principles," *Congressional Record* 102, 84th Cong., 2nd Sess., pt. 4:4459–60 (March 12, 1956); Anthony Lewis, *Portrait of a Decade: The Second American Revolution* (New York: Random House, 1964), 45; Greenberg, *Crusaders*, 226; Tushnet, *Making Civil Rights Law*, 268. See also Justin Driver, "Supremacies and the Southern Manifesto," *Texas Law Review* 92 (2014): 1053–135.

In the midst of the University of Alabama controversy, a journalist asked Marshall about the possibility of continuous litigation victories with no actual integration to show for it. "I don't know what we'd do," he responded. "That's something I can't even contemplate. It would be anarchy. It would be the end of the country. I can't imagine it coming to that." The journalist was struck by "the concreteness, the calm, the serene feeling of assurance that the law would eventually prevail." Bernard Taper, "A Meeting in Atlanta," *New Yorker*, March 17, 1956, 80–127, at 114, 123. It was this deep-seated faith in the power of the law that made subsequent failure to integrate the University of Alabama and repeated setbacks in the struggle to implement *Brown* in public schools such disillusioning experiences for Marshall and his colleagues. See Christopher W. Schmidt, "'Freedom Comes Only from the Law': The Debate over Law's Capacity and the Making of *Brown v. Board of Education*," *Utah Law Review* (2008): 1493–559.

8. Michael J. Klarman, *From Jim Crow to Civil Rights: The Supreme Court and the Struggle for Racial Equality* (New York: Oxford University Press, 2004), 348 ("first round"); Lewis, *Portrait of a Decade*, 46.

9. See Greenberg, *Crusaders*, 217–21; Klarman, *From Jim Crow*, 335–39; Walter F. Murphy, "The South Counterattacks: The Anti-NAACP Laws," *Western*

Political Quarterly 12 (1959): 371–90; Harry Kalven Jr., *The Negro and the First Amendment* (Chicago: University of Chicago Press, 1965); Christopher W. Schmidt, *"New York Times v. Sullivan* and the Legal Attack on the Civil Rights Movement," *Alabama Law Review* 66 (2014): 293–335, at 299–301.

10. Report of Robert L. Carter, General Counsel, Annual Meeting, NAACP, Jan. 4, 1960, NAACP Papers (microfilm), Part 22, Reel 22, Frame 402 ("forecast"); Wayne Phillips, "School Integration Has Passed Its Crisis, Negro Leader Says," *NYT*, January 3, 1960, 1 ("fast play"; "holding action"); "Deep South Firm on Segregation," *NYT*, January 10, 1960, 64 ("serious possibility").

11. "NAACP Sits Down," 24 ("by surprise"); John Morsell, Memorandum for Staff Discussion, May 2, 1960, NAACP Papers, Part III, Series A, Container 308, Folder: "Staff, Farmer, James, Memoranda, 1960–61" ("soul-searching"); Louis E. Lomax, "The Negro Revolt Against 'The Negro Leaders,'" *Harper's* (June 1960): 41–48, at 41.

     NAACP supporters predictably attacked Lomax's article. In the *Atlanta Daily World*, Louis Lautier described it as "a cleverly written piece, interlaced with half truths and innuendos which make it difficult to separate the true from the false." "In the Nation's Capitol: Absurd Conclusions," *ADW*, June 10, 1960, 6. See also George S. Schuyler, "Views and Reviews," *PC*, June 11, 1960, 13.

12. Robert L. Carter to John Morsell, May 5, 1960, NAACP Papers, Part III, Series A, Container 308, Folder: "Staff, Farmer, James, Memoranda, 1960–61" ("a 'me too'"); James Farmer to John Morsell, May 6, 1960, ibid. ("every discussion"). LDF staff attorney Constance Baker Motley later recalled: "To say that the students' boldness sent shock waves throughout the organized civil rights community is an understatement. . . . Stunned by the daring and lack of preparation of the students, neither the NAACP nor LDF initially offered legal assistance. We, like everybody else, had been caught off guard." Constance Baker Motley, *Equal Justice under Law* (New York: Farrar, Straus & Giroux, 1998), 131. See also Greenberg, *Crusaders*, 269.

13. Greenberg, *Crusaders*, 277 ("nearly impossible"); Juan Williams, *Thurgood Marshall: American Revolutionary* (New York: Times Books, 1998), 241, 245–52; Tushnet, *Making Civil Rights Law*, 301–13; "The Reminiscences of Thurgood Marshall," in *Thurgood Marshall: His Speeches, Writings, Arguments, Opinions, and Reminiscences*, ed. Mark V. Tushnet (Chicago: Lawrence Hill, 2001), 471 ("I used to have a lot of fights with [King] about his theory about disobeying the law. I didn't believe in that."); Motley, *Equal Justice*, 152; Raymond Arsenault, *Freedom Rides: 1961 and the Struggle for Racial Justice* (New York: Oxford University Press, 2006), 36–37.

14. Mary L. Dudziak, "Working toward Democracy: Thurgood Marshall and the Constitution of Kenya," *Duke Law Journal* 56 (2006): 721–80; Derrick Bell, "An Epistolary Exploration for a Thurgood Marshall Biography," *Harvard Blackletter Law Journal* 6 (1989): 51–67, at 55; Motley, *Equal Justice*, 149.

Motley recalled that only she and James Nabrit Jr. felt the students might have a viable legal claim, although she also noted, "We did not have a clue in 1960 as to a successful legal theory to end discrimination in places of public accommodation." Motley, *Equal Justice*, 132, 149.

15. The sit-ins were (and still are) often described as acts of civil disobedience. See, for example, Charles L. Black, "The Problems of the Compatibility of Civil Disobedience with American Institutions of Government," *Texas Law Review* 34 (1965): 492–506, at 497; Burke Marshall, "The Protest Movement and the Law," *Virginia Law Review* 51 (1965): 785–803, at 796. They do not obviously fit the category, however. In most cases, lunch counter operators did not choose to press charges and thus the sit-in protesters did not actually break any laws. Even when the students were charged with a crime, such as trespass, disorderly conduct, or disturbing the peace, they could be said to be engaging in only an *indirect* form of civil disobedience. The laws they were breaking were not the actual targets of the protest; the targets of the protest were segregation laws and practices. See Hugo A. Bedau, "On Civil Disobedience," *Journal of Philosophy* 58 (1961): 653–65, at 657; Carl Cohen, *Disobedience: Conscience, Tactics, and the Law* (New York: Columbia University Press, 1971), 51.

   Thoreau's refusal to pay taxes as an act of protest against U.S. foreign policy is the classic example of an indirect act of civil disobedience in which a "secondary" law is broken. This distinction can also be captured in the legal philosopher Ronald Dworkin's distinction between "integrity-based" civil disobedience (refusing to follow a law when doing so would violate one's conscience, such as an abolitionist ignoring the Fugitive Slave Act or a Jehovah's Witness refusing to salute the flag) and "justice-based" civil disobedience (breaking the law in order to demonstrate opposition to unjust policy or practices, such as lunch counter sit-ins or certain anti-war protests). Ronald Dworkin, *A Matter of Principle* (Cambridge, MA: Harvard University Press, 1985), 107.

   In his "Letter from Birmingham Jail," Martin Luther King Jr. addressed the question of whether breaking a secondary law, such as a trespass law or a parade permit requirement, is properly considered an act of civil disobedience. (He was in jail because he had led a protest march after local officials denied a parade permit and a local judge ordered him to call off the march.) "Sometimes a law is just on its face and unjust in application," he noted. *A Testament of Hope: The Essential Writings and Speeches of Martin Luther King, Jr.*, ed. James M. Washington (New York: HarperOne, 1986), 294. For King, a trespassing or disorderly conduct law used against lunch counter protesters was precisely this kind of law: facially just but applied to further discriminatory ends.

16. Bell, "Epistolary Exploration," 55–56; Tushnet, *Making Civil Rights Law*, 40, 310; Greenberg, *Crusaders*, 273.

17. The most recent cases in which courts had confronted the state action question in this context went against the students' constitutional claim.

See Williams v. Howard Johnson's Restaurant, 268 F.2d 845 (4th Cir. 1959); State v. Clyburn, 247 N.C. 455, 101 S.E.2d. 295 (1958).

Even as LDF lawyers were strategizing their response, a federal district court in Baltimore, in a suit brought by *Amsterdam News* reporter Sara Slack after she was denied service at a White Tower restaurant in 1957, came to the same conclusion: that a private restaurant, even if it was a branch of a national chain, was not a state actor under the Fourteenth Amendment. Slack v. Atlantic White Tower System, 181 F. Supp. 124 (D. Md. 1960). Slack's lawyers saw hope in defeat. "Great!" one responded. "This paves the way for a Supreme Court ruling." "Court Rules against Our Sara Slack," *AN*, February 20, 1960, 1, 35, at 35. As it turned out, this case went no further than a federal appeals court, which upheld the upheld the lower court's ruling, 284 F.2d 746 (4th Cir. 1960).

18. James Feron, "N.A.A.C.P. Plans Student Defense," *NYT*, March 18, 1960, 23 ("check the law"); "Negroes Plan Tests on Legal Fronts," *NYT*, March 20, 1960, E8 ("all the stops"); Thurgood Marshall, "The Cry for Freedom," *Crisis* (May 1960): 287–90 (speech before NAACP Meeting in Charlotte, North Carolina, March 20, 1960). See also "Lawyers Conference on Sit-In Protests Slated," *ADW*, March 12, 1960, 1; "Calls Lawyers Confab on 'Sit-In' Campaign," *CD*, March 19, 1960, 1; James E. Warner, "Lawyers Map Defense for South Sit-In," *NYHT*, March 20, 1960, 15; Jack Greenberg, "The Case against Jim Crow Eating," *New Leader*, March 14, 1960, 7–9.

19. "NAACP Sits Down," 24; Marsh v. Alabama, 326 U.S. 501, 506 (1946). See also Warner, "Lawyers Map Defense"; "Lauds Negro Students," *NYT*, April 4, 1960, 33; "NAACP Position on Jail, No Bail," n.d., NAACP Papers, Part III, Series A, Container 289, Folder: "Sit-Ins, General, 1960, June–Nov."

20. Shelley v. Kraemer, 334 U.S. 1 (1948); Marshall, "Cry for Freedom," 289 ("full strength"); "NAACP Sits Down," 24 ("violated"). See also "Lawyers Agree on Plan for Defense of 1,000 Arrested in South," *NYT*, March 20, 1960, 1, 46.

21. "Sitdowns Issue Faces Legal Test," *NYT*, February 29, 1960, 18.

22. "NAACP Sits Down," 24.

23. Gayle v. Browder, 352 U.S. 903 (1956); Harris Wofford, *Of Kennedys and Kings: Making Sense of the Sixties* (New York: Farrar, Straus & Giroux, 1980), 119 ("All that walking"). On the legal history of the bus boycott, see Randall Kennedy, "Martin Luther King's Constitution: A Legal History of the Montgomery Bus Boycott," *Yale Law Journal* 98 (1989): 999–1067; Robert Jerome Glennon, "The Role of Law in the Civil Rights Movement: The Montgomery Bus Boycott, 1955–1957," *LHR* 9 (1991): 59–112; Christopher Coleman, Laurence D. Nee, and Leonard S. Rubinowitz, "Social Movements and Social Change Litigation: Synergy in the Montgomery Bus Protest," *LSI* 30 (2005): 663–737.

24. Untitled, undated memorandum, NAACP Papers (microfilm), Part 22, Reel 3, Frames 374–75. On the growing costs of defending the students in

court, see Langston Hughes, *Fight for Freedom: The Story of the NAACP* (New York: Norton, 1962), 183–84. This financial strain lessened somewhat by the flow of contributions that came into the LDF offices in support of the protests. As a result of the sit-ins and then the Freedom Rides in 1961, the number of contributors to LDF shot up and its annual income went from $361,000 in 1959 to $500,000 in 1960 and $586,000 in 1961. Greenberg, *Crusaders*, 292.

25. "NAACP Position on Jail, No Bail" ("main objective"); Aldon D. Morris, *The Origins of the Civil Rights Movement: Black Communities Organizing for Change* (New York: Free Press, 1984), 317 n. 64 ("in the courtroom").

26. James R. Robinson, "The Meaning of the Sit-Ins," memorandum prepared for June 8, 1960, meeting of civil rights organizations, 4, NAACP Papers, Part III, Series A, Container 308, Folder: "Staff, Farmer, James, General, 1960, June–Sept." On the Atlanta sit-in movement, see C. Eric Lincoln, "The Strategy of a Sit-In," *Reporter*, January 5, 1961, 20–24; Jack L. Walker, "Protest and Negotiation: A Case Study of Negro Leadership in Atlanta, Georgia," *Midwest Journal of Political Science* 7 (1963): 99–124; Kevin Kruse, *White Flight: Atlanta and the Making of Modern Conservatism* (Princeton, NJ: Princeton University Press, 2005), 184; Brown-Nagin, *Courage to Dissent*, 143–58; Ted Lippman, "No More Sitdowns Now, Students Say," *AC*, March 17, 1960, 1, 12; Marion Gaines, "Negroes, Whites Picket Store Here," *AC*, March 26, 1960, 5; Martin Oppenheimer, *The Sit-In Movement of 1960* (New York: Carlson, 1989), 134–36; Maurice C. Daniels, *Saving the Soul of Georgia: Donald L. Hollowell and the Struggle for Civil Rights* (Athens: University of Georgia Press, 2013), 107.

27. Martin Luther King, Jr., "A Creative Protest," February 16, 1960, in *The Papers of Martin Luther King, Jr.*, vol. 5, ed. Clayborne Carson et al. (Berkeley: University of California Press, 1992), 369; Robinson, "Meaning of the Sit-Ins." King's vision of using the courtrooms and jails as a rallying tool for the movement was informed by his experience in the Montgomery bus boycott. See Kennedy, "Martin Luther King's Constitution," 1029, 1064–65.

28. Claude Sitton, "Racial Problems Put to President," *NYT*, April 18, 1960, 21; Helen Fuller, "Southern Students Take Over," *NR*, May 2, 1960, 14–16, at 16; Records from Raleigh Conference, Summary of Conclusions of Workshop on "Legalism," SNCC Papers, 1959–1972 (microfilm), Reel 1, Frame 7; Chafe, *Civilities and Civil Rights*, 94; Robinson, "Meaning of the Sit-Ins." Conference chairman Marion Barry explained that the student position was aimed at the pre-trial choice of bail versus jail, not necessarily to the choice of jail versus paying a fine after conviction. Sitton, "Racial Problems."

29. Robinson, "Meaning of the Sit-Ins"; untitled, undated memorandum, NAACP Papers (microfilm), Part 22, Reel 3, Frame 376.

30. "NAACP Position on Jail, No Bail." See also Charles H. Thompson, "Desegregation Pushed Off Dead Center," *JNE* 29 (1960): 107–11, at 110.

31. John Lewis with Michael D'Orso, *Walking with the Wind: A Memoir of the Movement* (New York: Simon and Schuster, 1998), 113–14.

32. Clarence Mitchell to Roy Wilkins, April 18, 1960, NAACP Papers, Part III, Series A, Container 289, Folder: "Washington Bureau"; Roy Wilkins, Remarks at a Mass Meeting of the Jackson, Mississippi, NAACP Branch, June 7, 1961, reprinted in *Black Protest Thought in the Twentieth Century*, 2nd ed., ed. August Meier, Elliott Rudwick, and Francis Broderick (Indianapolis: Bobbs-Merrill, 1971), 316–22 at 317, 321, 322. See also Robert Coles, "Serpents and Doves: Non-Violent Youth in the South," in *Youth: Change and Challenge*, ed. Erik Erikson (New York: Basic Books 1963), 200 (quoting an African American college student activist explaining, "When I go back to school I'll take law. . . . [I]t's the best way to fight them [segregationists] when you get older and have to settle down. . . . [I]t's the same thing, we're doing one part of the job and they're doing another. . . . [W]e need Negro lawyers in the South.").

33. Newton H. Fulbright, "2 Southern Negro Students Tell of Dining-Bias Fight," *NYHT*, March 1, 1960, 12 ("100 per cent"); "Urge NAACP to Back Sit-Downs," *CD*, February 27, 1960, 22 ("legitimate expressions"); John Morsell, Memorandum for Staff Discussion, n.d., NAACP Papers (microfilm), Part 22, Reel 9, Frame 216 ("amplify"); *The Day They Changed Their Minds*, NAACP pamphlet, March 1960, 4, available at www.loc .gov/exhibits/naacp/the-civil-rights-era.html#obj19; Special Report on Sitdowns, NAACP Branch Department, n.d., NAACP Papers (microfilm), Part 21, Reel 22, Frame 69 ("continuation"); Herbert L. Wright, memorandum to Roy Wilkins, Re: Report on Sit-Down Protests, March 2, 1960, NAACP Papers, Part III, Series A, Container 290, Folder: "Sit-Ins, North Carolina, 1960–61"; "The Role of the NAACP in the 'Sit-Ins,'" May 1960, ibid. See also Robert C. Weaver, "The NAACP Today," *JNE* 29 (1960): 421; Roy Wilkins, *Standing Fast: The Autobiography of Roy Wilkins* (New York: Viking, 1982), 259–60.

34. Annual Report of the General Counsel, January 1961, NAACP Papers (microfilm), Part 22, Reel 22, Frame 410 ("made inevitable"); "Sit-In Protests Hailed" (letter to the editor), *NYT*, April 26, 1960, 36.

35. "Plan Step-Up in Sit-In Protests," *CD*, March 23, 1960, 5. See also "Along the N.A.A.C.P. Battlefront: On the 'Sit-In' Strikes," *Crisis* (May 1960): 313–19.

36. James Q. Wilson, "The Strategy of Protest: Problems of Negro Civic Action," *Journal of Conflict Resolution* 5 (1961): 291–303, at 299–300; Ben H. Bagdikian, "Negro Youth's New March on Dixie," *Saturday Evening Post*, September 8, 1962, 15–19, at 18 ("loyalty"); Brown-Nagin, *Courage to Dissent*, 135; Thurgood Marshall to Marion Barry, August 4, 1960, NAACP Papers, Part III, Series A, Container 289, Folder: "Sit-Ins, General, 1960, June–Nov."

37. Morris, *Origins*, 39; Leslie Dunbar, "Reflection on the Latest Reform of the South," *Phylon* 22 (1961): 249–57, at 252–53.

38. Robinson, "Meaning of the Sit-Ins," 4; Roy Wilkins, memorandum to NAACP Branch Officers, April 1960, NAACP Papers, Part III, Series A, Container 289, Folder: "Sit-Ins, General, 1961–64." See also James R. Robinson, "To Achieve Integration" (letter to the editor), *NYT*, May 7, 1960, 22; Martin Luther King Jr., *Why We Can't Wait* (1964; repr., New York: Signet, 2000), 28–29; Wilkins, *Standing Fast*, 238.

39. See Brown-Nagin, *Courage to Dissent*, chap. 7; Francesca Polletta, "The Structural Context of Novel Rights Claims: Southern Civil Rights Organizing, 1961–1966," *Law & Society Review* 34 (2000): 367–406, at 380–81.

    Once past the initial trial stage, the litigation was largely out of the hands—and sometimes out of the minds—of the student protesters. Robert Mack Bell, the lead defendant in the most important of the sit-in cases, Bell v. Maryland, 378 U.S. 226 (1964), was not even following his case when it reached the U.S. Supreme Court. Peter Irons, *The Courage of Their Convictions: Sixteen Americans Who Fought Their Way to the Supreme Court* (New York: Free Press, 1988), 141–52; Kenneth W. Mack, "Civil Disobedience, State Action, and Lawmaking Outside the Courts: Robert Bell's Encounter with American Law," *Journal of Supreme Court History* 39 (2014): 347–71, at 366–67.

CHAPTER THREE

1. Editorial, "Negro Protests," *Commonweal* 72 (April 1, 1960): 4–5, at 4.
2. "The Sympathizers," *Time*, April 11, 1960, 66.
3. Martin Luther King Jr., Address to Charlotte, North Carolina, Branch of the NAACP, September 25, 1960, available at http://www.thekingcenter.org/archive/document/mlk-address-north-carolina-branch-naacp.
4. See Larry Kramer, *The People Themselves* (New York: Oxford University Press, 2004); Mark Tushnet, *Taking the Constitution Away from the Courts* (Princeton, NJ: Princeton University Press, 1999); Robert C. Post, "Foreword: Fashioning the Legal Constitution: Culture, Courts, and Law," *Harvard Law Review* 117 (2003): 4–112; Robert Post and Reva Siegel, "Popular Constitutionalism, Departmentalism, and Judicial Supremacy," *California Law Review* 92 (2004): 1027–44; Mark Tushnet, "Popular Constitutionalism as Political Law," *Chicago-Kent Law Review* 81 (2006): 991–1006; Christopher W. Schmidt, "Popular Constitutionalism on the Right: Lessons from the Tea Party," *Denver University Law Review* 88 (2011): 523–57; Sean Beienburg and Paul Frymer, "The People Against Themselves: Rethinking Popular Constitutionalism," *LSI* 41 (2016): 242–66.
5. Civil Rights Act of 1875, 18 Stat. 335; Civil Rights Cases, 109 U.S. 3 (1883). On racial justice activism at the turn of the century, see Susan D. Carle, *Defining the Struggle: National Organizing for Racial Justice, 1880–1915* (New York: Oxford University Press, 2013). On northern public accommoda-

tions laws and their limited enforcement, see Davidson M. Douglas, *Jim Crow Moves North: The Battle over Northern School Segregation, 1865–1954* (New York: Cambridge University Press, 2005), 134–35.

6. August Meier and Elliot Rudwick, *CORE: A Study of the Civil Rights Movement, 1942–1968* (New York: Oxford University Press, 1973), 31–33, 61–71; David J. Garrow, *Bearing the Cross: Martin Luther King, Jr., and the Southern Christian Leadership Conference* (New York: Morrow, 1986), 83–125; Taylor Branch, *Parting the Waters: America in the King Years, 1954–1963* (New York: Simon & Schuster, 1988), 206–71. As chapter 2 details, the NAACP national office and its local branches displayed some difference of opinion on this issue, with certain local branches more interested than the national office in challenging discrimination in public accommodations.

7. James E. Brown Sr., "An Injustice" (letter to the editor), *GDN*, February 27, 1960, A6. See also United States Commission on Civil Rights, *Freedom to the Free* (Washington, DC: Government Printing Office, 1963), 181–84.

8. Harold C. Fleming, "The Price of a Cup of Coffee," *Reporter*, May 12, 1960, 25–26, at 25.

9. Lerone Bennett Jr., "What Sit-Downs Mean to America," *Ebony*, June 1960, 35–40, at 35 ("zeal"); David Halberstam, "A Good City Gone Ugly," *Reporter*, March 31, 1960, 18 (quoting Rodney Powell) ("community movement"); Paul Laprad, "Nashville: A Community Struggle," in *Sit-Ins: The Students Report*, ed. James Peck (New York: CORE, 1960), 6–8, at 8; Ben H. Bagdikian, "Negro Youth's New March on Dixie," *Saturday Evening Post*, September 8, 1962, 15–19, at 19. On the support the students received from local black communities, see SRC, "The Student Protest Movement, Winter 1960," February 25, 1960, 9, available at http://www.thekingcenter.org/archive/document/student-protest-movement-special-report; Claude Sitton, "Negro Sitdowns Stir Fear of Wider Unrest in South," *NYT*, February 15, 1960; Harrison Salisbury, "Nashville Issue Is Full Equality," *NYT*, April 18, 1960, 1, 20, at 20; Paul Ernest Wehr, "The Sit-Down Protests: A Study of a Passive Resistance Movement in North Carolina" (MA thesis, University of North Carolina, Chapel Hill, 1960), 41, 84; William H. Chafe, *Civilities and Civil Rights: Greensboro, North Carolina, and the Black Struggle for Freedom* (New York: Oxford University Press, 1980), 131–35, 137; Aldon D. Morris, *The Origins of the Civil Rights Movement: Black Communities Organizing for Change* (New York: Free Press, 1984), 189–90, 210–12.

Wehr noted that the leaders of the black community tended to be "of upper-middle and upper-class standing, the NAACP member variety, and the demonstrators seemed, generally, to be members of the same strata in Negro society," a fact that may have helped explain the general sense of "pride" and "support" he found among older African Americans for the student activists. Wehr, "Sit-Down Protests," 41.

Even in places like Atlanta where there were clear divergences between the protesters and self-described "conservative" African American leaders, the difference was over tactics, not goals. One of these conservative blacks recognized that the sit-ins and boycotts produced "more integration in less than two years than we gained in ten," while also insisting that the students "will never get anything done on their own because they are cut off; they work in a righteous vacuum over there." Jack L. Walker, "The Functions of Disunity: Negro Leadership in a Southern City," *JNE* 32 (1963), 227–36, at 232. See also C. Eric Lincoln, "The Strategy of a Sit-In," *Reporter*, January 5, 1961, 20–24, at 22 ("Support from adult Negroes [in Atlanta] is firm and consistent.")

10. Letter from Savannah NAACP Branch to All Business Firms of Savannah and Chatham County, April 13, 1960, Information on Savannah Civil Rights Campaign, NAACP Papers, quoted in Maurice C. Daniels, *Saving the Soul of Georgia: Donald L. Hollowell and the Struggle for Civil Rights* (Athens: University of Georgia Press, 2013), 96. See also W. M. Phillips Jr., "The Boycott: A Negro Community in Conflict," *Phylon* 22 (1961): 24–30.

11. Willard Clopton, "Campuses Get Noisy in Behalf of Lunch Sit-Ins," *WP*, April 23, 1960, D1; Bennett, "What Sit-Downs Mean," 35 ("damned-up energy"); Nat Hentoff, "A Peaceful Army," *Commonweal*, June 10, 1960, 275–78, at 277 ("down to earth"); Martin Smolin, "The North: 'We Walk So They May Sit,'" *Sit-Ins: The Students Report*, 13–15, at 15 ("the awaited opportunity"). See also Ted Dienstfrey, "A Conference on the Sit-Ins," *Commentary* 30 (January 1960): 524–28, at 525; Stuart H. Loory, "Students Rally to Integration, Bent on Proving Themselves," *BG*, April 17, 1960, 14; Martin Oppenheimer, *The Sit-In Movement of 1960* (New York: Carlson, 1989), 49–51; McCandlish Phillips, "Campuses in North Back Southern Negro Students," *NYT*, March 20, 1960, 1.

12. "National Protest Reported," *NYT*, March 2, 1960, 28; Loory, "Students Rally to Integration"; "Negro Sitdown Protests Spread in South," *NYHT*, February 21, 1960, 21; Robert C. Albright, "Rights Protests Spreading," *WP*, February 28, 1960, A1; "Picket in Chicago," *CT*, March 1, 1960, 2; Phillips, "Campuses in North"; Les Mathews, "Sympathy and Support in New York," *CD*, April 5, 1960, 9; Claude Sitton, "Dr. King Favors Buyers' Boycott," *NYT*, April 16, 1960, 15; Smolin, "'We Walk So They May Sit,'" 15.

13. Thomas P. Lewis, "The Sit-In Cases: Great Expectations," *Supreme Court Review* (1963): 101–51, at 101; Bell v. Maryland, 378 U.S. 226, 243, 244 (1964) (Douglas, J., concurring in part).

14. Bennett, "What Sit-Downs Mean," 37 ("soul-searching"); Leslie Dunbar, "Reflection on the Latest Reform of the South," *Phylon* 22 (1961): 249–57, at 250 ("made firm").

15. "The Role of the NAACP in the 'Sit-Ins,'" May 1960, NAACP Papers, Part III, Series A, Container 290, Folder: "Sit-ins, North Carolina," LOC, Manuscript Division; "'Sit-Ins' Are Supported, *NYT*, March 23, 1960, 18; "Rocky Backs Sit-Ins, but Truman Is Silent," *AN*, April 16, 1960, 4; Lee D. Jenkins, "Jackie Robinson Blasts Civil Rights Patience Talk," *CD*, May 7, 1960, 23; Anthony Lewis, "Kennedy Salutes Negroes' Sit-Ins," *NYT*,

June 25, 1960, 13; "Democratic Party Platform," July 11, 1960, available at *The American Presidency Project*, http://www.presidency.ucsb.edu/ws/?pid=29602 (praising the sit-ins as "peaceful demonstrations for first-class citizenship" and "a signal to all of us to make good at long last the guarantees of our Constitution") "Republican Party Platform," July 25, 1960, available at *The American Presidency Project*, http://www.presidency.ucsb.edu/ws/?pid=25839 (affirming "the constitutional right to peaceable assembly to protest discrimination in private business establishments" and praising "the action of the businessmen who have abandoned discriminatory practices"); Brief for the United States as Amicus Curiae, 16–27, Boynton v. Virginia, 364 U.S. 454 (1960), October Term 1960 (No. 7), September 1960. See also "Democrats Map Plank on Rights," *NYT*, April 23, 1960, 21; "Mrs. Roosevelt Analyzes Trend," *NYT*, June 20, 1960, 16.

While John F. Kennedy brought relatively little personal interest in civil rights to his 1960 presidential campaign, his legal adviser Harris Wofford, a strong advocate for civil rights and outspoken supporter of the sit-in movement, helped awaken the candidate to the importance of the issue. In the summer of 1960, Kennedy wrote a letter to retired baseball great Jackie Robinson: "It is time for us to fulfill the promise of the Declaration of Independence—to make good the guarantee of the Constitution—to make equal opportunity a living reality in all parts of our public life," the candidate wrote. "I have called for an end to all discrimination—in voting, in education, in housing, in employment, in the administration of justice, and in public facilities including lunch counters." John F. Kennedy to Jackie Robinson, July 1, 1960, in *First Class Citizenship: The Civil Rights Letters of Jackie Robinson*, ed. Michael G. Long (New York: Times Books, 2007), 108. See James E. Clayton, "Kennedy Advisers on Civil Rights Urge More Active Presidential Aid," *WP*, August 10, 1960, A1; Harris Wofford, *Of Kennedys and Kings: Making Sense of the Sixties* (New York: Farrar, Straus & Giroux, 1981); Robert Dallek, *An Unfinished Life: John F. Kennedy, 1917–1963* (Boston: Little, Brown, 2003), 291–93.

16. National Student Association, Southern Project USNA Newsletter, n.d. [spring 1960], NCCHR Records, Folder 544, Southern Historical Collection, Wilson Library, University of North Carolina at Chapel Hill (listing groups and individuals who had expressed support for sit-ins); Bennett, "What Sit-Downs Mean," 36; "Presbytery Asks Woolworth Shift," *NYT*, May 7, 1960, 13; Leonard Buder, "Teachers Union Acclaims Sit-Ins," *NYT*, August 20, 1960, 10; Ross R. Barnett to Luther H. Hodges, April 18, 1960, Governor's Papers: Luther Hartwell Hodges, General Correspondence, 1960, Box 523, Folder: "Segregation—'Sit Down' Situations, A–F," North Carolina State Archives, Raleigh, North Carolina.

17. Louis E. Lomax, "The Negro Revolt against 'The Negro Leaders,'" *Harper's* (June 1960): 41–48, at 41, 42; Howard Zinn, "Finishing School for Pickets," *Nation*, August 6, 1960, 72. See also Hentoff, "A Peaceful Army"; Bennett,

"What Sit-Downs Mean"; Michael Walzer, "The Politics of the New
Negro," *Dissent* 7 (Summer 1960): 235–43, at 238.

18. "King Looks to Georgia Cafe Push," *AC*, February 23, 1960, 7; Martin
Luther King Jr., "The American Dream," in *A Testament of Hope: The
Essential Writings and Speeches of Martin Luther King, Jr.*, ed. James M.
Washington (New York: HarperOne, 1986), 214. See also Sitton, "Dr. King
Favors Buyers' Boycott," 15 (King praising students for "moving away from
tactics which are suitable merely for gradual and long-term change"); Mar-
tin Luther King Jr., "The Burning Truth in the South," *Progressive* 24 (May
1960): 8–10.

On Thurgood Marshall's oftentimes tense relationship with the civil
rights movement, see Mark V. Tushnet, *Making Civil Rights Law: Thurgood
Marshall and the Supreme Court, 1936–1961* (New York: Oxford University
Press, 1994), 301–13; Juan Williams, *Thurgood Marshall: American Revolutionary* (New York: Times Books, 1998), 245–52. On King's vision of the
law and its relation to social change, see Christopher W. Schmidt, "Conceptions of Law in the Civil Rights Movement," *UC Irvine Law Review* 1
(2011): 641–76, at 662–67.

19. King to Jackie Robinson, June 19, 1960, in *The Papers of Martin Luther King,
Jr.*, vol. 5, ed. Clayborne Carson et al. (Berkeley: University of California
Press, 1992), 578 ("sabotage") [hereinafter *King Papers*]; Stanley D. Levison
to Martin Luther King Jr., March 1960, in *King Papers*, 5:382. See also
Hentoff, "A Peaceful Army," 278 (quoting an unnamed "lieutenant of
King" who attacked the NAACP for "urg[ing] the students to call off the
demonstrations and rely entirely on the courts").

Tensions between the NAACP and SCLC predated the sit-ins. In 1959,
for example, NAACP official John Brooks attacked SCLC in an internal
report: "They hold emotional mass and prayer meetings, take up money
and do nothing on the civil rights front." John Brooks, Report, June 1,
1959, NAACP Papers, quoted in Manfred Berg, *"The Ticket to Freedom": The
NAACP and the Struggle for Black Political Integration* (Gainesville: University
Press of Florida, 2005), 168. At the same time, both the NAACP and SCLC
sought to avoid the public perception of conflict between the organizations. On the tense SCLC-NAACP relationship, see ibid., 168–72; Morris, *Origins*, 120–28; Roy Wilkins, *Standing Fast: The Autobiography of Roy
Wilkins* (New York: Viking, 1982), 237–38; Constance Baker Motley, *Equal
Justice under Law* (New York: Farrar, Straus & Giroux, 1998), 152.

NAACP leaders believed much of the public criticism of the NAACP—
such as Lawson's attack at a meeting of student activists in April or
Lomax's *Harper's* article—could be traced back to SCLC. King found
himself trying to mend bridges with the NAACP. Garrow, *Bearing the
Cross*, 134, 137–38; Branch, *Parting the Waters*, 297–99.

SNCC, too, became a target of NAACP suspicion, a feeling that the
students reciprocated. See, for example, Roy Wilkins to Kivie Kaplan,

April 24, 1961, NAACP Papers, Part III, Series A, Container 289, Folder: "Sit-Ins, General, 1961–64" (accusing SNCC leaders of "doing their best to downgrade the NAACP, to lure its young people and to set up a new, rival organization").

20. Ralph McGill, *The South and the Southerner* (Boston: Little, Brown, 1963), 16–17; "Protestant-Jewish-Roman Catholic Conversation on the Sit-Ins," *Presbyterian Outlook*, March 21, 1960, 5–6, at 6. One example of a southern racial moderate who was critical of the sit-in movement was the Mississippi journalist Hodding Carter. See, for example, Carter, "The Young Negro Is a New Negro," *NYT Magazine*, May 1, 1960, 11, 117–19.

21. James McBride Dabbs, "Out of Nazareth," *Presbyterian Outlook*, March 21, 1960, 6–7; Margaret Price, "Toward a Solution of the Sit-In Controversy" (SRC Report), May 31, 1960, 1, NAACP Papers, Part III, Series A, Container 289, Folder: "Sit-Ins, General, 1959, 1960, Jan.–May" ("conscience and self-interest"); SRC, "Postscript to Special Report of February 25: The Student Protest Movement, Winter 1960," March 14, 1960, ibid. ("mediation"); Dunbar, "Reflection," 249.

On the SRC and its work during this period, see Matthew Lassiter, *The Silent Majority: Suburban Politics in the Sunbelt South* (Princeton, NJ: Princeton University Press, 2006), chap. 1.

On the difficulty of fitting the school desegregation campaign into a social movement model, consider this comment King offered during his April 17, 1960, appearance on *Meet the Press*. When asked if his nonviolent direct action could work for school desegregation, King said, "I haven't thought through the strategy at this point . . . how nonviolent resistance can apply in the school integration struggle. I do think it can apply, and I think we need to think through some of these methods." *King Papers*, 5:433. This is a striking statement: six years after *Brown*, King had not found a way to advance this issue through his preferred protest strategy.

22. SRC, "A Follow-Up Report on the Student Protest Movement after Two Months," NCCHR Records, Folder 757.

23. See, for example, Harold C. Fleming to SRC Board Members, March 10, 1960, Marion Wright Papers, Folder 136, Southern Historical Collection, Wilson Library, University of North Carolina at Chapel Hill; Harold C. Fleming to SRC Executive Committee Members, September 19, 1960, ibid., Folder 138.

24. "Leadership at the Five and Ten," *GDN*, February 5, 1960, A6; "Common Sense at the Lunch Counters," *GDN*, February 15, 1960, A6; "Good Will and Bad Temper," *GDN*, February 17, 1960, A8; Clarence H. Patrick, *Lunch Counter Desegregation in Winston-Salem, North Carolina*, SRC pamphlet, 1960, 10–11 (*Sentinel* quotation at 10).

25. Wolff, *Lunch at the 5 & 10*, 49–53; Patrick, *Lunch Counter Desegregation*, 8 ("feed everyone"); Fleming, "Price of a Cup," 26 ("provoking discussion").

26. "Student Appeals Support for Unsegregated Eating Places," *Presbyterian Outlook*, March 21, 1960, 1; Special Bulletin, American Friends Service

Committee, Southeastern Regional Office, April 1960, NCCHR Records, Folder 758; "Southern Cleric Backs Negro Aims," *NYT,* March 28, 1960, 26.

27. David E. Sumner, "The Local Press and the Nashville Student Movement, 1960" (PhD diss., University of Tennessee, Knoxville, 1989), 70 ("catspaws"); "Vandiver's Statement on Student Ad," *AC,* March 10, 1960, 15 ("left-wing statement"); Clayton Knowles, "Truman Believes Reds Lead Sit-Ins," *NYT,* April 19, 1960, 21. See also Fleming, "Price of a Cup," 25 (quoting comments by Senator Richard B. Russell and Georgia governor Ernest Vandiver); Wehr, "Sit-Down Protests," 28–30 (noting that the southern press often made a point of emphasizing the presence of white CORE field secretary Gordon Carey at sit-ins as an indication of outside influence on the protest movement); Kevin Kruse, *White Flight: Atlanta and the Making of Modern Conservatism* (Princeton, NJ: Princeton University Press, 2005), 181–82; J. Mills Thornton, *Dividing Lines: Municipal Politics and the Struggle for Civil Rights in Montgomery, Birmingham, and Selma* (Tuscaloosa: University of Alabama Press, 2002), 113–14.

28. "Negroes Extend Sitdown Protest," *NYT,* February 10, 1960, 21 ("did not consult"); Oppenheimer, *Sit-In Movement,* 121 ("keep themselves free"; "no intention"). On anti-communist commitments among sit-in leaders, see Clayborne Carson, *In Struggle: SNCC and the Black Awakening of the 1960s,* 2nd ed. (Cambridge, MA: Harvard University Press, 1995), 13; Simon Hall, "The Sit-Ins, SNCC, and Cold War Patriotism," in *From Sit-Ins to SNCC: The Student Movement in the 1960s,* ed. Iwan Morgan and Philip Davies (Gainesville: University Press of Florida, 2012), 135–52.

The students sometimes leveraged Cold War politics for their own cause. One popular picket sign read, "Khrushchev can eat here, why can't we?" Wehr, "Sit-Down Protests," 56.

Sympathizers of both races saw the sit-ins as a potential antidote to black radicalism, particularly the Black Muslims, who were gaining adherents during this period. The students, noted one approving reporter, channeled their frustration into a "traditional patterns of protest, reform and ultimate cooperation," rather than the "bitter and destructive" program of the Black Muslims. Bagdikian, "Negro Youth's New March," 19.

29. James H. Laue, *Direct Action and Desegregation, 1960–1962: Toward a Theory of Rationalization of Protest* (Brooklyn: Carlson, 1989) (reprint of PhD diss., Harvard University, 1965), 81, 346 n. 24 (SRC and "sit-ins"); "Will Negroes Win in South?" *U.S. News & World Report,* March 14, 1960, 41–45, at 45 ("their own show"); "Suggested Protest Procedures," NAACP National Office memorandum, n.d. [Spring 1960], NAACP Papers, Part III, Series A, Container 289, Folder: "Sit-In Branches, 1960" ("Other elements"); SRC, "Student Protest Movement, Winter 1960," 2; SRC, "Postscript: Events February 26–March 13," n.d., NCCHR Records, Folder 757 ("spirit of emulation"). See also Anthony Lewis, "Since the Supreme Court Spoke," *NYT Magazine,* May 10, 1964, 92; Helen Fuller, " 'We Are All So Happy,' " *NR,* April 25, 1960, 13–16; Harry S. Jones, letter to Members and Friends of the

North Carolina Council on Human Relations, February 19, 1960, NCCHR Records, Folder 757.

30. See, for example, "Movement by Negroes Growing," *GDN*, February 4, 1960, B1 (describing North Carolina attorney general Malcolm Seawell's reaction to the sit-ins); State v. Avent, 253 N.C. 580, 118 S.E. 2d 47 (1961); Williams v. Howard Johnson's Restaurant, 268 F.2d 845 (4th Cir. 1959); State v. Clyburn, 247 N.C. 455, 101 S.E.2d. 295 (1958). I examine these arguments in more detail in the next chapter.

31. Daniel H. Pollitt, "Dime Store Demonstrations: Events and Legal Problems of First Sixty Days," *Duke Law Journal* (1960): 315–65, at 320 (quoting *Durham Morning Herald*, February 11, 1960) ("in one hand"); *Raleigh News and Observer*, March 16, 1960, 8 ("now extends"); "Javits Ask Strong GOP Rights Plank," *WP*, July 18, 1960, A2.

32. New Orleans City Park Improvement Ass'n v. Detiege, 358 U.S. 54 (1958) (per curiam) (parks); Gayle v. Browder, 352 U.S. 903 (1956) (buses); Holmes v. City of Atlanta, 350 U.S. 879 (1955) (per curiam) (golf courses); Mayor and City Council of Baltimore v. Dawson, 350 U.S. 877 (1955) (per curiam) (beaches); Louis H. Pollak, "The Supreme Court and the States: Reflections on *Boynton v. Virginia*," *California Law Review* 49 (1961): 15–55, at 20 n. 23; Arthur Krock, "The Issue of 'Rights' in the Southern Sit-Ins," *NYT*, March 22, 1960, 36. See also Anthony Lewis, "Court Broadens Desegregation: Bus Ruling Points up Fact That Issue Is Wider than Schools," *NYT*, December 11, 1960, E6.

33. Martin Luther King Jr., "A Creative Protest," February 16, 1960, *in King Papers*, 5:368 (emphasis added) ("whether in eating places"); Brown v. Board of Education, 347 U.S. 483, 495 (1954) ("Separate educational facilities are inherently unequal."); Interview on *Meet the Press*, April 17, 1960, in *King Papers*, 5:430–31 ("dignify the law"); "Heed Their Rising Voices," *NYT*, March 29, 1960. Rustin's advertisement sparked a libel lawsuit that led to the famous Supreme Court First Amendment ruling in *New York Times v. Sullivan*, 376 U.S. 254 (1964).

For other descriptions of the students claiming a right that was grounded in the Constitution, see L. F. Palmer Jr., "Uprising for Freedom," *CD*, March 22, 1960, 9, 11, at 11 (defining as a goal of the movement letting "the world know that young Negro America is 'sick and tired' of waiting for the rights which the U.S. Constitution guarantees ALL citizens"); "Ministers Reaffirm Appeal to Reason," *AC*, March 12, 1960, 4 (white Atlanta ministers praising the students for embracing "the spirit of our Constitution"); North Carolina Council on Human Relations, "Statement on the Negro Protest Movement," February 19, 1960, NCCHR Records, Folder 757. (The sit-ins "are the result of accumulated frustrations on the part of students who are aware of their rights as American citizens and who believe that recognition of these rights is long overdue.")

34. Dwight D. Eisenhower, "The President's News Conference," March 16, 1960, *The American Presidency Project*,

http://www.presidency.ucsb.edu/ws/index.php?pid=12157; Dwight D. Eisenhower, "The President's News Conference," May 11, 1960, ibid., http://www.presidency.ucsb.edu/ws/?pid=11778; "Ike Asks Mixed Teams to End South's Tensions," *CD*, March 17, 1960, A2.

Eisenhower's confused and confusing statements predictably (perhaps intentionally) led to divergent interpretations of the president's actual position on the sit-ins. The *Amsterdam News*, a black newspaper, ran the front-page headline "White House OK's Student Sit-Ins" (March 16, 1960), and South Carolina governor Ernest F. Hollings criticized the president for being confused about the law and warned of the "great damage to peace and good order" that would result from Eisenhower's approval of the protests. "Judge Brands Sitdowns as a Negro Blot," *CT*, March 17, 1960, 15. Writers at the *New York Times* saw nothing so ambitious in the president's remarks, parsing them as tracking existing state action doctrine, whereby only publicly owned operations were constitutionally prohibited from discriminating. James Reston, "What Kind of President Do You Want?" *NYT*, March 18, 1960, 24; Arthur Krock, "Local Licenses and the Fourteenth Amendment," *NYT*, March 17, 1960, 32; Anthony Lewis, "President Advises South to Set Up Biracial Talks," *NYT*, March 17, 1960, 37.

35. Eugene Patterson, "Sit-In Question Needs Examining," *AC*, July 5, 1960, 4.
36. "Diner Push Sets Off New Race Flareups," *AC*, February 18, 1960, 15.
37. John F. Kennedy, "Special Message to the Congress on Civil Rights," February 28, 1963, *The American Presidency Project*, http://www.presidency.ucsb.edu/ws/?pid=9581; John F. Kennedy, "Radio and Television Report to the American People on Civil Rights," June 11, 1963, ibid., http://www.presidency.ucsb.edu/ws/?pid=9271; Clay Risen, *The Bill of the Century: The Epic Battle for the Civil Rights Act* (New York: Bloomsbury Press, 2014), 93 (quoting July 9, 1963, statement).
38. *Congressional Record* 110, 88th Cong., 2nd sess., pt. 5:6553 (March 30, 1964); Lyndon B. Johnson, "Radio and Television Remarks upon Signing the Civil Rights Bill," July 2, 1964, *The American Presidency Project*, http://www.presidency.ucsb.edu/ws/?pid=26361. I look more closely at the Fourteenth Amendment and the Civil Rights Act in chapter 6.

CHAPTER FOUR

1. Quoted in Claude Sitton, "Negroes Press for Faster Desegregation," *NYT*, February 21, 1960, E3. Whether they approved of the trend toward desegregation or not, at the time of the sit-ins, most white southerners (like most black southerners) agreed that the South was indeed heading in this direction. Donald R. Matthews and James W. Prothro, "Southern Racial Attitudes: Conflict, Awareness, and Political Change," *Annals of the American Academy of Political and Social Science* 344 (1962): 108–21, at 120.
2. For recent scholarship that emphasizes the divisions among southern segregationists, see Kevin Kruse, *White Flight: Atlanta and the Making of*

Modern Conservatism (Princeton, NJ: Princeton University Press, 2005); *Massive Resistance: Southern Opposition to the Second Reconstruction*, ed. Clive Webb (New York: Oxford University Press, 2005); Jason Sokol, *There Goes My Everything: White Southerners in the Age of Civil Rights, 1945–1975* (New York: Knopf, 2006); Matthew Lassiter, *The Silent Majority: Suburban Politics in the Sunbelt South* (Princeton, NJ: Princeton University Press, 2006); Joseph Crespino, *In Search of Another Country: Mississippi and the Conservative Counterrevolution* (Princeton, NJ: Princeton University Press, 2007); Clive Webb, *Rabble Rousers: The American Far Right in the Civil Rights Era* (Athens: University of Georgia Press, 2010); Jason Morgan Ward, *Defending White Democracy: The Making of a Segregationist Movement and the Remaking of Racial Politics, 1936–1965* (Chapel Hill: University of North Carolina Press, 2011).

3. On the centralization of authority in southern states after *Brown*, see Anders Walker, *The Ghost of Jim Crow: How Southern Moderates Used* Brown v. Board of Education *to Stall Civil Rights* (New York: Oxford University Press, 2009); Numan V. Bartley, *The Rise of Massive Resistance: Race and Politics in the South During the 1950's* (Baton Rouge: Louisiana State University Press, 1969).

4. Clarence Lee Harris Scrapbook #1, 19 (1980), Clarence Lee Harris Papers, Martha Blakeney Hodges Special Collections and University Archives, UNCG University Libraries, Greensboro, North Carolina; Miles Wolff, *Lunch at the 5 & 10* (1970; rev. ed., Chicago: Ivan Dee, 1990), 15.

5. Harris Scrapbook, 19, 28–29; "Negroes in South in Store Sitdown," *NYT*, February 3, 1960, 22; Wolff, *Lunch at the 5 & 10*, 16.

6. Harris Scrapbook, 22–23, 29, 30, 37; Wolff, *Lunch at the 5 & 10*, 17, 48; "Movement by Negroes Growing," *GDN*, February 4, 1960, B1 ("go along").

Other chain stores took the same line as Woolworth. "Our practices are governed by local customs, which we cannot control and which existed long before our stores were opened," stated the president of W.T. Grant Company. "New School Plan Urged in Georgia," *NYT*, April 29, 1960, 12. See also Claude Sitton, "Negroes Extend Store Picketing," *NYT*, February 11, 1960, 22.

7. C. L. Harris to Governor Hodges, February 29, 1960, Hodges Papers, General Correspondence, 1960, Box 523, Folder: "Segregation—'Sit Down' Situations, A–F."

8. Nelson Strawbridge, Chairman, Mayor's Committee on Human Relations, Durham, North Carolina, to Floyd McKissick, May 12, 1960, Floyd B. McKissick Papers, Southern Historical Collection of the University of North Carolina at Chapel Hill and the African American Resources Collection of North Carolina Central University, Subseries 3.3.1: "Correspondence, 1949–1974 and undated," Folder 7133l; Harrison Salisbury, "Nashville Issue Is Full Equality," *NYT*, April 18, 1960, 1, 20; David Halberstam, "A Good City Gone Ugly," *Reporter*, March 31, 1960, 17–19, at 19. On the

fear of economic competition from suburban stores, see "Sit-In Results," *NYT*, May 15, 1960, E12.

9. Harris Scrapbook, 43, 47, 49–50; Wolff, *Lunch at the 5 & 10*, 122; Salisbury, "Nashville Issue." According to Edward R. Zane, a white businessman in Greensboro who led the Mayor's Advisory Committee on Community Relations, Harris was a primary obstacle in getting businesses to abandon their segregation policies. "He appears concerned with only economic factors," Zane wrote at the time. William H. Chafe, *Civilities and Civil Rights: Greensboro, North Carolina, and the Black Struggle for Freedom* (New York: Oxford University Press, 1980), 379 n. 29. Harris would later claim that he was urging his fellow restaurant owners to desegregate with him, but they refused. Harris Scrapbook, 50, 52–53.

10. Harris Scrapbook, 80 ("stepped in"); Halberstam, "Good City Gone Ugly," 17; Gavin Wright, *Sharing the Prize: The Economics of the Civil Rights Revolution in the American South* (Cambridge, MA: Harvard University Press, 2013), 78 (quoting *Women's Wear Daily*, May 10, 1960) ("defenseless"); Ben Gordon, "The Hostages," *Chain Store Age*, April 1960 [excerpted and distributed on stationery of North Carolina Chain Store Council], Hodges Papers, General Correspondence, 1960, Box 523, Folder: "Segregation—'Sit Down' Situations" ("a higher judgment"). See also Kruse, *White Flight*, chap. 7 (describing response of Atlanta businessmen to the sit-ins).

    A Knoxville store owner was able to persuade a local judge to issue an injunction prohibiting the leaders of the sit-in movement and their organization from protesting or "attempting to be served food or sitting down" at his store. "White Man Beaten in Knoxville Sit-In," *NYT*, June 30, 1960, 19.

11. Margaret Price, " 'Sit-In' Drive Changing State," *CD*, June 25, 1960, 5A; Harris Scrapbook, 47, 53, 56, 70; George Roach interview with Eugene E. Pfaff, November 17, 1978, Greensboro Voices/Greensboro Public Library Oral History Project [hereinafter Roach interview]; Michael T. Kaufman, "C.L. Harris, 94; Allowed Lunch Counter Sit-In," *NYT*, July 15, 1999, B9 (quoting from 1998 interview).

    For the first three days of the protest, sales at the Greensboro Woolworth held above the previous year's sales. Then, from the fourth day onward, sales plummeted. Harris Scrapbook, 40–44.

12. Harris to Governor Hodges, February 29, 1960.

13. "Memorandum on conversation between Governor [Luther H. Hodges] and Mr. Harvin, President of Rose's Stores, Henderson," March 10, 1960, Hodges Papers, General Correspondence, 1960, Box 523, Folder: "Segregation—'Sit Down' Situations"; Michael Walzer, "A Cup of Coffee and a Seat," *Dissent* 7 (1960): 111–20, at 117; Claude Sitton, "Negro Sitdowns Stir Fear of Wider Unrest in South," *NYT*, February 15, 1960, 1; "S.S. Kresge Says Its Southern Stores Don't File 'Sit-In' Complaints," *WSJ*, May 16, 1960, 9.

In correspondence with NAACP executive director Roy Wilkins in 1963, the vice president of Woolworth proudly noted that his company "has not caused the arrest of a single 'sit in' demonstrator and our local managers have treated them with dignity and respect." E. F. Harrigan to Roy Wilkins, May 28, 1963, NAACP Papers, Part III, Series A, Container 289, Folder: "Sit-Ins, General, 1961–64."

14. Howell Raines, *My Soul Is Rested: The Story of the Civil Rights Movement in the Deep South* (New York: Putnam, 1977), 77.

15. For instances of white southerners referencing segregation laws to intimidate protesters, see Susanna McBee, "More Dining Places Drop Racial Bars," *WP*, June 24, 1960, A1; Statement Submitted by the Student Nonviolent Coordinating Committee to the Platform Committee of the National Democratic Convention, July 7, 1960, available at http://www.crmvet.org/docs/6007_sncc_demconv-platform.pdf.

16. "Negroes Extend Sitdown Protest," *NYT*, February 10, 1960, 21 ("no violence"); "Sit-Down Strike Here Closes Lunch Counters," *Raleigh Times*, February 10, 1960 ("answer requests"); "Police Keep Close Watch for Trouble," *GDN*, February 18, 1960, A1, A7 ("not taking sides").

17. "77 Negroes Arrested Here as Cafeteria Sitdowns Start," *AC*, March 16, 1960, 1, 9. The official police bulletin spelling out enforcement procedures was clearly written with some knowledge of the state action doctrine and potential equal protection constraints. The policy "gives the owner, or the manager of any establishment, the authority to control their own premises . . . but it puts the responsibility on the owner and not on the police department." "Police Get Rule Giving Business Expelling Power," *ADW*, February 24, 1960, 1.

18. See Garner v. Louisiana, 368 U.S. 157 (1961); Brief for Petitioners, 11, Garner v. Louisiana, 368 U.S. 157 (1961), October Term 1961 (Nos. 26, 27, 28), August 25, 1961.

19. J. W. Anderson, "Open Lunch Counters Set Precedent," *WP*, June 26, 1960, E2; United States Civil Rights Commission, *Civil Rights '63* (Washington, DC: Government Printing Office, 1963), 112–14.

20. Wolff, *Lunch at the 5 & 10*, 43 ("explode").

21. "Bombing Rips House, Hosp. in Nashville," *ADW*, April 20, 1960, 1 ("negotiation and conciliation"); "Complete Text of Mayor's Statement," *GDN*, February 7, 1960 ("peace and good order"); Roach interview; Anderson, "Open Lunch Counters"; "Reaction to Sit-Down Is Praised," *WP*, June 26, 1960, A13.

22. Gene Britton, "Vandiver, Hartsfield Differ on Negro Students' Appeal," *AC*, March 10 1960, 1; "Mayor Asks End to Sitdowns," *AC*, March 31, 1960, 9; Elsie Carper, "Rights-Ad Signers Face Georgia Law Test," *WP*, April 26, 1960, A24; Kruse, *White Flight*, 181.

23. "Eight Negroes Chose Jail in Sitdown Case," *CT*, March 19, 1960, 12; Patricia Stephens, "Tallahassee: Through Jail to Freedom," in *Sit-Ins: The Students Report*, ed. James Peck (New York: Core, 1960), 2–4; Lewis M.

Killian, "Organization, Rationality and Spontaneity in the Civil Rights Movement," *ASR* 49 (1984): 770–83, at 777.

24. Paul Ernest Wehr, "The Sit-Down Protests: A Study of a Passive Resistance Movement in North Carolina" (MA thesis, University of North Carolina, Chapel Hill, 1960), 67; Halberstam, "Good City Gone Ugly."

25. "When Lunch Counters Reopen, They Should Serve All Customers," *Winston-Salem Sentinel*, March 17, 1960, quoted in SRC, "A Follow-Up Report on the Student Protest Movement After Two Months," NCCHR Records, Folder 757, Southern Historical Collection, Wilson Library, University of North Carolina at Chapel Hill; "Needed: A 'Just and Honorable' Answer," *GDN*, February 8, 1960, 6. In a subsequent editorial, the *Greensboro Daily News* clarified, or perhaps qualified, its assertion that the lunch counter operators had a "sound legal position" in their choice to racially discriminate by noting that "arresting for trespass customers they invite into parts of their stores and repel in other parts" may put them on "shaky legal grounds." Editorial, "Common Sense and the Public Safety," *GDN*, February 20, 1960, 6.

Urging a resolution of the sit-in issue that did not rely on legal mandates was not limited to moderates in the South. The *New York Times* editorial board seemed to adopt a similar approach. The editorial "Laws and Folkways" contrasted the debate over voting rights legislation in the Senate (a matter of "law") with the sit-in demonstrations (a matter of "folkways"). The Senate debate concerned the enforcement of civil rights; the sit-ins concerned outdated "white community folkways." In confronting southern folkways, "the utmost patience is certainly required by both sides," and the best hope for resolution can be found in "effective interracial committees in the South," which "are normally composed of moderate persons of both races, who are able to put the welfare of the whole community above their private prejudices and resentments." Editorial, "Laws and Folkways," *NYT*, February 16, 1960, 36.

26. Editorial, "Making It Their Business," *Raleigh News & Observer*, February 13, 1960; Editorial, "Common Sense at the Lunch Counters," *GDN*, February 15, 1960, A6. See also Editorial, "Of Civil Rights and Civilities," *GDN*, March 2, 1960, A6 (differentiating "civil rights" [desegregation in schools and public facilities] from "civilities" ["the right of businesses to invite their own customers and the fairness of business practices"] and arguing that dealing with "civilities" required "both sides . . . to sit down and work out an answer unimpeded by the threat of force or the worry of economic reprisal"); Editorial, "We Urge an End to Atlanta Sit-Ins," *AC*, October 20, 1960, 4 (condemning both lunch counter segregation ["an antique" that "is dying, as it should, of legitimate pressure"] and the sit-ins ["unwise and destructive"]).

27. "Vandiver's Statement on Student Ad," *AC*, March 10 1960, 15; John Britton, "Students Bound Over to a Higher Court After Food Service

Appeal," *ADW*, March 16, 1960, 1; "77 Negroes Arrested," 1; "State Probe in Sitdowns Ordered," *AC*, March 17, 1960, 14; "3 Laws Bar Sitdowns, Cook Says," *AC*, March 2, 1960, 11; "State Leaders Silent on Negro Stand," *AC*, March 9, 1960, 7; "Bill Bars Sitdowns in Restaurants," *AC*, February 11, 1960, 10; "9 Students Arrested," *NYT*, March 30, 1960, 25 ("a good mule").

On Vandiver's strength among rural voters, see C. Eric Lincoln, "The Strategy of a Sit-In," *Reporter*, January 5, 1961, 20–24, at 20. On state legislative malapportionment as a contributing factor to racial extremism in the civil rights era, see Michael J. Klarman, *From Jim Crow to Civil Rights: The Supreme Court and the Struggle for Racial Equality* (New York: Oxford University Press, 2004), 415.

28. "35 Negroes Arrested in Texas, Louisiana," *AC*, March 29, 1960, 12; "Protest Scheduled," *NYT*, March 1, 1960, 20; Thomas Gaither, "Orangeburg: Behind the Carolina Stockade," in *Sit-Ins: The Students Report*, 9–11.

29. Martin Oppenheimer, *The Sit-In Movement of 1960* (New York: Carlson, 1989), 131; "Anti-Sitdown Bills Passed," *GDN*, February 25, 1960, B14; "Stricter Laws of Trespass Approved," *GDN*, February 26, 1960, A3; "Legal Aspects of the Sit-In Movement," *Race Relations Law Reporter* 5 (1960): 935–47, at 939; William M. Kunstler, "Law and the Sit-Ins," *Nation*, November 4, 1961, 351–354, at 352; Adam Fairclough, *Race and Democracy: The Civil Rights Struggle in Louisiana, 1915–1972* (Athens: University of Georgia Press, 1995), 271–72.

Some cities in the Deep South also joined in this wave of new trespass regulation. Montgomery, Alabama, passed its own criminal trespass ordinance along with a stricter disorderly conduct ordinance and new parade ordinances in March 1960. "Legal Aspects," 939.

30. "Police Get Rule"; "Atlanta Stores Agree to End Lunch Counter Segregation," *NYHT*, March 8, 1961, 17.

31. "200 Negro Students Parade in Columbia," *AC*, March 4, 1960, 6 ("illegal and dangerous"); SRC, "A Follow-Up Report" (quoting Collins address); "Floridian with Gavel: LeRoy Collins," *NYT*, July 13, 1960, 19 ("essence of his stand").

The governor's speech received national attention. It was "a heartening reminder that there are still rational and moderate men in the South who cherish ideals of justice and morality," wrote the *Washington Post*. "Moral Leadership," *WP*, March 23, 1960, A14. See also "The Pattern of High Ground Set for Other Governors," *ADW*, March 22, 1960, 6; "Three Cheers for Gov. Collins," *CD*, March 30, 1960, A10; "South's Mood: Florida's Governor Sounds New Integration Note," *NYT*, March 27, 1960, E8. According to the governor's office, it was also received strong support among Floridians. Robert Giles to Luther Hodges, April 12, 1960, Hodges Papers, General Correspondence, 1960, Box 523, Folder: "Segregation—'Sit Down'

Situations"; McCandlish Phillips, "Floridians Back Racial Proposal," *NYT*, March 28, 1960, 25.

32. Luther H. Hodges to C. L. Harris, March 2, 1960, Hodges Papers, General Correspondence, 1960, Box 523, Folder: "Segregation—'Sit Down' Situations, A–F." On North Carolina's racial politics, see Chafe, *Civilities and Civil Rights*.

33. Hodges Statement on Sit-ins, Hodges Papers, General Correspondence, 1960, Box 523, Folder: "Segregation—'Sit Down' Situations"; Luther H. Hodges to R. C. Kirkwood, March 24, 1960, Hodges Papers, General Correspondence, 1960, Box 523, Folder: "Segregation—'Sit Down' Situations, G–Z."

34. Thomas Wade Bruton to Luther H. Hodges, March 9, 1960, Hodges Papers, General Correspondence, 1960, Box 523, Folder: "Segregation—'Sit Down' Situations."

35. Luther H. Hodges to C. M. Purdy, March 24, 1960, Hodges Papers, General Correspondence, 1960, Box 523, Folder: "Segregation—'Sit Down' Situations, G–Z"; Hodges to Kirkwood, March 24, 1960; Hodges to Harris, March 2, 1960, ibid.; Robert E. Giles to William C. Allred Jr., March 18, 1960, Hodges Papers, General Correspondence, 1960, Box 523, Folder: "Segregation—'Sit Down' Situations, A–F."

36. Untitled draft of statement on sit-ins by Woolworth's [labeled "not used"], n.d., Hodges Papers, General Correspondence, 1960, Box 522, Folder: "Segregation—Lunch Counters (Negro) 1960." An excerpt of this draft was included in Hodges to Kirkwood, March 24, 1960.

37. Wehr, "Sit-Down Protests," 65 ("It is impossible"); F. B. Williams, "The Christian Way" (letter to the editor), *GDN*, February 12, 1960, A8.

38. "Police Keep Close Watch"; "The Sitdowns," *Richmond News Leader*, February 22, 1960. On the limits of white supremacy as an ideological defense against the civil rights movement, see David L. Chappell, *A Stone of Hope: Prophetic Religion and the Death of Jim Crow* (Chapel Hill: University of North Carolina Press, 2004); Keith M. Finley, *Delaying the Dream: Southern Senators and the Fight Against Civil Rights, 1938–1965* (Baton Rouge: Louisiana State University Press, 2008).

   In North Carolina, the sit-in movement energized segregationist fervor and helped launch the gubernatorial campaign of I. Beverly Lake, who made an attack on integration and the NAACP the centerpiece of his campaign. Although Terry Sanford eventually defeated him in the Democratic primary, Lake ran a strong second. Wehr, "Sit-Down Protests," 79–80.

39. Kruse, *White Flight*, 196 (Maddox quotation); "Klan Pickets; Boycott Talked by Maddox," *AC*, December 11, 1960, 1, 26; Editorial, "Seditious Sit-Downs," *Citizens' Council* (March 1960): 1–2; Frank Wells, "Talmadge Likens Sit-In to Mob Rule," *AC*, October 20, 1960, 29; *Congressional Record* 106, 86th Cong., 2nd sess., pt. 5:6777 (March 29, 1960) (comments of Richard Russell).

From the beginning of the sit-ins, Maddox had been threatening that protests and boycotts would result in white businesses "boycotting" black employees. "Pickrick Says" (advertisement), *AC*, March 12, 1960, 12. (Maddox also suggested that a solution to the problem would be for department stores to get out of the food service business and leave it to restaurants. Ibid.) One of Maddox's group's first actions was to collect information on black employees in segregated facilities, so they could be fired as retaliation for a black boycott of their businesses. "It may be necessary to resort to the principle of fighting fire with fire," Maddox explained. "Klan Pickets." The group also threatened to boycott any store that desegregated. "Maddox Group Threatens to Boycott Stores," *AC*, November 15, 1960, 17. On Maddox, see Sokol, *There Goes My Everything*, 182–87, 231–35; Kruse, *White Flight*, 194–203.

40. "The Sitdowns."

41. Kruse, *White Flight*, 201. I explore this topic in more depth in Christopher W. Schmidt, "Defending the Right to Discriminate: The Libertarian Challenge to the Civil Rights Movement," in *Signposts: New Directions in Southern Legal History*, ed. Sally Hadden and Patricia Minter (Athens: University of Georgia Press, 2013), 417–46. See also Kevin M. Kruse, "The Fight for 'Freedom of Association': Segregationist Rights and Resistance in Atlanta," in *Massive Resistance: Southern Opposition to the Second Reconstruction*, ed. Clive Webb (New York: Oxford University Press, 2005), 99–114.

42. Lochner v. New York, 198 U.S. 45 (1905); Schmidt, "Defending the Right," 421–27; Wallace F. Caldwell, "State Public Accommodations Laws, Fundamental Liberties and Enforcement Programs," *Washington Law Review* 40 (1965): 841–72, at 853–62.

43. Roger K. Newman, *Hugo Black: A Biography*, rev. ed. (New York: Fordham University Press, 1997), 541–43; *The Supreme Court in Conference, 1940–1985*, ed. Del Dickson (New York: Oxford University Press, 2001), 720 (quoting Hugo Black); "Truman Formula for Sitdowners: Throw 'Em Out," *BG*, March 20, 1960, 18; "Truman Reiterates Views on Sitdowns," *NYT*, March 25, 1960, 12; NAACP Press Release, April 19, 1960, NAACP Papers (microfilm), Part 21, Reel 21, Frame 707; Harry S. Truman to Edward Turner and Art Johnson (telegram), n.d., NAACP Papers (microfilm), Part 21, Reel 21, Frame 594. Truman went on to explain that although he was not saying the students were themselves Communists, the sit-in tactic was "the kind of program [Communists] like to put on" and the movement was "pushed on by a Communist program." "Truman Repeats Charge on Sit-Ins," *NYT*, June 13, 1960, 20.

44. On the suppression of dissent among southern whites as a key component of defending Jim Crow in the civil rights era, see, for example, Bartley, *Rise of Massive Resistance*.

45. John Ehle, *The Free Men* (New York: Harper & Row, 1965), 139; "Statement by Atlanta Restaurant Association," *AC*, January 27, 1964, 20; "Stricter Laws of Trespass Approved."

46. State v. Clyburn, 247 N.C. 455, 101 S.E.2d 295 (1958); State v. Avent, 253 N.C. 580, 591, 118 S.E. 2d 47, 55 (1961); Peterson v. City of Greenville, 373 U.S. 244, 250 (1963) (Harlan, J., concurring and dissenting).

    There is a large scholarly literature on the role of aspirational rights in the American constitutional tradition. See, for example, Robert Post and Reva Siegel, "*Roe* Rage: Democratic Constitutionalism and Backlash," *Harvard Civil Rights–Civil Liberties Law Review* 42 (2007): 373–433; Jack M. Balkin, *Constitutional Redemption: Political Faith in an Unjust World* (Cambridge, MA: Harvard University Press, 2011); George I. Lovell, *This Is Not Civil Rights: Discovering Rights Talk in 1939 America* (Chicago: University of Chicago Press, 2012). Although most of this literature focuses on rights talk from the ideological left, the same dynamics operated on the other end of the ideological spectrum.

47. "The Revolt of the Negro Youth," *Ebony* (May 1960): 38; Editorial, "Justifiable Recalcitrance," *Shaw Journal* (March–April 1960): 4.

CHAPTER FIVE

1. Bell v. Maryland, 378 U.S. 226, 243 (1964) (Douglas, J., concurring).
2. Alexander M. Bickel, "The Proper Role of the United States Supreme Court in Civil Liberties Cases," *Wayne Law Review* 10 (1964): 473–77, at 477.
3. *The Supreme Court in Conference, 1940–1985*, ed. Del Dickson (New York: Oxford University Press, 2001), 718 (Warren quotation) [hereinafter *In Conference*]. On the Warren Court, see, for example, Morton J. Horwitz, *The Warren Court and the Pursuit of Justice* (New York: Hill and Wang, 1998); Lucas A. Powe Jr., *The Warren Court and American Politics* (Cambridge, MA: Harvard University Press, 2000).

    This formulation of the constitutional issue is somewhat simplified and overbroad. The particular question the justices considered was whether the state could enforce race-neutral laws, such as those regulating trespass or breach of peace, when these enforcement actions had the effect of protecting discrimination in public accommodations. As a formal legal matter, the equal protection challenges in the sit-in cases targeted state or local governments, not private businesses. Yet since removing the ability of the state to protect private discrimination would largely (if not completely) remove the ability of public accommodations to maintain discriminatory policies, the constitutional claim was often described, inside and outside the courtrooms, in this broader way, as a right to nondiscriminatory access to public accommodations. See, for example, Bell v. Maryland, 378 U.S. 226, 286 (1964) (Goldberg, J., concurring) ("The Constitution guarantees to all Americans the right to be treated as equal members of the community with respect to public accommodations."); Andrew Glass, "High Court Upsets Sit-In Convictions," *BG*, June 23, 1964, 1; Robert C. Toth, "Supreme Court Becoming Nation's Conscience," *Los Angeles Times*, June 28, 1964, F1.

4. Charles Whalen and Barbara Whalen, *The Longest Debate: A Legislative History of the 1964 Civil Rights Act* (Cabin John, MD/Washington, DC: Seven Locks Press, 1985), 155; Herbert H. Hyman and Paul B. Sheatsley, "Attitudes toward Desegregation," *Scientific American* 195 (1956): 35–39, at 35; "How Whites Feel about Negroes: A Painful American Dilemma," *Newsweek*, October 21, 1963, 45; Bell v. Maryland, 378 U.S. 226, 284 (1964) (opinion of Douglas, J.) (appendix listing state public accommodations laws); "Survey Shows Rights Laws Now Cover 65% of Nation," *WP*, December 26, 1963, A17; William E. Blundell, "30 States, Some Cities Bar Discrimination in Public Accommodations," *WSJ*, October 22, 1963, 1, 14; Louis Harris, "South Joins Opposition to Rights Bill Filibuster," *WSJ*, April 27, 1964, A1.

5. Benjamin Cardozo, *The Nature of the Judicial Process* (New Haven, CT: Yale University Press, 1921), 168. On the responsiveness of the Supreme Court to public opinion and political pressure, see Barry Friedman, *The Will of the People: How Public Opinion Has Influenced the Supreme Court and Shaped the Meaning of the Constitution* (New York: Farrar, Straus & Giroux, 2009); Michael J. Klarman, *From Jim Crow to Civil Rights: The Supreme Court and the Struggle for Racial Equality* (New York: Oxford University Press, 2004); Powe, *Warren Court*; David Cole, *Engines of Liberty: The Power of Citizen Activists to Make Constitutional Law* (New York: Basic Books, 2016). Klarman analyzes the role played by the justices' culturally elite values in *From Jim Crow to Civil Rights*, 6, 250–52. For an insightful discussion of the distinctive nature of judicial decision making, see Gordon Silverstein, *Law's Allure: How Law Shapes, Constrains, Saves, and Kills Politics* (New York: Cambridge University Press, 2009), chap. 3.

6. Louis H. Pollak, "The Supreme Court and the States: Reflections on *Boynton v. Virginia*," *California Law Review* 49 (1961): 15–55, at 18; Boynton v. Virginia, 361 U.S. 958 (1960) (granting certiorari); 364 U.S. 454, 455–56 (1960). Earlier Supreme Court rulings holding that racial discrimination while traveling on interstate railroads violated the Interstate Commerce Act include *Mitchell v. United States*, 313 U.S. 80 (1941) (exclusion of blacks from first-class coaches), and *Henderson v. United States*, 339 U.S. 816 (1950) (segregated dining cars).

   When the Court first accepted the *Boynton* case for review, *New York Times* Supreme Court reporter Anthony Lewis predicted that a victory for the plaintiff "would be a long legal step toward ending discrimination against Negroes in private facilities such as restaurants and hotels." Anthony Lewis, "Court Backs N.A.A.C.P. on Secrecy in Little Rock," *NYT*, February 24, 1960, 1.

7. Brief for Petitioner, Boynton v. Virginia, 364 U.S. 454 (1960), October Term 1960 (No. 7), August 25, 1960.

8. Brief for the United States as Amicus Curiae, 16–27, Boynton v. Virginia, 364 U.S. 454 (1960), October Term 1960 (No. 7), September 1960. Why

did the Justice Department under the Eisenhower administration (an administration not known for being particularly pro–civil rights) make such a bold state action argument, while the Justice Department under Kennedy (an administration that was generally more supportive of civil rights issues than its predecessor) did not? The best explanation is probably that the lawyers in Eisenhower's Justice Department simply did not struggle with the doctrinal implications of a broad state action ruling the way their successors would. Solicitor General Rankin sympathized with the cause of the sit-ins, and he believed the Fourteenth Amendment prohibited the use of state authority to protect racial discrimination in public accommodations. Like Chief Justice Fred Vinson, a moderate at best on racial issues who in 1948 wrote the *Shelley* opinion with little apparent appreciation of its potentially radical implications for the state action doctrine, Rankin was focused on the problem before the Court, and not the myriad future issues that might be raised by a broad constitutional ruling for the students.

9. Boynton v. Virginia, 364 U.S. 454, 464 (1960); Anthony Lewis, "Court Broadens Desegregation: Bus Ruling Points up Fact That Issue Is Wider than Schools," *NYT*, December 11, 1960, E6.

10. Brown v. Board of Education, 347 U.S. 483 (1954); Sweatt v. Painter, 339 U.S. 629 (1950); McLaurin v. Oklahoma State Regents, 339 U.S. 637 (1950); Cooper v. Aaron, 357 U.S. 566 (1958); Shelley v. Kraemer, 334 U.S. 1 (1948); Anthony Lewis, "Bus Terminal Segregation Curbed by Supreme Court," *NYT*, December 6, 1960, 1; see also Pollak, "Reflections on *Boynton*."

11. Burton v. Wilmington Parking Authority, 150 A.2d 197 (Del. Chan. Ct. 1959), reversed by Wilmington Parking Authority v. Burton, 157 A.2d. 894 (Del. 1960). The Delaware Supreme Court used its decision as an opportunity to rail against *Brown* and other Supreme Court civil rights decisions that have "erode[d] our local law." 157 A.2d, 902. On civil rights in Delaware, see Brett Gadsden, *Between North and South: Delaware, Desegregation, and the Myth of American Sectionalism* (Philadelphia: University of Pennsylvania Press, 2013).

12. Burton v. Wilmington Parking Authority, 365 U.S. 715, 722 (1961).

13. Ibid., 725. For a discussion of *Burton* and its critics, see Christopher W. Schmidt, "On Doctrinal Confusion: The Case of the State Action Doctrine," *Brigham Young University Law Review* (2016): 575–628, at 594–95. On the "permission" theory of state responsibility in the context of the state action doctrine, see, for example, Roger Paul Peters, "Civil Rights and State Non-Action," *Notre Dame Law Review* 34 (1959): 303–34, at 320–34; Pamela Brandwein, *Rethinking the Judicial Settlement of Reconstruction* (New York: Cambridge University Press, 2011); Bell v. Maryland, 378 U.S. 226, 311 (1964) (Goldberg, J., concurring); Reitman v. Mulkey, 387 U.S. 369, 394–95 (1967) (Harlan, J., dissenting).

14. *Burton*, 365 U.S., at 725–26.

15. Ibid., 728 (Harlan, J., dissenting). Whittaker joined Harlan's dissent, and Frankfurter wrote his own dissent.

16. Editorial, "Jim Crow by Lease," *WP*, April 24, 1961, A14; "Editorials: Defeat in Victory," *PC*, April 29, 1961, A6; Jerre S. Williams, "The Twilight of State Action," *Texas Law Review* 41 (1963): 347–90, at 382 ("vague and obscure"). See also Thomas P. Lewis, *"Burton v. Wilmington Parking Authority*—a Case without Precedent," *Columbia Law Review* 61 (1961): 1458–67. Wilmington responded to the ruling by passing an ordinance prohibiting racial discrimination in all licensed eating establishments. "Legislatures: Public Accommodations: Restaurants—Delaware," *Race Relations Law Reporter* 6 (1961): 885.

17. Lewis, "Court Broadens Desegregation"; Anthony Lewis, "Court on 'Private Bias,'" *NYT*, April 23, 1961, 189.

18. Lewis, "Court Broadens Desegregation."

19. Garner v. Louisiana, 368 U.S. 157 (1961); Conference notes, March 17, 1961, re: Nos. 617, 618, 619, William O. Douglas Papers, Washington, D.C., Box 1269, Folder: "Nos. 26, 27, 28(c) Garner v. Louisiana, Misc. Memos, Certs.," LOC, Manuscript Division.

20. Douglas, draft dissent from denial of certiorari, March 17, 1961, Douglas Papers, Box 1269, Folder: "Nos. 26, 27, 28(c) Garner v. Louisiana, Misc. Memos, Certs." Two other appeals of disturbing-the-peace convictions from the Baton Rouge sit-ins were consolidated with *Garner*: Briscoe et al. v. Louisiana, No. 27; Hoston et al. v. Louisiana, No. 28.

21. Motion for Leave to File Brief and Brief Amicus Curiae for the Committee on the Bill of Rights of the Association of the Bar of the City of New York, 2–3, 7, Garner v. Louisiana, 368 U.S. 157 (1961), October Term 1961 (Nos. 26, 27, 28).

22. Oral Arguments, Garner v. Louisiana, 368 U.S. 157 (1961), October 18–19, 1961, available at https://www.oyez.org/cases/1961/26; Brief on Behalf of Respondent State of Louisiana, Garner v. Louisiana, 368 U.S. 157 (1961), October Term 1961 (Nos. 26, 27, 28), October 4, 1961 [hereinafter *Garner* Louisiana Brief]; Brief for Petitioners, 8–9, Garner v. Louisiana, 368 U.S. 157 (1961), October Term 1961 (Nos. 26, 27, 28), August 25, 1961.

23. *Garner* Oral Arguments; *Garner* Louisiana Brief.

24. *Garner* Oral Arguments; *Garner* Louisiana Brief, 52.

25. *Garner* Oral Arguments; *Garner* Louisiana Brief, 50; Supplemental Brief on Behalf of Respondent State of Louisiana, Garner v. Louisiana, 368 U.S. 157 (1961), October Term 1961 (Nos. 26, 27, 28), October 19, 1961.

26. Douglas conference notes, October 20, 1961, Douglas Papers, Box 1269, Folder: "Nos. 26, 27, 28(c) Garner v. Louisiana, Misc. Memos, Certs"; Douglas, Memorandum re: No. 26, Nov. 6, 1961, ibid. (comparing the issue to *Plessy* and identifying Warren and Brennan as his only sure allies on this issue); Bernard Schwartz, *Super Chief: Earl Warren and His Supreme Court—A Judicial Biography* (New York: New York University Press, 1983), 402–4. Although Douglas believed Warren to be sympathetic to his argu-

ments, by the end of the *Garner* conference, Warren appeared to have settled on a narrower approach. Douglas conference notes, October 20, 1961.

27. Douglas conference notes, October 20, 1961; *In Conference*, 708; Frankfurter to Warren, December 4, 1961, Earl Warren Papers, Box 600, Folder: "Nos. 26, 27 & 28—Garner, etc. v. Louisiana," LOC, Manuscript Division; Earl Warren to Felix Frankfurter, December 6, 1961, ibid.; Brief for the United States as Amicus Curiae, 4, Garner v. Louisiana, 368 U.S. 157 (1961), October Term 1961 (Nos. 26, 27, 28), September 11, 1961; *Garner*, 368 U.S., at 163.

    In a letter to Harlan, Frankfurter derided "the extreme Warren-Douglas-Brennan constitutional views regarding the sit-ins," referring to their willingness to decide in favor of the protesters on both First and Fourteenth Amendment grounds. Schwartz, *Super Chief*, 403.

28. 368 U.S., at 163, 170. See "No Evidence to Support a Conviction," *University of Pennsylvania Law Review* 110 (1962): 1137–46. The Court's *Garner* decision relied on its recent ruling in *Thompson v. Louisville*, 362 U.S. 199 (1960). On *Thompson*, see Risa Goluboff, *Vagrant Nation: Police Power, Constitutional Change, and the Making of the 1960s* (New York: Oxford University Press, 2016), chap. 3.

29. 368 U.S., at 174–76 (Frankfurter, J., concurring); ibid., 177 (Douglas, J., concurring); ibid., 201, 203 (Harlan, J., concurring).

30. Ibid., 177, 181.

31. Ibid., 181–85.

32. Kenneth L. Karst and William W. Van Alstyne, "Comment: Sit-Ins and State Action—Mr. Justice Douglas Concurring," *Stanford Law Review* 14 (1962): 762–76, at 762, 763; Anthony Lewis, "High Court Voids Sit-In Conviction in Louisiana," *NYT*, December 12, 1961, 1 ("new day"); Major Johns and Ronnie Moore, *It Happened in Baton Rouge, U.S.A.*, CORE pamphlet (1962), available at http://www.crmvet.org/info/61_batonrouge.pdf; Adam Fairclough, *Race and Democracy: The Civil Rights Struggle in Louisiana, 1915–1972* (Athens: University of Georgia Press, 1995), 289–90; Eugene Patterson, "Supreme Court, Lincoln and Lee," *AC*, December 12, 1961, 4; Anthony Lewis, "Sit-Ins Pose Basic Legal Question," *NYT*, December 17, 1961, E10; "Negroes in South Hail Sit-In Ruling," *NYT*, December 12, 1961, 50; Elsie Carper, "Court Decision on Sit-Ins Not Expected to Affect Area Trespass Cases," *WP*, December 13, 1961, A10.

33. James E. Clayton, "16 'Sit-In' Convictions Reversed," *WP*, December 12, 1961, A1; "Tribunal Faces New Woes in 'Sit-In' Edict," *CD*, December 13, 1961, 3.

34. Karst and Van Alstyne, "Mr. Justice Douglas Concurring," 763; "The Nation," *NYT*, December 17, 1961, E2; "Equality of Use," *WP*, December 14, 1961, A24. See also Lewis, "Sit-Ins Pose Basic Legal Question" (describing the Douglas and Harlan concurrences as "open[ing] large legal vistas for the future").

35. Philip B. Kurland, "Egalitarianism and the Warren Court," *Michigan Law Review* 68 (1970): 629–82, at 654.

36. Jack Greenberg, *Crusaders in the Courts: How a Dedicated Band of Lawyers Fought for the Civil Rights Revolution* (New York: Basic Books, 1994), 309–10; Victor S. Navasky, *Kennedy Justice* (New York: Atheneum, 1971), 289–93 (Greenberg quotation at 289); Archibald Cox Oral History, June 19, 2000, Columbia University, Oral History Research Office, available at http://www.columbia.edu/cu/lweb/digital/collections/oral_hist/cox/interview.html; Ken Gormley, *Archibald Cox: Conscience of a Nation* (New York: Da Capo, 1997), 189; Brief of the United States, 42, Avent v. North Carolina, 373 U.S. 375 (1963), October Term 1962 (No. 11).

37. Anthony Lewis, "Court Weighs Sit-In Rights," *NYT*, November 11, 1962, 208; Warren conference notes, 1962 Term sit-in cases, November 9, 1962, Warren Papers, Box 604, Case File: "sit-in cases"; Douglas conference notes, Lombard v. Louisiana, November 9, 1962, Douglas Papers, Box 1291, Case File: "No. 58"; Douglas conference notes, Peterson v. City of Greenville, November 9, 1962, Douglas Papers, Box 1281, Case File: "No. 71."

38. Peterson v. Greenville, 373 U.S. 244, 248 (1963); see also Gober v. City of Birmingham, 373 U.S. 374 (1963) (per curiam) (reversing convictions based on *Peterson*); Avent v. North Carolina, 373 U.S. 375 (1963) (same); Shuttlesworth v. Birmingham, 373 U.S. 262 (1963) (reversing conviction for inciting sit-in demonstrations, based on previous holding in *Gober* that sit-ins were not illegal).

   Following the 1963 rulings, the Court vacated sit-in convictions from Virginia and requested the Virginia courts to reconsider them in light of *Peterson*. Randolph v. Virginia, 374 U.S. 97 (1963); Henry v. Virginia, 374 U.S. 98 (1963); Thompson v. Virginia, 374 U.S. 99 (1963); Wood v. Virginia, 374 U.S. 100 (1963); Daniels v. Virginia, 374 U.S. 500 (1963).

39. Lombard v. Louisiana, 373 U.S. 267, 273–74 (1963).

40. Ibid., 276–83.

41. 373 U.S. 244, 249 (Harlan, J., concurring and dissenting).

42. Ibid., 250.

43. Ibid., 252–53.

44. Ibid., 253–58.

45. Arthur Goldberg, Draft Concurrence, Peterson v. Greenville, n.d., Supreme Court Papers of Arthur J. Goldberg, Pritzker Legal Research Center Special Collections, Northwestern Law School, available at http://plrc.omeka.net/items/show/113.

46. Warren to Douglas, May 18, 1963, Douglas Papers, Box 1281, Case File: "court memoranda"; Memorandum from the Chief Justice, re: The Sit-In Cases Remaining on the Docket of the Court, May 1963, ibid.

47. Opinions of William J. Brennan, October Term 1963, xii, William J. Brennan Papers, Box II: 6, Folder 6, LOC, Manuscript Division (memorandum prepared by Justice Brennan and law clerks) [hereinafter Brennan Memo].

On June 10, 1963, the Court accepted four new sit-in cases for review: Barr v. Columbia, 374 U.S. 804 (1963); Bell v. Maryland, 374 U.S. 805 (1963); Bouie v. City of Columbia, 374 U.S. 805 (1963); and Robinson v. Florida, 374 U.S. 803 (1963). These were considered alongside *Griffin v. Maryland*, 370 U.S. 935 (1962), an appeal of a trespass conviction for a June 1960 protest at a segregated amusement park, which the Court held over from the previous term.

48. Brief of Respondents, 3, Bell v. Maryland, 378 U.S. 226 (1964), October Term 1963 (No. 12), September 25, 1963 [hereinafter *Bell* Respondents Brief]; Bell v. Maryland, 227 Md. 302, 176 A. 2d 771 (1962). See also Kenneth W. Mack, "Civil Disobedience, State Action, and Lawmaking Outside the Courts: Robert Bell's Encounter with American Law," *Journal of Supreme Court History* 39 (2014): 347–71.

49. *Bell* Respondents Brief, 5–6.

50. Brief for the United States as Amicus Curiae, 5, 23–25, Griffin v. Maryland, 378 U.S. 130 (1964), October Term 1963 (Nos. 6, 9, 10, 12, 60), September 1963.

51. Douglas handwritten note, on JGC [law clerk] cert memo, Bell v. Maryland, June 5, 1963, Douglas Papers, Box 1315, Folder: "No. 12—Bell v. Maryland: Misc. Memos, Cert Memo."

52. Oral Argument, October 14, 1963, Bell v. Maryland, 378 U.S. 226 (1964), in *Landmark Briefs and Arguments of the Supreme Court of the United States: Constitutional Law*, vol. 59, ed. Philip B. Kurland and Gerhard Casper (Arlington, VA: University Publications of America, 1975), 541–42, 579 [hereinafter *Bell* Oral Argument].

53. Ibid., 555.

54. Warren conference notes, 1963 Term sit-in cases, October 23, 1963, Warren Papers, Box 510, Case File: "sit-in cases"; Black conference notes, October 23, 1963, in A. E. Dick Howard and John G. Kester, "The Deliberations of the Justices in Deciding the Sit-In Cases of June 22, 1964," 3, Hugo L. Black Papers, Box 376, "Oct. Term 1963: Sit-In Cases," LOC, Manuscript Division [hereinafter Deliberations].

55. Brennan Memo, xiii; William O. Douglas, Memorandum to Conference, re: No. 9—Barr v. City of Columbia, Oct. 26, 1963, Douglas Papers, Box 1311, Folder: "O.T. 1963: Opinions: No. 9 Barr v. City of Columbia; No. 10 Bouie and Neal v. Columbia; No. 12 Bell et al. v. State of Maryland."

56. Brennan Memo, xiii–xiv, xvi; Black conference notes, October 23, 1963; Hugo L. Black and Elizabeth Black, *Mr. Justice and Mrs. Black* (New York: Random House, 1986), 112; *In Conference*, 722 (comments of Justice Goldberg); Roger K. Newman, *Hugo Black: A Biography*, rev. ed. (New York: Fordham University Press, 1997), 546 (quoting Brennan interview).

It is likely that the justices' fears about the negative consequences of affirming the sit-in convictions were overstated. See Powe, *Warren Court*,

228; Monrad G. Paulsen, "The Sit-In Cases of 1964: 'But Answer Came There None,'" *Supreme Court Review* (1964): 137–70, at 146. Inside the Kennedy administration, some advisers actually saw a potential Court ruling against the sit-in protesters as an additional justification for the civil rights legislation. Clay Risen, *The Bill of the Century: The Epic Battle for the Civil Rights Act* (New York: Bloomsbury Press, 2014), 48.

57. Brennan Memo, xiv; *In Conference*, 722–23; Douglas, Memorandum to the Conference, October 21, 1963, Douglas Papers, Box 1315, "No. 12—Bell v. Maryland: Law Clerks—3"; Black conference notes, October 23, 1963.

58. Brennan Memo, xiv–xv; Bell v. Maryland, 375 U.S. 918 (1963); Anthony Lewis, "Supreme Court to Survey Power of States in Sit-Ins," *NYT*, November 19, 1963, 1, 24.

59. Greenberg, *Crusaders*, 313.

60. Supplemental Brief, Griffin v. Maryland, 378 U.S. 130 (1964), October Term 1963 (Nos. 6, 9, 10, 12, 60), January 17, 1964; Robinson v. Florida, 378 U.S. 153 (1964).

61. Brennan Memo, xv–xvi; Deliberations, 9, 13; Clark to Black, March 9, 1964, ibid., 10; Harlan to Black, March 9, 1964, ibid., 11.

62. Black draft opinion for the Court, No. 12: Bell v. Maryland, March 12, 1964, reprinted in Bernard Schwartz, *The Unpublished Opinions of the Warren Court* (New York: Oxford University Press, 1985), 149–63, quotation at 160–61.

63. Douglas, draft dissent, No. 60: Robinson v. Florida, 1, 6, March 11, 1964, Douglas Papers, Box 1314, Folder: "No. 12—Bell v. Maryland: Galley Proofs-2."

64. Earl Warren, draft dissent in Barr v. City of Columbia, May 7, 1964, Warren Papers, Box 510, Folder: "Sit-in cases, O.T. 1963; No. 9—Barr v. City of Columbia." Warren's draft dissent is also reprinted in Schwartz, *Unpublished Opinions*, 164–72.

65. Brennan Memo, xvi–xvii. The justices were actually aware of these laws all along, as LDF lawyer Jack Greenberg had mentioned them at oral argument. *Bell* Oral Argument, 540.

66. Brennan Memo, xvii; Harlan to Black, April 16, 1964, in Deliberations, 16; ibid., 17; Black to Goldberg, April 23, 1964, ibid., 18.

67. William Brennan, Draft Dissenting Opinion in Bell v Maryland, May 5 Draft, Brennan Papers, Box I:97, Folder 8; Brennan Memo, xix–xxi; Black and Black, *Mr. Justice*, 92.

68. Hugo Black, opinion of the Court, Bell v. Maryland, May 15, 1964, Black Papers, Box 377.

69. Brennan Memo, xxi.

70. Tom C. Clark, Memorandum to Conference, Re Nos. 9, 10, 12—Barr, Bouie and Bell, May 27, 1964, Douglas Papers, Box 1311, Folder: "O.T. 1963: Opinions: No. 9 Barr v. City of Columbia; No. 10 Bouie and Neal v. Columbia; No. 12 Bell et al. v. State of Maryland" [hereinafter Clark *Bell* memorandum]; Brennan Memo, xxii.

71. Clark *Bell* memorandum; Deliberations, 25; Douglas to Conference, May 27, 1964, ibid., 25; Douglas to Conference, May 28, 1964, ibid., 27; Douglas to Brennan, June 3, 1964, "re: sit-in cases," Douglas Papers, Box 1315, "No. 12—Bell v. Maryland: Misc. Memos, Cert Memo"; Brennan Memo, xxii–xxiv; Douglas, memorandum for the files, June 20, 1964, Douglas Papers, Box 1315, "No. 12—Bell v. Maryland: Misc. Memos, Cert Memo" [hereinafter Douglas *Bell* Memorandum].

72. Harlan to Black, June 2, 1964, in Deliberations, 29; Brennan Memo, xxvi; Deliberations, 32.

73. Warren, Memorandum to the Brethren, June 11, 1964, Douglas Papers, Box 1315, "No. 12—Bell v. Maryland: Misc. Memos, Cert Memo"; Brennan Memo, xxvi; Schwartz, *Unpublished Opinions*, 188–89.

74. Clark, draft opinion in *Bell v. Maryland*, June 11, 1964, 14, Earl Warren Papers, Box 512, "No. 12—Bell v. Maryland, Opinion by Justice Clark" [hereinafter Clark *Bell* draft opinion]; Douglas *Bell* Memorandum. Clark's draft opinion is reprinted in Schwartz, *Unpublished Opinions*, 173–86. The "fabric of society" quotation is from Thomas P. Lewis, "The Sit-In Cases: Great Expectations," *Supreme Court Review* (1963): 101–51, at 144. Brad Ervin offers a strong case for the bluff interpretation (i.e., that Clark did not actually believe the arguments he put into his opinion and never intended to release it) in "Result or Reason: The Supreme Court and Sit-In Cases," *Virginia Law Review* 93 (2007): 181–233, at 232–33.

75. Clark *Bell* draft opinion. Legal scholar Bruce Ackerman writes, "Clark's opinion for the Court would have provided Title II with a constitutional foundation worthy of the Second Reconstruction, sweeping away the remnants of the limited notions of state responsibility inherited from the nineteenth century." Bruce Ackerman, *The Civil Rights Revolution* (Cambridge, MA: Harvard University Press, 2014), 146.

76. Warren to Conference, June 11, 1964, in Deliberations, 34.

77. Reynolds v. Sims, 377 U.S. 533 (1964); Lucas v. Forty-Fourth General Assembly of Colorado, 377 U.S. 713, 747–48 (1964) (Stewart, J., dissenting); Brennan Memo, xxvii; Schwartz, *Super Chief*, 524; Brennan to Conference, June 16, 1964, in Deliberations, 35.

78. *Bell*, 378 U.S., at 230, 235; Greenberg, *Crusaders*, 314. On the same day the Court decided *Bell*, it also reversed convictions in several other sit-in cases on narrow grounds. Barr v. Columbia, 378 U.S. 146 (1964) (disturbing-the-peace conviction overturned for lack of evidence); Robinson v. Florida, 378 U.S. 153 (1964) (trespassing charge overturned based on existence of state regulation requiring segregated restrooms in public accommodations); Bouie v. City of Columbia, 378 U.S. 347 (1964) (overturning trespassing conviction on due process grounds because South Carolina courts reinterpreted law subsequent to sit-in protest). See also Griffin v. Maryland, 378 U.S. 130 (1964) (enforcement of discrimination policy by deputy sheriff working as a security guard at an amusement park consti-

tutes state action). The Court vacated a number of other sit-in convictions for reconsideration in light of this most recent round of decisions. Green v. Virginia, 378 U.S. 550 (1964); Harris v. Virginia, 378 U.S. 552 (1964); Williams v. North Carolina, 378 U.S. 548 (1964); Fox v. North Carolina, 378 U.S. 587 (1964); Mitchell v. City of Charleston, 378 U.S. 551 (1964); Drews v. Maryland, 378 U.S. 547 (1964).

79. For an elaboration of this point, see Christopher W. Schmidt, "The Sit-Ins and the State Action Doctrine," *William & Mary Bill of Rights Journal* 18 (2010): 767–829, at 798–802.

80. *Bell*, 378 U.S., at 244–45. According to Douglas, Warren had been willing to join Douglas's opinion until he added the language attacking the Court for not deciding the case on its merits. Douglas *Bell* Memorandum. The language of Douglas's denunciation of the Court for avoiding an issue that he believed should have been decided was strong, but it had been even stronger. In a draft opinion he circulated, Douglas accused the Court of "irresponsible judicial management of the foremost issue of our time" and "abdication of judicial responsibility." He softened this language somewhat in the final draft. Brennan Memo, xxvii.

81. Douglas to Goldberg, May 8, 1964, Douglas Papers, Box 1315, "No. 12— Bell v. Maryland: Misc. Memos, Cert Memo"; Douglas *Bell* Memorandum.

82. Brennan Memo, xxviii; *Bell*, 378 U.S., at 327–28, 346.

83. Anthony Lewis, "High Court Voids Sit-In Convictions of 42 in 3 States," *NYT*, June 23, 1964, 1, 16.

84. Editorial, "Apartheid at Home," *WP*, June 26, 1964, A18; Editorial, "The Nine Caesars," *CT*, June 28, 1964, 22; William Buckley, "Supreme Court's Latest Actions Hurt Nation's Defensive Ability," *Los Angeles Times*, June 29, 1964, A5; "Justice Black: Defense of Property Rights," *Montgomery Advertiser*, July 1, 1964, 4.

85. Clippings of these articles can be found in Black Papers, Box 376, "Oct. Term 1963: Sit-In Cases": Stephens Broening, "12 Pickets Thrown Out of Store," *WP*, March 3, 1964, A1; "Pickets Back at Annapolis After Talks," *Evening Star*, March 3, 1964, A1; "Police Club Negroes in Motel Pool," *WP*, June 19, 1964, A1, A2; "Harlem: The Tension Underneath," *NYT*, May 29, 1964, 1, 13. Cox v. Louisiana, 379 U.S. 559, 583–84 (1965) (Black, J., concurring in part, dissenting in part) ("street multitudes"); Black and Black, *Mr. Justice*, 92. See also Christopher W. Schmidt, "Hugo Black's Civil Rights Movement," in *Transformations in American Legal History: Essays in Honor of Professor Morton J. Horwitz*, ed. Daniel W. Hamilton and Alfred L. Brophy (Cambridge, MA: Harvard Law School, 2009), 246–66; McKenzie Webster, "The Warren Court's Struggle with the Sit-In Cases and the Constitutionality of Segregation in Places of Public Accommodation," *Journal of Law and Politics* 17 (2001): 373–407.

86. Black's most significant state action opinion is *Marsh v. Alabama*, 326 U.S. 501, (1946), discussed in chapter 2. Black also joined the Court's opinion in

Shelley, the Court's extension of *Shelley* in *Barrows v. Jackson,* 346 U.S. 249 (1953), and he was prepared to do the same in *Rice v. Sioux City Memorial Park Cemetery, Inc.,* 349 U.S. 70 (1955). *In Conference,* 703. Black wrote a sweeping majority opinion in *Terry v. Adams,* 345 U.S. 461 (1953), a decision extending the seminal white primary decision, *Smith v. Allwright,* 321 U.S. 649 (1944). He also signed on to Justice Douglas's dissent in *Black v. Cutter Laboratories,* 351 U.S. 291 (1956), a case in which the majority distinguished *Shelley* and refused to find state action when a court enforced a private employment contract that, had it been with the state, would have raised due process and First Amendment concerns. Black also had expressed skepticism toward the *Civil Rights Cases,* describing that opinion in 1950 as "not true to the purposes of [the] Fourteenth Amendment." *In Conference,* 639.

87. Newman, *Hugo Black,* 541–43.
88. Byron R. White, unpublished draft dissent, Bell v. Maryland, June 17, 1964, 1, Warren Papers, Box 512, "No. 12—Bell v. Maryland, Opinion by Justice White." Several years later, Justice Stewart wrote the most powerful condemnation of civil disobedience of the civil rights era in *Walker v. City of Birmingham,* 388 U.S. 307 (1967). See Christopher W. Schmidt, " 'The Civilizing Hand of Law': Defending the Legal Process in the Civil Rights Era," in *Rhetorical Process and Legal Judgments,* ed. Austin Sarat (New York: Cambridge University Press, 2016), 12–30.

CHAPTER SIX

1. Editorial, "When Judges Disagree," *WP,* December 20, 1964, E6.
2. Among the shelves of sources on the 1964 Civil Rights Act, some of the best include the following: Charles Whalen and Barbara Whalen, *The Longest Debate: A Legislative History of the 1964 Civil Rights Act* (Cabin John, MD/Washington, DC: Seven Locks Press, 1985); Hugh Davis Graham, *The Civil Rights Era: Origins and Development of National Policy, 1960–1972* (New York: Oxford University Press, 1990); Rebecca E. Zietlow, *Enforcing Equality: Congress, the Constitution, and the Protection of Individual Rights* (New York: New York University Press, 2006); Todd S. Purdum, *An Idea Whose Time Has Come: Two Presidents, Two Parties, and the Battle for the Civil Rights Act of 1964* (New York: Henry Holt, 2014); Clay Risen, *The Bill of the Century: The Epic Battle for the Civil Rights Act* (New York: Bloomsbury Press, 2014).
3. Earl Lawrence Carl, "Reflections on the 'Sit-Ins,' " *Cornell Law Quarterly* 46 (1961): 444–57, at 455. See also Editorial, "Some Racial Facts and Fallacies," *WSJ,* March 25, 1960, 8; Milton R. Konvitz, *A Century of Civil Rights* (New York: Columbia University Press, 1961), vii. On Johnson and the Civil Rights Acts of 1957 and 1960, see Robert Caro, *Master of the Senate* (New York: Knopf, 2002).
4. John F. Kennedy, "Special Message to the Congress on Civil Rights," February 28, 1963, available at *The American Presidency Project,* http://www

.presidency.ucsb.edu/ws/?pid=9581; Purdum, *An Idea Whose Time Has Come*, 29; Gavin Wright, *Sharing the Prize: The Economics of the Civil Rights Revolution in the American South* (Cambridge, MA: Harvard University Press, 2013), 90; Risen, *Bill of the Century*, 40.

5. Graham, *Civil Rights Era*, 76; Risen, *Bill of the Century*, 60.

6. Editorial, "Transition by Law," *WP*, July 3, 1963, A14; Wright, *Sharing the Prize*, 90–96; Marion A. Wright, "The Sit-In Movement: Progress Report and Prognosis," *Wayne Law Review* 9 (1963): 445–57, at 445; Clifford M. Lytle, "The History of the Civil Rights Bill of 1964," *JNE* 51 (1966): 275–96, at 289–91; Risen, *Bill of the Century*, 192–93.

7. Martin Luther King Jr., *Why We Can't Wait* (1964; New York: Signet, 2000), 33–45; Glenn T. Eskew, *But for Birmingham: The Local and National Movements in the Civil Rights Struggle* (Chapel Hill: University of North Carolina Press, 1997).

8. John F. Kennedy, "The President's News Conference," May 22, 1963, *The American Presidency Project*, http://www.presidency.ucsb.edu/ws/?pid=9233; Alexander M. Bickel, "The Civil Rights Act of 1964," *NR*, August 1, 1964, 33–39, at 33. See also Alexander M. Bickel, "After the Civil Rights Act," *NR*, May 9, 1964, 11; Risen, *Bill of the Century*, 42–45; Kenneth T. Andrews and Sarah Gaby, "Local Protest and Federal Policy: The Impact of the Civil Rights Movement on the 1964 Civil Rights Act," *Sociological Forum* 30 (2015): 505–27. On national security concerns as a factor in Kennedy administration civil rights policy, see Mary L. Dudziak, *Cold War Civil Rights: Race and the Image of American Democracy* (Princeton, NJ: Princeton University Press, 2000), 169–87; Michael J. Klarman, *From Jim Crow to Civil Rights: The Supreme Court and the Struggle for Racial Equality* (New York: Oxford University Press, 2004), 433–39.

9. Risen, *Bill of the Century*, 47–48 ("frustrations and anger"); Kennedy, "President's News Conference"; Anthony Lewis, "Kennedy Studies New Legal Steps for Integration," *NYT*, May 23, 1963, 1.

10. As one news report explained, "Congressional leaders of both parties . . . agreed that [President Kennedy] had virtually no chance of getting the authority he seeks to enforce desegregation of privately owned public accommodations." E. W. Kenworthy, "One Rights Plea Expected to Fail," *NYT*, June 20, 1963, 1. See also Memorandum from Deputy Attorney General Nicholas deB. Katzenbach to the Attorney General [Robert F. Kennedy], June 29, 1963, in *Securing the Enactment of Civil Rights Legislation: Civil Rights Act of 1964*, ed. Michal R. Belknap (New York: Garland, 1991), 42 (noting newspapers reporting that the public accommodations provision "is dead, and this view is shared by some Congressmen").

11. E. W. Kenworthy, "Cooper Questions Rights Bill Basis," *NYT*, July 4, 1963, 38; Arthur Krock, "When Justices and Law Professors Disagree," *NYT*, July 16, 1963, 30 (Gunther quotation). See also Arthur Krock, "Rights Bill Strategy," *NYT*, June 30, 1963, 115. Even Solicitor General Archibald Cox, a staunch defender of the commerce clause approach, described the

Fourteenth Amendment as "a more natural source of power" for Title II. Archibald Cox, *The Warren Court: Constitutional Decision as an Instrument of Reform* (Cambridge, MA: Harvard University Press, 1968), 54.

12. Joseph L. Rauh Jr., "The Role of the Leadership Conference on Civil Rights in the Civil Rights Struggle, 1963–1964," in *The Civil Rights Act of 1964: The Passage of the Law That Ended Racial Segregation*, ed. Robert D. Loevy (Albany: State University of New York Press, 1997), 51; Anthony Lewis, "Kennedy Presses G.O.P. to Support Civil Rights Drive," *NYT*, June 14, 1963, 1, 18; Gerald Griffin, "Extent of Accommodations Bill Argued in Congress," *BS*, June 27, 1963, 6; Cabell Phillips, "Russell Charges Socialism in Bill," *NYT*, August 12, 1963, 12; Whalen and Whalen, *Longest Debate*, 107; Ken Gormley, *Archibald Cox: Conscience of a Nation* (New York: Da Capo, 1997), 189; Risen, *Bill of the Century*, 88–90.

13. John F. Kennedy, "Special Message to the Congress on Civil Rights and Job Opportunities," June 19, 1963, *The American Presidency Project*, http://www.presidency.ucsb.edu/ws/?pid=9283; Senate Committee on Commerce, *A Bill to Eliminate Discrimination in Public Accommodations Affecting Interstate Commerce: Hearings on S. 1732*, 88th cong., 1st sess., 1:17–28 (1963) (remarks of Attorney General Robert F. Kennedy) [hereinafter Senate Commerce Committee Hearings].

14. Whalen and Whalen, *Longest Debate*, 4; Graham, *Civil Rights Era*, 90; Risen, *Bill of the Century*, 55 ("judicial words").

15. Burke Marshall, Legislative Possibilities, May 20, 1963, in *Securing the Enactment*, 26–27; Victor S. Navasky, *Kennedy Justice* (New York: Atheneum, 1971), 280–81; Gormley, *Archibald Cox*, 156–59; Risen, *Bill of the Century*, 48.

16. Brief of Professor Paul A. Freund, Senate Commerce Committee Hearings, 2:1183–90, at 1187–88.

17. John F. Kennedy, "The President's News Conference," May 22, 1963, *The American Presidency Project*, http://www.presidency.ucsb.edu/ws/?pid=9233; "2 Senators Propose Desegregation Bill," *NYT*, May 23, 1963, 21; Graham, *Civil Rights Era*, 88–89; Senate Commerce Committee Hearings, 1:66–71 (discussion between Senator Mike Monroney and Attorney General Kennedy); Donald G. Morgan, *Congress and the Constitution: A Study of Responsibility* (Cambridge, MA: Harvard University Press, 1966), 299.

On the question of which of the two options would give the more expansive coverage, Harvard Law School dean Erwin Griswold responded: "I think both of them are strong and embracing. I think that the commerce clause reaches a little further in some ways. I think the 14th amendment reaches a little further in other ways." Senate Commerce Committee Hearings, 2:776 (remarks of Erwin N. Griswold). Amidst the frequent posturing, positioning, and hyperbole that characterized the congressional debate over the constitutional basis for Title II, Griswold's response, almost anticlimactic in its commonsense simplicity, was exceptional.

18. Arthur Krock, "When Legislation Rests on a 'Moral' Basis," *NYT,* July 4, 1963, 16; Herbert Wechsler, "Basis for Rights Law" (letter to the editor), *NYT,* July 10, 1963, 28; Krock, "When Justices and Law Professors Disagree." See also Arthur Krock, "The Advancing Prospect of the Sit-In Decisions," *NYT,* May 23, 1963, 34; Arthur Krock, "Rationing the Ban on Discrimination," *NYT,* June 6, 1963, 32; Herbert Wechsler to Warren G. Magnuson, July 18, 1963, in Senate Commerce Committee Hearings, 2:1193–94; Herbert Wechsler, "The Courts and the Constitution," *Columbia Law Review* 65 (1965): 1001–14, at 1013.

19. Whalen and Whalen, *Longest Debate,* 34–37; H.R. Rep. No. 914, 88th Cong., 1st sess., pt. 2 (1963), Additional Majority Views of Hon. Robert W. Kastenmeier, in *The Civil Rights Act of 1964: Text, Analysis, Legislative History* (Washington, DC: Bureau of National Affairs, 1964), 174.

20. Press Conference of Attorney General Robert F. Kennedy, Oct. 15, 1963, in *Securing the Enactment,* 88, 90. See also Burke Marshall, "Address before Executive Board of the American Jewish Congress," November 2, 1963, ibid., 109–10.

21. Memorandum for the President from the Attorney General, October 23, 1963, ibid., 96–99.

22. Morgan, *Congress and the Constitution,* 327; Civil Rights Act of 1964, Pub. Law 88-352, 78 Stat. 241, Sec. 201(b). ("Each of the following establishments which serves the public is a place of public accommodation within the meaning of this title if its operations affect commerce, or if discrimination or segregation by it is supported by State action. . . .") Title II includes a broad definition of when the operations of an establishment "affect commerce," ibid., Sec. 201(c), while adopting a traditional, narrow definition of when a discrimination by an establishment is "supported by State action," ibid., Sec. 201(d).

23. Morgan, *Congress and the Constitution,* 295.

24. Phillips, "Russell Charges Socialism in Bill" ("66 words"); H.R. Rep. No. 914, 88th Cong., 1st sess., pt. 2 (1963), Minority Report upon Proposed Civil Rights Act of 1963, Committee on Judiciary Substitute for H.R. 7152, in *Civil Rights Act of 1964,* 202; Bernard Schwartz, ed., *Statutory History of the United States: Civil Rights, Part II* (New York: Chelsea House, 1970), 1129 ("free and uncontrolled"), 1305 ("would deny"). See also H.R. Rep. No. 914, 88th Cong., 1st sess., pt. 2 (1963), Additional Views of Hon. George Meader, in *Civil Rights Act of 1964,* 185–86; "Deep South Reacts," *ADW,* June 20, 1964, 1; George Wallace, "The Civil Rights Movement: Fraud, Sham, and Hoax," Atlanta, Georgia, speech, July 4, 1964, available at http://xtf.lib.virginia.edu/xtf/view?docId=modern_english/uvaGenText/tei/WalCivi.xml;brand=default; Risen, *Bill of the Century,* 79.

25. Rick Perlstein, *Before the Storm: Barry Goldwater and the Unmaking of the American Consensus* (New York: Hill and Wang, 2001), 363. By the point that his and Goldwater's paths crossed, Rehnquist had already developed

a skepticism toward government regulation of private discrimination. When he was a law clerk to Supreme Court Justice Robert H. Jackson in the early 1950s, he wrote a memorandum arguing that the Constitution "most assuredly did not appoint the Court as a sociological watchdog to rear up every time private discrimination raises its admittedly ugly head. To the extent that this decision advances the frontier of state action and 'social gain,' it pushes back the frontier of freedom of association and majority rule." Cert memo from William Rehnquist to Justice Robert Jackson on *Terry v. Adams* (undated), Jackson Papers, Box 179, Folder 9, reprinted in Nomination of Justice William Hubbs Rehnquist: Hearings Before the Senate Committee on the Judiciary, 312–13, quotation at 313, 99th Cong. 2nd sess. (July 31, 1986). Rehnquist later testified against a proposed Phoenix public accommodations ordinance. Charles Lane, "Head of the Class," *Stanford Magazine*, July/August 2005.

26. Robert Bork, "Civil Rights—A Challenge," *NR*, August 31, 1963, 21–24.
27. Barry Goldwater, "Discrimination Is a Moral Problem," *Human Events* 22 (September 21, 1963), 10; "Text of Goldwater Speech on Rights," *NYT*, June 19, 1964, 18.
28. Sam J. Ervin Jr., "The United States Congress and Civil Rights Legislation," *North Carolina Law Review* 42 (1964): 3–15, at 3–4, 9–10; Sam J. Ervin Jr., "The Role of the Supreme Court as the Interpreter of the Constitution," *Alabama Lawyer* 26 (1965): 389–99. See also Virginia Commission on Constitutional Government, *Civil Rights and Legal Wrongs* (Richmond, VA: Virginia Commission on Constitutional Government, 1963), 11–12.
29. Schwartz, *Statutory History*, 1114.
30. §201(e); §201(b)(1). On exemptions to coverage as a way to attract moderate Republicans to Title II, see Ted Lippman, "Sen. Russell and Mrs. Murphy," *AC*, June 30, 1963, 16; Robert C. Albright, "Rights Bill Alterations Indicated," *WP*, August 6, 1963, A1, A11; Robert D. Loevy, *To End All Segregation: The Politics of the Passage of the Civil Rights Act of 1964* (Lanham, NY: University Press of America, 1990), 51–53. The exemption received majority support in public opinion polls. George Gallup, "Equal Right Favored in Accommodations," *Los Angeles Times*, September 4, 1963, A2.
31. Robert C. Albright, "Right Bill Optimism Is Rising," *WP*, June 22, 1963, A1, A2 (Aiken quotation); House Committee on the Judiciary, *Civil Rights: Hearings on H.R. 7152 as Amended by Subcommittee No. 5*, 88th Cong., 1st sess., pt. 4:2700 (1963) (statement of Attorney General Kennedy); ibid., 3:1881 (statement of Joseph Rauh, Vice Chairman, Americans for Democratic Action). Rauh wrote a report for the Leadership Conference on Civil Rights in which he argued that any exemptions from Title II's coverage should be based on Mrs. Murphy's "right of privacy," not the size of her business. "It is just as immoral for a little place to discriminate as it is for a big one." "Rights Group Opens Office For Lobbying," *WP*, July 28, 1963, B1.

32. John F. Kennedy, "The President's News Conference," July 17, 1963, *The American Presidency Project*, http://www.presidency.ucsb.edu/ws/?pid=9348; "Mrs. Murphy's Impact Is Felt at News Session," *NYT*, July 18, 1963, 8.

33. *Congressional Record* 110, 88th Cong., 2nd sess., pt. 5:6534 (March 30, 1964) ("truly personal"); Schwartz, *Statutory History*, 1154 ("balancing"). See also Bickel, "Civil Rights Act of 1964," 36; Harry T. Quick, "Public Accommodations: A Justification of Title II," *Western Reserve Law Review* 16 (1965): 660–710, at 672–73.

Bruce Ackerman argues that the Mrs. Murphy exemption is best understood as an acknowledgment that in these situations the victim of discrimination does not suffer the humiliation—which he argues is the central target of Title II—she would in a larger establishment. Bruce Ackerman, *The Civil Rights Revolution* (Cambridge, MA: Harvard University Press, 2014), 142. Although Ackerman's focus on humiliation as a key component of civil rights law captures much of the impetus behind Title II, defenders of the exemption emphasized the privacy and associational rights of Mrs. Murphy, not any sort of lesser form of humiliation experienced by the person Mrs. Murphy denied service. Further, there is little evidence that the African Americans who would benefit from Title II saw Mrs. Murphy's discrimination as less humiliating. At the March on Washington, several speakers received rousing applause when they denounced the Mrs. Murphy exemption. A. Philip Randolph said, "We must destroy the notion that Mrs. Murphy's property rights include the right to humiliate me because of the color of my skin." Susanna McBee, "Restrained Militancy Marks Rally Speeches," *WP*, August 29, 1963, A14. See also Editorial, "Civil Rights," *CD*, March 21, 1964, 8 (condemning Mrs. Murphy exemption).

34. James C. Tanner, "Civil Rights Test," *WSJ*, July 2, 1962, 1, 16.

35. Richard C. Cortner, *Civil Rights and Public Accommodations: The Heart of Atlanta Motel and McClung Cases* (Lawrence: University Press of Kansas, 2001), 35; Heart of Atlanta Motel, Inc. v. U.S., 231 F. Supp. 393 (N.D. Ga., July 22, 1964).

36. Cortner, *Civil Rights and Public Accommodations*, 65–66. On McClung, see also Michael Durham, "The Right to Refuse Service," *Life*, October, 9, 1964.

37. Cortner, *Civil Rights and Public Accommodations*, 72; McClung v. Katzenbach, 233 F. Supp. 815, 825 (D.C.N.D. Ala., September 17, 1964).

38. Heart of Atlanta Motel v. United States, 379 U.S. 241 (1964); Katzenbach v. McClung, 379 U.S. 294 (1964).

39. *Heart of Atlanta*, 379 U.S., at 250.

40. *The Supreme Court in Conference, 1940–1985*, ed. Del Dickson (New York: Oxford University Press, 2001), 712 [hereinafter *In Conference*]; Bell v. Maryland, 378 U.S. 226, 331, 343, 345 (1964); Clark, draft opinion in Bell v. Maryland, June 11, 1964, 14, Earl Warren Papers, Box 512, "No. 12— Bell v. Maryland, Opinion by Justice Clark," LOC, Manuscript Division

[hereinafter Clark *Bell* draft opinion]; Byron R. White, unpublished draft dissent, Bell v. Maryland, June 17, 1964, 2, Warren Papers, Box 512, "No. 12—Bell v. Maryland, Opinion by Justice White" ("I find nothing in §1 of the Fourteenth Amendment in the way of public accommodations or fair employment provisions which justifies action by this Court. These are legislative tasks which, in my opinion, are within the congressional powers of the Congress and of the state legislatures.").

Black's position revolved around the sharp distinction he drew between the courts and legislatures in regulating private racial discrimination. "If these businesses can be regulated by the Court in this way, so can private homes," he warned during deliberations on the sit-in cases. "I have no objection to regulation by a proper body of rights of policy, but we are not the proper agency to do it." *In Conference*, 720. Black also repeatedly told the other justices that he would be willing to overrule the *Civil Rights Cases*, meaning its holding on congressional authority, not its definition of the state action doctrine as applied to judicially enforceable rights. Ibid., 719, 727; Earl Warren, Conference Notes, n.d., Warren Papers, Box 510, "Sit-in cases, O.T. 1963; Combined Cases."

41. William O. Douglas, Memorandum to the Conference, October 21, 1963, William O. Douglas Papers, Box 1315, "No. 12: Bell v. Maryland: Law Clerks-3," LOC, Manuscript Division; Black conference notes, October 23, 1963, in A. E. Dick Howard and John G. Kester, "The Deliberations of the Justices in Deciding the Sit-In Cases of June 22, 1964," 3, Hugo L. Black Papers, Box 376, "Oct. Term 1963: Sit-In Cases," LOC, Manuscript Division; William O. Douglas, draft dissent, Bell v. Maryland, March 24, 1964, 27, Douglas Papers, Box 1314, "No. 12: Bell v. Maryland: Galley Proofs."

42. Brief for Appellees, 15, Heart of Atlanta Hotel v. United States, 379 U.S. 241 (1964), October Term 1964 (No. 515), September 28, 1964; Oral Argument, October 5, 1964, Heart of Atlanta Hotel v. United States, 379 U.S. 241 (1964), in *Landmark Briefs and Arguments of the Supreme Court of the United States: Constitutional Law*, vol. 60, ed. Philip B. Kurland and Gerhard Casper (Arlington, VA: University Publications of America, 1975), 561–62.

43. *In Conference*, 726–28. Harlan told the other justices that he did not believe Congress asserted an independent definition of state action. Rather, "Congress, by use of 'state action,' has adopted the *Civil Rights Cases* and has used it in the judicial sense of the term." It was, Harlan argued, because the legislation accepted the traditional state action definition that the Fourteenth Amendment alone was not a sufficient basis for Title II. *In Conference*, 727. Harlan was elaborating on a point he made during oral arguments, when he noted: "The Civil War amendments . . . provided that the Federal power to deal with local state action with reference to discrimination is limited to discrimination that is applied to state action; and, for whatever it is worth, Congress in this bill seems to have accepted

that view of the *Civil Rights Cases* in the judicial construction that is put on state action by the courts." These comments suggested the possibility that Congress held some interpretive authority under the Fourteenth Amendment—that Congress had the option *not* to accept the "judicial construction"—but that it had not chosen to exercise it in passing Title II. *Heart of Atlanta* Oral Argument, 573.

44. WOD [William O. Douglas], Memorandum [for Conference], re: Heart of Atlanta, McClung, Oct. 12, 1964, Black Papers, Box 382, Folder: "Oct. Term 1964: No. 515: Atlanta Motel v. U.S"; *In Conference*, 728; *Heart of Atlanta*, 379 U.S., at 286–91 (Douglas, J., concurring); ibid., 291–93 (Goldberg, J., concurring); Arthur Goldberg to William O. Douglas, December 14, 1964, Douglas Papers, Box 1348, Folder: "Nos. 515, 543: Atlanta Motel v. U.S., U.S. v. McClung, O.T. 1964."

45. Brief for Appellees, 32, Katzenbach v. McClung, 379 U.S. 294 (1964), October Term 1964 (No. 543), October 2, 1964. See also Willis v. Pickrick Restaurant, 231 F. Supp. 396 (D.C. Ga. 1964); Christopher W. Schmidt, "Defending the Right to Discriminate: The Libertarian Challenge to the Civil Rights Movement," in *Signposts: New Directions in Southern Legal History*, ed. Sally Hadden and Patricia Minter (Athens: University of Georgia Press, 2013), 417–46 (discussing Lester Maddox's challenge to Title II).

46. Jurisdictional Statement and Brief, 8, 14, 51–58, Heart of Atlanta Motel v. United States, 379 U.S. 241 (1964), October Term 1964 (No. 515), September 21, 1964.

47. Appellate Brief, 61, Heart of Atlanta Motel v. United States, 379 U.S. 241 (1964), October Term 1964 (No. 515), September 28, 1964; Civil Rights Act of 1866, 14 Stat. 27; George Rutherglen, *Civil Rights in the Shadow of Slavery: The Constitution, Common Law, and the Civil Rights Act of 1866* (New York: Oxford University Press, 2013).

48. Robert H. Williams, "Legal Scholar Alfred Avins Dies at Age 64; Founder of Law Schools in Northern Va. and Delaware and Author of 4 Books," *WP*, June 11, 1999, 6; Alfred Avins, "Maybe It's Time to Look at the Antislavery Amendment: Is It Unconstitutional to Require a White Employee to Serve Negro Customers in 'Places of Public Accommodation'?" *U.S. News & World Report*, May 11, 1964, 82–84; Alfred Avins, "Freedom of Choice in Personal Service Occupations: Thirteenth Amendment Limitations on Antidiscrimination Legislation," *Cornell Law Quarterly* 49 (1964): 228–56; Senate Commerce Committee Hearings, 2:1202–19 (statement of Alfred Avins on behalf of the Liberty Lobby).

49. Senate Commerce Committee Hearings, 1:118 (remarks of Senator Strom Thurmond); Senate Report No. 88-872 (1964), 52–53 (Individual Views of Senator Strom Thurmond); Arthur Krock, "Intolerance in Pursuit of Tolerance," *NYT*, May 14, 1964, 34 ("intolerance"); Arthur Krock, "The 13th Amendment and the Equal Rights Bill," *NYT*, May 7, 1964, 36 ("neglected").

50. *Heart of Atlanta*, 379 U.S., at 261; ibid., 278 n. 12 (Black, J., concurring). See also Willis v. Pickrick Restaurant, 231 F. Supp. 396, 401 (D.C. Ga. 1964) (dismissing Thirteenth Amendment claim); Linda C. McClain, "Involuntary Servitude, Public Accommodations Laws, and the Legacy of *Heart of Atlanta Motel, Inc. v. United States*," *University of Maryland Law Review* 71 (2011): 83–162, at 136–41.

51. *Heart of Atlanta*, 379 U.S., at 258, 261; ibid., 277 (Black, J., concurring).

52. Hamm v. City of Rock Hill, 379 U.S. 306 (1964). Consolidated with *Hamm* was Lupper v. Arkansas, 236 Ark. 596, 367 S.W.2d 750 (1963).

53. 379 U.S., at 315–16; Jack Greenberg, "The Supreme Court, Civil Rights and Civil Dissonance," *Yale Law Journal* 77 (1968): 1520–44, at 1532.

54. 379 U.S., at 318–20 (Black, J., dissenting); ibid., 328 (White, J., dissenting). Lucas Powe has described *Hamm* as "a free shot at justice unencumbered by technicalities—such as constitutional power." Lucas A. Powe Jr., *The Warren Court and American Politics* (Cambridge, MA: Harvard University Press, 2000), 237.

55. "Sit-In Cases Die," *NYT*, December 15, 1964, 1, 48; "New Legislation by the Supreme Court," *CT*, December 15, 1964, 20; "When Judges Disagree," *WP*, December 20, 1964, E6; "Ruling on Sit-Ins May Free 3,000, Mostly in the South," *NYT*, December 15, 1964, 1, 48.

56. "Constitutional Law: How to Change Laws You Don't Like," *Time*, July 17, 1964.

57. "'Socialistic State' Foreseen," *NYT*, December 15, 1964, 48; "The Supreme Court: Beyond a Doubt," *Time*, December 25, 1964; John Herbers, "Civil Rights: The South Slowly Yields," *NYT*, December 20, 1964, E3.

58. "Civil Rights: Hoss Unhorsed," *Time*, August 14, 1964; Herbers, "South Slowly Yields"; Wright, *Sharing the Prize*, 97–98; Adam Fairclough, *Race and Democracy: The Civil Rights Struggle in Louisiana, 1915–1972* (Athens: University of Georgia Press, 1995), 339–40.

59. On the general trend toward compliance, see Peter Millones, "Negroes in South Test Rights Act; Resistance Light," *NYT*, July 4, 1964, 1; Alexander M. Bickel, "What Has Been Done Is Prologue: Carrying Out the Civil Rights Act," *NR*, January 9, 1965, 16–17; John Herbers, "Whites Say Compliance Has Been Achieved with Little Strife," *NYT*, January 24, 1965, 1; Wright, *Sharing the Prize*, 97–101; Risen, *Bill of the Century*, 192–93, 244–49; Brian K. Landsberg, "Public Accommodations and the Civil Rights Act of 1964: A Surprising Success?," *Hamline Journal of Public Law and Policy* 36 (2015): 1–25, at 13–15.

60. Wright, *Sharing the Prize*, xi. For an illuminating analysis of the economics of segregation and desegregation in public accommodations, see ibid., chap. 3.

61. Herbers, "South Slowly Yields"; Bayard Rustin, "From Protest to Politics: The Future of the Civil Rights Movement," *Commentary*, January 1965, 25–31, at 25; Bruce Headlam, "For Him, the Political Has Always Been Comical," *NYT*, March 14, 2009, 1, 7.

"Oh, public accommodations is nothing!" President Kennedy once said when white southern leaders challenged him for going too far by backing federal public accommodations legislation. He noted that the issue was much less significant than the challenge of desegregating schools. After noting the problem of white flight in Washington, D.C., he reiterated his point: "Public accommodations is nothing! My God, it's whether you can go into a store or a hotel." Taylor Branch, *Parting the Waters: America in the King Years, 1954–1963* (New York: Simon & Schuster, 1988), 897 (quoting civil rights briefing, September 23, 1963, audiotape 112.5, JFK Library).

Another line of critique of the limits of this victory has emphasized gaps in the coverage of Title II. See, for example, Joseph William Singer, "No Right to Exclude: Public Accommodations and Private Property," *Northwestern University Law Review* 90 (1996): 1283–497.

CONCLUSION

1. Alvin C. Adams, "'And Then We'll Win,' Vows Sit-In Students," *CD*, March 29, 1960, 7.
2. Henry David Thoreau, "Resistance to Civil Government" (1849), reprinted in *Thoreau: Political Writings*, ed. Nancy L. Rosenblum (New York: Cambridge University Press, 1996), 8.
3. Ella Baker, "Bigger than a Hamburger," *Southern Patriot* 18 (June 1960): 4; James Baldwin, "A Negro Assays the Negro Mood," *NYT Magazine*, March 12, 1961, 25, 103–4, at 25.

Index

abatement, 144, 174–75

Ackerman, Bruce, 239n75, 246n33

Aiken, George, 166–67

Alabama, University of, 50, 209n7

American Friends Service Committee, 81

Amsterdam News, 33, 212n17, 223n34

anti-colonialism, 15, 27

arrests: business operators' avoidance of, 10, 93–97, 113, 226n13; of segregationist counter-protesters, 20; of sit-in protesters, 4, 7, 22, 24, 55, 57–61, 65, 66, 80–81, 84, 93, 98–99, 101, 102, 135. *See also* bail; jail; police

Associated Council for Full Citizenship (Knoxville), 44

Associated Press (AP), 82, 98

Atlanta, GA: condemnation of sit-ins, 100, 102, 108, 111; desegregation of lunch counters, 104; police, 98; sit-in protests, 58–59, 64, 87, 102; student leaders 15, 81, 100, 102, 216n9. *See also* Hartsfield, William; Patterson, Eugene; Rolleston, Moreton; Vandiver, Ernest

Atlanta Constitution, 78, 87, 128

Atlanta Daily World, 204n51, 210n11

Avins, Alfred, 172–73

Bagdikian, Ben, 73

bail: fund-raising for, 23, 73, 74; NAACP payment of, 57–58, 63; refusal to pay, 4, 34, 57, 59–61, 213n28. *See also* arrests; jail

Baker, Ella, 22, 39, 45, 182, 205n60

Baldwin, James, 182

Baltimore, MD, 135, 140, 144

Barnett, Ross R., 76

Barrows v. Jackson, 240n86

Barr v. Columbia, 239n78

Barry, Marion, 43, 213n28

Baton Rouge, LA, 98–99, 123–28, 234n20

Bell, Derrick, 52

Bell, Robert Mack, 215n39

Bell v. Maryland, 117, 134–50, 170, 174, 215n39, 231n3, 238n65, 239n75, 239n78, 240n80

Bevel, James, 40

Bible, 3, 84, 88, 89, 103, 108, 162

Bickel, Alexander, 114, 122, 156

Biggs, Michael, 205n58

Birmingham, AL: church bombings, 161; 1963 protests, 11, 30, 155–56; Restaurant Association, 168; sit-in cases involving, 130–33. *See also* Ollie's Barbecue

Black, Hugo, 123–24, 126, 131; *Bell* case, 135–50; *Boynton* opinion, 119; on congressional enforcement power (Fourteenth Amendment), 169–71, 246n40; criticism of protests, 130, 146, 148–50, 175; defense of property rights, 110, 130–31, 139–40, 150; *Hamm* dissent, 175; *Heart of Atlanta* concurrence,

THE CHICAGO SERIES IN LAW AND SOCIETY
Edited by John M. Conley and Lynn Mather

Series titles, continued from front matter: